NEW TESTAMENT

Chapter By Chapter

DANIEL GOEPFRICH

Daniel Goepfrich
2 Peter 3:18

TRUSTHOUSE
PUBLISHERS

New Testament: Chapter by Chapter
by Daniel Goepfrich
www.DanielGoepfrich.com

www.TheologyIsForEveryone.com

Printed in the United States of America
ISBN: 978-1-945774-15-7

Trust House Publishers
P.O.Box 3181
Taos, NM 87571

www.trusthousepublishers.com

Ordering Information: Special discounts are available on quantity purchases by churches,
associations, and retailers. For details, contact the publisher at the address above or call toll-free
1-844-321-4202.

For all who love the Scriptures
and desire a faithful and accurate interpretation
so they can know the Savior better and love him more

Table of Contents

Introduction

This book (and its anticipated companion on the Old Testament) was born out of the desire to help Christians build confidence in their knowledge of the Bible. The best method is to read the Bible passage first, followed by the corresponding chapter in this book. I hoped to benefit the most people possible by writing with several types of readers in mind.

Some readers may want an overview of the entire New Testament, so each book begins with an introduction which may include information on the author, the recipients, or the historical situation surrounding the book which prompted its writing. Together these introductions provide a brief survey of the entire New Testament.

Other readers want a short, simple summary of an individual chapter to supplement their Bible reading or study. They will find the notes to be succinct yet full of principles and applications.

Certain readers may desire insight on some of the more difficult passages without going into as much detail as a full exegetical commentary does. I have attempted to address these passages by at least mentioning, if not explaining, some of the more prominent views offered by other scholars. The footnotes often contain more information for those who want to study further.

Finally, although this is not a technical commentary, some readers will appreciate where I have included advanced terminology and information. This is often related to passages where the Greek language of the New Testament is indispensable for proper interpretation. Again, the footnotes often contain additional information to assist with this type of study.

The notes and interpretation come from a worldview that embraces these key foundational truths:

1. God meant the Bible to be understood and interpreted in its plain, natural sense within the original languages and context in which he gave it. The Bible is a unique work which, as God's very Word, has final authority over every area of faith and life.

2. God has worked with his creation in various ways with various people groups over the centuries and has given his revelation cumulatively so we must carefully interpret every passage of Scripture considering those differences.

3. God has two chosen people groups – Israel and the Church – which are distinct in every way, including their beginning, present relationship with God, and their future. The two are not to be conflated or confused in any way.

4. Just as past prophecy was fulfilled literally, future prophecy will also be fulfilled literally, including a seven-year Tribulation on the Earth, which will be preceded by Jesus removing the Church to be with him in Heaven and followed by Jesus' literal, physical reign on the Earth from Jerusalem.

5. Jesus' death and resurrection are the only terms by which any man, woman, or child can be made right with God. Any individual who attempts to earn God's free gift of salvation or utterly refuses it will be separated from God for eternity. Those who embrace God's

terms for the forgiveness of their sin will spend eternity with him.

Charles Ryrie once wrote, "Everyone is a theologian—of one sort or another." No matter what type or level of theologian you think you are, I hope you will find this book beneficial for your personal study and spiritual growth. For further discussion or to ask specific questions about a passage or topic, please join our Facebook group, "Theology is For Everyone" (facebook.com/theologyisforeveryone), or visit DanielGoepfrich.com or TheologyIsForEveryone.com for additional resources.

Many people contributed to this book with their questions and suggestions, but I owe a great deal of gratitude to my wife, Saralynn, for her involvement in helping prepare this book. Not only did she read the entire manuscript once, but she also read several sections multiple times, and her input was invaluable in bringing clarity that I would have otherwise missed. Any errors or confusing statements are solely mine.

Matthew

Matthew is the opening book of the New Testament, the first gospel written, and possibly the first New Testament book written (mid-40s AD). Academia in the 20th century saw a wide rejection that Matthew was the first gospel written, preferring to believe instead that Matthew borrowed heavily from Mark, Luke, and other (unknown) sources. However, the language and purpose of Matthew's account, along with his apostolic significance over Mark and Luke and his primarily Jewish audience, make that an unlikely scenario. Additionally, throughout the Early Church, Matthew was consistently placed first in the New Testament canon.

It seems obvious by looking at the flow of the Gospel that Matthew's primary goal in writing was to present Jesus as the Messiah, the "Anointed One" for whom the Jewish people had been waiting for 1,500 years. He was the promised King of the Jews. Beginning with Abraham, Matthew recounted much of Jewish history, quoted heavily from the Hebrew prophets, set the stage for the Church Age, and recorded detailed prophecy about the coming Tribulation and Messianic Kingdom. Matthew's gospel is the crucial bridge between the Old and New Testaments, probably the most important transition book in all of Scripture.

One significant point to note is that Matthew bookended the body of his Gospel with fulfillments of Old Testament prophecy. In the first three chapters, there are no fewer than six direct quotes or allusions to Messianic prophecies, and the last three chapters (concerning Jesus' death, burial, and resurrection) contain at least another half-dozen. No first-century Jew reading or hearing Matthew's work could escape his blatant declaration that Jesus was their long-awaited Deliverer.

Chapter one introduces Jesus from Joseph's perspective. The genealogy given in verses 1-17 traces Joseph's family tree from Abraham through David to show that Jesus was the rightful heir to the Messianic throne. However, Joseph was a descendant of Jeconiah, whom God had cursed so that he would never have an heir on the throne. Had Jesus been Joseph's biological son, he would have been unable to be the Messiah (Jeremiah 22:24-30). This created a tension in the story that only the Virgin Birth could resolve.

A point that is frequently brought up concerning this genealogy is the repeated mention of "FOURTEEN GENERATIONS" in verse 17. The significance is in the fact that the Hebrew letters, דוד, (*dvd*, "David"), represent the number "14."[1] By repeating this number, Matthew was blatantly invoking David by subtly insisting that Jesus was the promised heir of David's throne, though not through Joseph.

Whereas Luke wrote Mary's story, Matthew recorded Joseph's experiences around Jesus' conception and birth. Although they both learned the truth by angelic messages, Joseph received specific commands in a series of dreams. He must have been upset and crushed when Mary returned to Nazareth approximately three months pregnant (Luke 1:42, 56), but he decided to grant her a private divorce (rather than having her executed, which was his right), since she apparently loved someone else (vs. 19). Instead, the angel commanded him to marry his pregnant fiancée immediately and raise Jesus as his own son. Curiously, Matthew never recorded a single word uttered

---

1 Each Hebrew letter also acts as a numeral, and these three letters together are 4+6+4 or 14.

by Joseph. This righteous man simply obeyed every command God gave him.

Chapter two opens with the first Gentile recognition of Jesus as Messiah. Somehow, using the stars as the language they would understand, God revealed to Eastern astrologers that a new Jewish king had been born. Since Daniel had Jeremiah's writings available to him in Persia (Daniel 9:2), it is possible that they had access to other Hebrew Scriptures as well, including Numbers 24:17: "A STAR WILL MARCH FORTH OUT OF JACOB, AND A SCEPTER WILL RISE OUT OF ISRAEL." If this newborn was to fulfill the ancient Hebrew prophecies of the coming Deliverer, they would naturally want to make a political ally by celebrating his birth with a grand procession. However, their reception was not what they expected (vs. 1-3). After pressing for further information from them, Herod attempted to kill Jesus, who was a threat to his own reign. Both the Magi and Joseph received direction by God in a series of dreams, instructing them how to save Jesus' life, and each time they obeyed him immediately.

Matthew was careful to note that Jesus' birth in Bethlehem fulfilled an ancient prophecy, specifically Micah 5:2, which clearly points to his deity as the eternal God. In the rest of the chapter Matthew directly quoted or referred to Hosea, Jeremiah, and Isaiah. Matthew's not-always-literal application of Hebrew prophecy has caused trouble for many scholars, but Dr. Arnold Fruchtenbaum notes that Matthew followed the four-fold interpretation method of the rabbis of the day.[2] These are *Literal Prophecy Plus Literal Fulfillment* (vs. 5-6); *Literal Plus Typical* (vs. 15); *Literal Plus Application* (vs. 17-18); and *Summation* (vs. 23). Dr. Christopher Cone has also addressed the usage of Old Testament quotes in the New Testament by emphasizing the fact that fulfillment does not require a direct prophecy. In other words, a New Testament writer can interpret an Old Testament event or statement

---

2 Arnold Fruchtenbaum, "How the New Testament Quotes the Old Testament", http://arielb.org/archives/794.

as foreshadowing a future situation without requiring it to be a formal Old Testament prophecy and without changing or ignoring the meaning of the original passage.[3]

The chapter ends with Jesus probably as a toddler or pre-school-aged child, back in Nazareth, where Luke wrote that he "GREW AND BECAME STRONG, FILLED WITH WISDOM, AND THE FAVOR OF GOD WAS UPON HIM" (Luke 2:40).

Chapter three skips approximately 28-30 years of Jesus' life, moving directly to the beginning of his ministry. The reason is that there was nothing in Jesus' early life that added value to Matthew's purpose of presenting Jesus as Messiah, including Jesus' first Temple visit as told by Luke. Matthew also did not find the need to introduce John the Baptist, since his readers would have likely still remembered him. However, to reinforce his point that Jesus was the anticipated Messiah, Matthew did identify John as the one Isaiah said would "PREPARE THE WAY FOR THE LORD" (Isaiah 40:3). Matthew also used John's story to connect his writing to Malachi, the last of the ancient Hebrew prophets. Malachi ended with a promise that God would send his messenger before Messiah came (Malachi 3:1). This is further internal support that Matthew was the first New Testament book written and served as the bridge between the Old and New Testaments.

Strictly speaking, John the Baptist was the last of the Hebrew prophets, and in the fashion of his predecessors, he excoriated the religious leaders for being false shepherds who led the people away from God instead of toward him (vs. 7-12; see Ezekiel 34). He preached of the coming Messiah and his judgment, offering the nation a chance to repent. Water baptism was the method by which they publicly identified with John's message and displayed their heart change.

---

3 For further examples and explanation, see Christopher Cone, "Foreshadowing and Fulfillment: The New Testament Use of the Old Testament in John", http://www.drcone.com/2016/09/16/foreshadowing-fulfillment-new-testament-use-old-testament-john.

What John did not expect is that Jesus would ask to be baptized himself. After a brief discussion in which John nearly refused, he finally did baptize Jesus. At this moment John recalled that God the Father spoke his approval of Jesus (vs. 16-17). It seems this was audible only to Jesus and John (see John 1:32-34).

In these first three chapters, Matthew offered six witnesses to Jesus as Messiah: the Hebrew prophets, angels, Herod and his advisors, the Magi, John the Baptizer, and the full Trinity.

Chapter four introduces Matthew's final external witness to Jesus' true identity: Satan. Immediately after his baptism, the Holy Spirit led Jesus into the desert to be tested and tempted by Satan (vs. 1). Although Matthew focuses on only three temptations, Luke noted that the temptation period lasted for the entire 40 days, concluded by the "big three" (Luke 4:1-2). The writer of Hebrews said that Jesus "HAD TO BE MADE LIKE HIS BROTHERS AND SISTERS IN EVERY RESPECT," including temptation, "SO THAT HE COULD BECOME A MERCIFUL AND FAITHFUL HIGH PRIEST" (Hebrews 2:17-18). Successfully passing this 40-day, nothing-held-back barrage convincingly proved Jesus to be the sinless Son of God.

While Satan watched for a more opportune time to attack Jesus again (Luke 4:13), Jesus began to present himself and his kingdom to the public in Galilee, headquartering his ministry in Capernaum (vs. 13). His message was essentially the same as John's: "REPENT, FOR THE KINGDOM OF HEAVEN IS NEAR" (vs. 17), a general call for people to repent of their sins and follow him, recognizing him as their Messiah. The proof of his message and offer included the healings and miracles that Isaiah said Messiah would do in his Kingdom (Isaiah 61:1-3; see Luke 4:16-30).

This was neither the first nor the final call Jesus made to Peter, Andrew, James, and John (vs. 18-22), nor was it their commissioning as apostles. A comparison with the other gospels indicates that he called and they followed him temporarily multiple times before he commissioned them full-time to be his apostles.

Chapters five through seven contain the first of five major discourses or lengthy speeches that Matthew recorded. Jesus delivered this address, traditionally called "the Sermon on the Mount," to hundreds or thousands of early "disciples," people who had followed him to learn more about him and his Kingdom.

Chapter five focuses on the requirements necessary to gain entrance into the Kingdom and the Kingdom law-code. Jesus was clear that entry into his Kingdom was basely solely on personal righteousness (5:3-12, 20). Simply put, the Kingdom will not be a place where sinners are comfortable, and those who choose to live in sin will suffer the consequences for it.

It is important to clarify that, although there are some principles that apply to the Church, this teaching was not directed to the Church but to Israel (specifically) and all Kingdom residents (generally). The Church will be glorified before entering the Kingdom to reign alongside Christ (Revelation 20:6), so we will not be subject to this law code.

In the rest of the chapter Jesus provided a series of examples of Kingdom law in practice. Because God's perfect standard cannot change, Kingdom law often sounds like the Mosaic Law. A major difference in the Kingdom, however, is that Jesus will judge based on a person's heart as well as on actions. Just as sinners will not enter the Kingdom, sin will not be tolerated in his Kingdom. Jesus summarized this section by saying, "Just be perfect like God" (5:48).

Chapter six, the second section of the Sermon on the Mount, focuses on the personal spiritual life of Kingdom citizens. Jesus addressed the proper heart attitude that he required to be behind giving alms to the poor, private prayer, and fasting (vs. 1-18). He taught that the wrong attitude toward wealth or money was the single greatest enemy of a person's allegiance to God (vs. 19-24). The antidote to relying on personal wealth in the face of need was to focus on God and his provision.

In one of the most important sections with application to the Church as well, Jesus used nature as his example to show that God is able and willing to take care of those who are his, Because of this we are to not worry about anything. Paul taught this frequently to Christians as well. The proper attitude in Jesus' kingdom is to prioritize the Kingdom (God's work is to be first) and let God take care of the details (vs. 25-34).

Chapter seven, part three of the Sermon on the Mount, focuses on Kingdom citizens' personal interaction and ministry. In verses 1-6, the infamous "judge not" passage, Jesus taught that one's judgment of another's personal righteousness is to be withheld in fear that God will judge as harshly. This is obviously not a Church-age truth, as God's judgment of believers is based solely on the cross. People frequently use the "measure" in Luke 6:38 to refer to financial reward for giving. The context there and in Matthew 7 proves this to be bad exegesis. It refers to giving and receiving judgment, not financial blessings.

Jesus again emphasized God's provision as a natural result of his goodness, kindness, and love for his people, as any good father does for his children (vs. 7-12). Verses 13-14 are often mistaken for a Church-age salvation message. However, the context is about one's personal righteousness, so they refer to entering the Kingdom rather than coming to the cross. In the Kingdom, there will still be false prophets; however, they will be immediately evident, not by their prophecies but by their lack of righteousness (vs. 15-20).

Lest his audience think, based on all of Jesus' teaching about personal righteousness, that they could be "good enough" on their own to enter the Kingdom, Jesus insisted that good deeds were not the same as righteousness. Their righteousness would never exceed "THAT OF THE EXPERTS IN THE

LAW AND THE PHARISEES" (5:20). Entrance into the Kingdom still requires personal knowledge of the Son (7:21-23), which will be evidenced by personal righteousness and good deeds. The Olivet Discourse reflects this same truth in more detail (Matthew 25:31-46).

Chapters eight and nine contain a series of examples of the many miracles and teachings to which Matthew had started to allude at the end of chapter four. Although Israel had seen two previous periods of miracles in their history (Moses/Joshua and Elijah/Elisha), what they experienced during Jesus' early ministry was unprecedented. Both Matthew 12:15 and Luke 6:19 state that, regardless of how many people were there, Jesus "HEALED THEM ALL." It is likely that a person could not walk anywhere in Galilee or Jerusalem without encountering a person who had been healed. There may not have been even one family which did not have a personal experience with Jesus' power.

In chapter eight Jesus displayed his power over leprosy, demons, and the weather. Though Jesus was sent first to the Jews, his interaction with a humble Gentile army commander showed that Jesus was fulfilling the part of the Abrahamic Covenant that "ALL OF THE FAMILIES OF THE EARTH" would be blessed, not just the Jews (Genesis 12:3). In verse 17, Matthew quoted Isaiah to show that Jesus' healing miracles proved his Messiahship. The little bit of teaching that Matthew recorded in this chapter was that Jesus demanded total allegiance and true humility from those who wanted to follow him.

Chapter nine continues with more samples of Jesus' miracles and his first minor run-in with the local Pharisees (vs. 1-8). It was one thing to cleanse a man from leprosy (8:3); it was a different matter to make a paralytic move. However, rather than healing him right away, Jesus forgave his sins, claiming the ability to do something that only God could do. As was true with all his miracles, the healing was done to prove his claim. It was at this point that the Pharisees began to realize that Jesus thought he was more than just another rabbi, and they began their opposition against him.

Throughout the chapter, Matthew also recorded Jesus' ability to raise the dead, heal long-term internal diseases, restore the blind and mute, and exercise more authority over demons. The more he did, the more the opposition rose against him (vs. 11, 24, 34).

It was during this time that Jesus came to Matthew's workplace to call Matthew to follow him (vs. 9). The chapter concludes with Jesus' statement that he needed more workers to continue and expand his ministry, the main message of which was still "THE GOSPEL OF THE KINGDOM" (vs. 35-38).

Chapter ten opens with Jesus' initial solution to the ministry needs he expressed at the end of chapter nine and is presented as the second of the five major discourses in Matthew. Out of his huge group of followers, Jesus chose only twelve to be his official "APOSTLES," those authorized to speak and act on his behalf. To these Twelve he gave the temporary and limited ability to work some of the same miracles that Jesus did and commissioned them to preach the gospel of the Kingdom, including the command to repent and follow Jesus.

This chapter is often mistakenly applied to the Church, especially by those who believe in the continuation of signs and wonders (vs. 8) and by those who lean toward a social gospel (vs. 40-42).[4] However, there are three points they ignore that clarify the interpretation. First, Matthew was clear that these powers were granted only to the Twelve. The "TWELVE" are mentioned specifically three times in 10:1-5 and again in 11:1. Nowhere in the Church epistles are these powers given, commanded, or instructed. On the contrary, 2 Corinthians 12:12 and Hebrews 2:3-4 more than imply that they

---

4   "Social gospel" is a term used to describe charitable ministry such as feeding the hungry, helping the poor, etc. that does not include a call to repentance for sin or the presentation of Jesus' death and resurrection for salvation. It is based in the assumption that our goal is to relieve needs rather than preach the gospel.

were limited to the apostles, even after the beginning of the Church. Second, this temporary ministry was clearly limited to only the Jewish people (vs. 5-6), whereas the Church mission is to "MAKE DISCIPLES OF ALL NATIONS" (28:19). Third, the message they preached was the gospel of the Kingdom (vs. 7), not the gospel of salvation. Modern liberal theology (including the Covenant and Replacement forms) has resurrected the gospel of the Kingdom, making the cross simply a means to the end. Sadly, even evangelicals tend to preach a "gospel of heaven," making heaven, rather than Christ, the goal. Paul, on the other hand, preached only "THE MESSAGE ABOUT THE CROSS...[AND] ABOUT A CRUCIFIED CHRIST...[TO] BOTH JEWS AND GREEKS" (1 Corinthians 1:18, 23-24).

Thus, there are several passages throughout this chapter which cause contention between churches and denominations that could be eliminated with a proper understanding of the context. Some of these will have future fulfillment during the Tribulation, when the gospel of the kingdom is preached again (Matthew 24:14).

Chapter eleven records that John the Baptizer expressed surprise, concern, and possibly even doubt when he was imprisoned by Herod and sentenced to death (vs. 2-3). Naturally, he fully expected to see Jesus establish his Kingdom, but his question of Jesus' identity proved his misunderstanding of Jesus' whole ministry. Jesus' answer was neither scolding nor ridiculing. Instead, he told John to trust the promises God made in the Scriptures. The prophets said that Messiah would do certain things which Jesus did (vs. 4-6).

Additionally, Jesus used the opportunity to tell the crowd his estimation of John, that he was the "Elijah" that Malachi foresaw (vs. 7-19; Malachi 3:1). By this, Jesus once again clearly identified himself as that Messiah whom "Elijah" would announce. This doubled as a denouncement of the religious leaders who rejected John and his message (vs. 16-19), further widening the gap between Jesus and the religious establishment.

At this time Jesus offered his first public condemnation of those who did not accept him. In verse 20 it is important to note that he "BEGAN TO CRITICIZE OPENLY." Rather than being just a one-time statement to the immediate crowd, as he traveled throughout Galilee, Jesus began to couple his gospel of the kingdom with harsh condemnation toward his detractors. His comparison of unbelieving Israel to Tyre and Sidon (vs. 21), Hades (vs. 23), and Sodom (vs. 24) are the words of a fiery evangelist who recognized that the religious and political machine against him was just starting up. Yet, at the same time, he continued to offer his hand out to all who would humble themselves to receive it (vs. 28-30).

Chapter twelve is truly the climax of Matthew's narrative, the show-down between rebellious Israel and her Messiah. In response to the Pharisees' accusations that Jesus and his disciples had violated the Mosaic Law by "harvesting" on the Sabbath, Jesus asserted his deity again with four bold claims. First, Jesus is greater than the Temple. This necessarily includes the entire Mosaic Law code, sacrificial system, the priests, and the interpreters and enforcers of the Law (12:6). This means that he made the Law and cannot possibly break it. Second, Jesus is greater than the Sabbath, because he is the lord over it (12:8). This means that he has full rights to use the Sabbath however he wants. Third, Jesus is greater than the prophet Jonah (vs. 41). There was no question in their minds that Jonah was a true prophet. As with all the prophets, only God was greater than they were. Fourth, Jesus is greater than Israel's greatest king, Solomon (12:42).[5] This means that he has full ruling rights over all of Israel. In Jewish estimation, nothing was greater than these things, yet Jesus claimed complete superiority over them all. Interestingly, one can see a shadow of Jesus' three roles in these claims. He is <u>Priest</u> over the Temple; he is <u>Prophet</u>, speaking God's truth about the Sabbath and

---

5   Spiritually speaking, David was a much greater king than Solomon, but in the context, Jesus was referring to Solomon's wealth and influence, including the fact that he was the one who built the Temple.

the condemnation of the religious leaders; and he is the promised <u>King</u> of David's dynasty. Indeed, Matthew explained, Jesus was the Chosen *Servant of Jehovah* prophesied by Isaiah (vs. 17-21; Isaiah 42:1-4) who would bring justice and victory to both Israel and the Gentiles.

In response to his blatant claims of deity, the local Pharisees declared Jesus to be the pawn of Satan, acting under his power rather than that of the Holy Spirit (vs. 24). Jesus declared that they were not just being illogical or irrational (vs. 25-30), but rather they had committed a sin against the Holy Spirit that was unforgiveable (vs. 31-32). He noted that this attitude solidified their rejection of him as their Messiah, and they would be judged appropriately (vs. 33-37). Since Jesus had focused much of his ministry thus far in Galilee, this local rejection was representative of the rejection by the entire nation, which would come soon.

In the final dozen verses of the chapter Jesus made his first (although subtle) prophecy of his own death. Comparing himself to Jonah in the great fish, Jesus claimed that he would "BE IN THE HEART OF THE EARTH"(vs. 40). Some commentators have used this to prove that Jonah was dead while in the fish, although that is unlikely but debatable. In Jesus' condemnation on unbelieving Israel (vs. 43-45), he likened that generation to a person who was cleansed from demonic power, only to have the demon return even stronger. Finally, in verses 46-50, Jesus began to distance himself even from those in his family who would have quieted him. As he prepared to head toward Jerusalem, the demands of his followers increased as well.

Chapter thirteen contains the first of two drastic changes to Jesus' teaching ministry. First, quoting Isaiah 6:9-10 as his foundation (vs. 13-15, 34-35), following his rejection and for the remainder of his ministry, Jesus did all his public teaching only in parables. According to Isaiah and Jesus, these parables had two purposes. For unbelievers, they would hide new truths so as to not heap further judgment upon those who refused to believe, which was in reality a wonderful act of grace. For believers, the parables would reveal new truths about the Kingdom, including its postponement into the unspecified future.

Each of the parables in chapter 13 is related to the "KINGDOM OF HEAVEN." Although there is often confusion between "the kingdom of heaven" and "the kingdom of God," the former was used only by Matthew, and it always referred to the Messianic Kingdom, Heaven's rule on earth. Those who attempt to apply these parables to the Church must deal with the explanation in vs. 36-43, where the end of the kingdom of heaven is described in terms vastly different than the Rapture of the Church.

The second change in Jesus' teaching was that, beginning in chapter thirteen, neither Jesus nor the apostles announced again that the kingdom was at hand. That offer was rescinded and replaced with the command to drop everything and follow Jesus. The rejection that began with the religious leadership in Capernaum (a central city in Galilee) began to spread, overtaking public opinion even in the small villages like Nazareth, Jesus' hometown (vs. 53-58).

Chapter fourteen contains a wonderful demonstration of God's grace toward those who were still undecided about Jesus. As Jesus had grown in popularity, Herod began to take notice (vs. 1-2). Although Matthew had mentioned John's imprisonment in chapter 11, he had not mentioned the outcome until this point, when he gave the detail of how Herod's wife connived to have John murdered (vs. 3-12). Superstitiously, Herod thought that Jesus was John who had been resurrected and was haunting him. Not wanting a political run-in yet, Jesus moved away from Herod, toward the mountains, to focus on training his apostles. Still, people continued to follow him.

It is amazing that, even though the religious opinion had started to shift against him, many of the common people still wanted to hear and see more. (This is likely an indication of how weak the Pharisees' influence outside of the cities was). Jesus continued to show his compassion for the common people of Israel in his miracle of feeding a crowd of more than 10,000 people (vs. 13-21). Other than the resurrection itself, this is the only miracle Jesus did that was recorded in all four Gospels (Mark 6:30-44; Luke 9:10-17; John 6:1-13).

After this great miracle and the resulting attempt by the crowd to make him their king right then (see John 6:15), Jesus needed to spend time alone in prayer (vs. 23), so he sent the people and the apostles away. During the night, a storm came over the Sea of Galilee that even the experienced fishermen could not handle. Jesus used this as an opportunity to prove his power to the Twelve again by easily walking through the torrential storm on top of the lake. In a great statement of faith, Peter asked for the power to do the same thing, which Jesus granted (vs. 28-29). Only when he began to fear the sea rather than focus on the Savior did Peter begin to sink. Jesus rescued him, and, upon entering the boat, he calmed the storm immediately, without even saying a word (vs. 32).

Chapter fifteen records Jesus' first major run-in with Pharisees from Jerusalem. To this point, his opposition was primarily localized to the Pharisees from Galilee. However, he had apparently become infamous enough in their circles that the "big shots" from Jerusalem made their way to Galilee to investigate for themselves. Their first encounter with him was an argument over a ceremonial hand-washing ritual that was not part of the original law code (vs. 1-9). In his reply, Jesus accused them of twisting the law for their own purposes, disobeying the clear commands while holding others to things that God never said. This made them hypocrites, the very issue Isaiah, the great prophet they claimed to follow, had denounced 700 years earlier. Jesus used this interaction to teach the crowd that the ceremonial rituals never made someone truly clean or unclean. Rather it was the person's heart that was defiled, something ritual could never correct (vs. 10-20).[6]

After this encounter, Jesus spent the rest of the chapter in Gentile territory (vs. 21). Not only did this put him outside of the jurisdiction of the Pharisees (since it was not yet his time to be arrested and killed), this also impressed on the apostles that Gentile ministry would continue to grow, even as Israel continued to reject him. First, he conversed with a Canaanite woman. This was scandalous because of her gender and ethnicity (see also John 4:9, 7). She had obviously heard of his miracles and healings and wanted a demon cast out of her daughter (vs. 22). Addressing him as "Son of David" revealed her belief that he was the promised Messiah, even though she was not even Jewish. After a short dialogue (probably for the sake of the apostles), Jesus commented on the woman's great faith and healed her daughter. Like the centurion of chapter eight, her humility showed that her faith was genuine.

The second part of this ministry outside of Israel included a great number of healings (vs. 29-31). Matthew's comment that "THEY PRAISED THE GOD OF ISRAEL" points to the fact that they were Gentiles. Similar to the event in chapter fourteen, the crowd would not leave him, and his compassion for them included their stomachs. As before, Jesus told the apostles to get food for the people (vs. 33). Did this not feel like *déjà vu*? Should they not have responded immediately by asking someone for a small lunch to bring to Jesus, instead of him having to repeat the whole scenario over again?

Occasionally it is suggested that this was just a repeat of the previous miracle when he fed 5,000. However, this simply cannot be the case as there are at least six differences recorded. First, the crowd and location were Gentile, not Jewish. Second, the number of men was 4,000 not 5,000. Third, the starting amount was "SEVEN [LOAVES] AND A FEW SMALL FISH" (vs. 34) not "FIVE LOAVES AND TWO FISH" (14:17). Fourth, the leftovers filled "SEVEN BASKETS" (vs. 37) not "TWELVE BASKETS" (14:20). Fifth, both Matthew and

---

6 It is important to remember that, although Jesus often did not follow the Pharisees' traditions, he never violated the actual Law given by God, which would have been sin.

Mark used the exact same words for "BASKET" in their accounts, but the words describing the two accounts are different. Sixth, after the event, Jesus and the apostles all got into the boat and left at the same time, which did not happen after the previous miracle. If all that is not enough, Jesus himself referred to them as distinct events (16:9-10).

Chapter sixteen marks a significant shift in Matthew's writing. To this point, Matthew has been careful to support his presentation of Jesus as Messiah with a barrage of quotes from the Hebrew Scriptures, the Old Testament. However, for the next five chapters (chapters sixteen through twenty), there is not a Messianic quote to be found. Instead, we find Jesus preparing his apostles for the next phase of ministry that would come shortly. Significantly, the quotations start again in chapter 21, when Jesus presented himself to Jerusalem as her King, followed by his death and resurrection.

Returning to Jewish territory after feeding more than four thousand Gentiles, Jesus was once again accosted by the religious leaders. Although he had already said he would give no more signs until his resurrection (12:39-40), they continued to ask for a sign proving his authority from heaven (vs. 1). Jesus replied that they could make weather predictions based on the color of the sky but still refused to believe what he had already shown them. He then reiterated his policy of no signs for them (vs. 2-4).

In verses 5-12, Jesus used the examples of his feeding five and four thousand to show that he was unconcerned about physical food compared with spiritual malnourishment. He warned his disciples about the "LEAVEN" that the Pharisees and Sadducees laced in their teaching and questions. Their "leaven" was false teaching which led people away from the Messiah rather than toward him.

This interaction set up Jesus to ask the most important question of all time: *Who is Jesus?* When he posed this to the apostles, they responded first with the general response to Jesus. He was obviously a great prophet, maybe

John the Baptist (like Herod thought), Elijah (who was promised to come), or Jeremiah (vs. 13-15). However, when he asked for their own understanding, Peter responded with the famous line: "YOU ARE THE CHRIST [MESSIAH], THE SON OF THE LIVING GOD" (vs. 16). Jesus noted that this realization cannot come without enlightenment from God himself (vs. 17). This continues to be the question that everything hinges on.

It was at this moment that Jesus made his first mention of the Church. In verse 18 Jesus gave five hints about this yet-unknown entity. First, it was still future ("I WILL BUILD"). This means that it could not be the same as Israel, which already existed. Second, it would be his ("MY CHURCH"). This is different than Israel being called Jehovah's people throughout the Hebrew Scriptures. Third, it would be a congregation, the meaning of "church." This means that the Church is a group of people, distinct from those who are not included. Fourth, the Church would be built on Christ himself, the referent of "THIS ROCK." This is clarified by Peter in 1 Peter 2:8 and Paul in Ephesians 2:20. Fifth, the Church will never die. Although members of the Church would die throughout the centuries, "THE GATES OF HADES" (the grave) will never cause her to go extinct. Physical death does no harm to Jesus' congregation.

The chapter ends with Jesus' first major prophecy of his death and resurrection and the ramifications of what that means to someone who would choose to truly follow him. Although it was difficult for them to understand (vs. 22), the disciples would come to learn the true meaning of following Jesus, when he was no longer admired by the crowds. There would be similarities between following him and being despised by the world ("TAKE UP HIS CROSS"). Yet the benefits of following Jesus are far beyond what this world could ever offer (vs. 26-27).

Chapter seventeen records one of the greatest events that could happen to a person. In verses 1-8 Jesus allowed Peter, James, and John to see him in his full glory. They were, naturally, overwhelmed. Additionally, being able to see heroes they had only heard about, Moses and Elijah, must have been an unspeakable honor. In their writings, both Peter and John referred to the Transfiguration as an actual event that they witnessed (see 2 Peter 1:16-18 and John 1:14). It seems that this was to help solidify in their minds who Jesus was, since his teaching and ministry were about to change and as he began to talk about his death. These two would end up being the most influential of the Twelve once the Church began (Galatians 1:18; 2:9; Acts 4:1-22; 8:14-17; Revelation 1:9-11).

While those three were on the mountain, the other nine apostles attempted to cast a demon out of a man's son but were unable to do it (vs. 16). It seems that they had relied on their own ability to do this rather than God's power, which they had been given temporarily in chapter ten (vs. 20). Out of compassion for the man and son, Jesus cast out the demon immediately.

In verses 22-23, Matthew recorded a second prophecy of Jesus' death and resurrection. Likely, this was not only the second time Jesus said it, because 16:21 states that "HE BEGAN" to tell his disciples about it, indicating that this could have been a regular discussion topic.

The final verses (24-27) record another brief encounter between the religious leaders and Jesus; this time they used the unwitting Peter as their proxy. Jesus deftly told Peter that, although he was not subject to their laws by nature, he voluntarily subjected himself during his temporary earthly ministry. This is a great example of the balanced perspective Christians should have of our obligation to both God and the State.

Chapter eighteen divides naturally into two sections, each containing two parts. In the first section (vs. 1-14), Jesus gave another teaching on the kingdom of heaven. In response to the apostles' question, Jesus insisted that the kingdom would be characterized by humility and innocence (vs. 3-5) rather than arrogance and sin (vs. 6-9). The thought of cutting off an arm or gouging out an eye was a hyperbolic way to show that anything that prohibits a person from being righteous should be eradicated from our lives. Because the gospel of salvation through Jesus' death and resurrection was not yet preached at this point, this illustration should not be used as support to teach that our works will determine our destiny.

Verses 10-14 seem to be a shorter version of the full parable found in Luke 15, when Jesus told of the lost sheep, the lost coin, and the lost son. Since children were considered part of the Israelite covenant people of God (due to Old Testament circumcision and sacrifice), this was a warning again regarding the Pharisees and Sadducees whose teaching was leading people away from Jesus rather than toward him.

The second section (vs. 15-35) contains a teaching on forgiveness and relational restoration. In his second mention of the coming Church (vs. 15-22), Jesus taught that repentance, forgiveness, and restoration is to be the purpose of Christian discipline. Multiple chances are to be offered an erring brother, rather than the three that the rabbis required or even the seven that Peter "graciously" offered (vs. 21). Jesus assured the apostles that, whether the result was discipline or restoration, doing it God's way carried God's authority (vs. 18-20). The common teaching that these verses refer to prayer meetings and the like is wrong and has no foundation in the context.

Jesus applied his desire for grace and forgiveness to business and personal relationships outside the Church as well in verses 23-35. Although the slave was forgiven an enormous amount by his master (vs. 27; roughly $3.5 billion at today's minimum wage), he refused to write off a $6,000 debt owed him by a co-worker (vs. 30). Naturally, the master was enraged at the disparity and took back his pardon (vs. 34). Jesus' statement in verse 35 should not be taken as how God deals with Christians today. His Jewish audience had been granted much by God, but they were brutal toward each other. Jesus said that they could not expect God's favor when they withheld it themselves. Notice that Jesus called God "*my* heavenly Father" not "*your* heavenly Father."

Chapter nineteen contains two main parts, both of which are frequently misunderstood and misapplied. In the first section (vs. 1-12) Jesus gave a direct answer to a direct question about marriage and divorce. Since Paul added to this later (see 1 Corinthians 7), it is essential that we not think this to be the full biblical doctrine on the topic, as some often do. However, in his statement, Jesus did enforce at least three significant principles. First, God created gender (vs. 4). Second, God instituted marriage (vs. 5-6). Third, divorce is a concession, allowed by God on his terms, but not required or preferred (vs. 8-9). Fourth, marriage is to be done God's way or not at all (vs. 11-12).

The second major section is the account of Jesus' interaction with the rich young man and his subsequent teaching about it (vs. 16-30). The man approached Jesus wondering what he still had to do to enter the kingdom. When Jesus pressed him about his obedience to the law (the standard for God's blessing in the Old Testament and the Sermon on the Mount), he was confident in his personal righteousness, but he somehow knew he needed something more (vs. 20).

Jesus' response that he should sell his possessions and give them to the poor has been misconstrued by many who think this applies to Christians. They believe that we should not have many possessions and that not selling what we have and giving it away, or at least not making a habit of supporting the poor, puts us in jeopardy of discipline or even loss of salvation. Obviously, this could not be Jesus' meaning, as he was not talking with a Christian. It also misses the most important part of his command to the young man: "FOLLOW ME" (vs. 21). It was his heart, an unwillingness to follow Jesus at possible financial loss, not his money that was at issue.

Even the disciples missed this point. Picking up on the theme that allegiance to God and money is mutually exclusive (6:24), Jesus taught that wealth can keep a person from following him. Yet, again, wealth itself is not the culprit. Jesus and Paul both said that wealth can be used for eternal purposes (vs. 21) and earthly enjoyment (1 Timothy 6:17-19).

Chapter twenty continues Jesus' teaching from chapter nineteen. It was common then, as it is now, to believe that wealth was proof of God's favor. Not only did Jesus refute that concept, in his parable of the vineyard workers, he insisted that God was free to reward his workers as he saw fit rather than according to a human concept of "fairness." This story is often taught to mean that no matter when a person believes in Christ, all believers will receive full salvation. While that is certainly true, given the context and audience, a better interpretation is that God "WILL GIVE...WHATEVER IS RIGHT" (vs. 4) to all his servants and that he alone has the right to make that determination (vs. 14-15). Inheritance in the kingdom is not necessarily based on time in the field.

As he made his final approach to Jerusalem, Jesus gave his apostles one more clear statement on his impending death and resurrection (vs. 17-19). That they still did not get it is clearly demonstrated by the argument that broke out in verses 20-28. Apparently, they were so enthralled with Jesus' promise that they would rule in the kingdom (19:28) that they were already making plans for that. It can be proven that James and John were probably Jesus' cousins, so it seems they hoped their familial connection would gain them a greater inheritance (vs. 20-21), specifically contradicting what Jesus had just taught in the parable. Naturally, this upset the others, leading to Jesus' sternest warning to them yet, that his ministry was one of serving not being served (vs. 28).

In his final recorded act before entering Jerusalem, Matthew wrote that Jesus healed two blind men outside of Jericho (vs. 29-34). The significance of this event is less in the healing (he had healed many blind people before this) and more in their identification of Jesus as the "SON OF DAVID," a clear reference to his Messiahship. The one who was about to be rejected by those who claimed to be enlightened was wholly accepted by those who were blind.

Chapter twenty-one introduces the final major section of Matthew. As noted in chapter sixteen, Messianic references in the Hebrew Scriptures return in full force as Jesus offered himself formally as Israel's Messiah and King.

A comparison of the four gospel accounts shows that Jesus' entry into Jerusalem took place on Monday. He spent Monday, Tuesday, and Wednesday teaching in the Temple but spending the night outside of the jurisdiction of the religious leaders. Other than the entry itself, not much is recorded about what he did on Monday. Contrary to most common opinion, it was a small group of Jesus' followers, not the large Jerusalem and Temple crowds, who shouted, "HOSANNA!" (vs. 9).

On Tuesday morning, Jesus cursed a fig tree on his way into Jerusalem. Mark 11 notes that this occurred on the morning before Jesus cleansed the Temple, and the disciples noticed it the following morning (Wednesday) on the way back into Jerusalem. There is sometimes confusion regarding when Jesus cleansed the Temple. He actually did this twice – once at the beginning of his ministry, when he was still unknown (John 2:12-22), and once during Passion Week.

Like a lamb being offered as a sacrifice needed to be examined for purity, Jesus' official presentation of himself in Jerusalem was met with examination by the religious leaders. Multiple times Jesus' authority and teaching were questioned (vs. 23); each time he proved himself to be exactly who he claimed to be.

Jesus responded to this questioning with three parables. The first (vs. 28-32) told of two sons given a job by their father. One outright refused but later repented and obeyed; the other promised to obey but never did. Jesus condemned the religious leaders for saying that they obeyed God but did not, while he commended the "SINNERS" who had broken God's law but repented in response to Messiah.

The second parable (vs. 33-44) showed a landowner who leased his vineyard to some tenants then left. When he sent servants to collect his rent, the tenants beat and killed them. He finally sent his own son with the same result. The servants represented the Hebrew prophets who were killed for speaking God's truth; the Son, of course, was Jesus, who was killed for the same reason. Jesus' point was that the owner would certainly come in judgment upon the wicked tenants, including taking away their rights to the land, symbolizing the kingdom. The religious leaders clearly understood these parables and began looking for an opportunity to arrest Jesus (vs. 45-46).

Chapter twenty-two contains the third parable, the wedding banquet (vs. 1-14). Jesus compared the kingdom to a wedding banquet given by a king in honor of his son. However, the special guests the king invited refused the invitation due to their apathy (vs. 5). Like the tenants in the second parable (21:33-41), some of the invited guests even killed the king's servants. In this case, the king acted immediately, executing the ungrateful invitees and inviting every other person. Many who did not receive an initial invitation attended and enjoyed the banquet. In an interesting twist, Jesus included a guest who showed up without the proper attire, meaning he sneaked in rather than coming through the accepted entrance. This one was ejected from the banquet, representing all who try to come to God in ways other than through Jesus (John 14:6).

In response to these parables, the Pharisees (vs. 15-22, 34-40) and Sadducees (vs. 23-33) attempted to trick and trap Jesus in his own words (vs. 15) with three distinct attacks. First, the Pharisees used politics against him. If he supported paying the Roman tax, the masses would reject him as the Messiah sent to overthrow the Roman occupation. If he rejected the tax, Rome would certainly view him as inciting rebellion. He responded that they should keep things in proper priority, both to God and government.

Second, the Sadducees used <u>a hypothetical situation</u> against him. Due to a custom called "levirate marriage," a man could marry his widowed sister-in-law if she had not born the man's brother a son to continue his family name. In their hypothetical scenario, a woman did not bear a son for seven brothers, so in the resurrection, whose wife would she be? There are a lot of details we could get into with this, but Jesus cut to the center. They, he claimed, did not understand Scripture at all, so he simply told them that relationships in heaven will not match those in this life. Additionally, because they did not believe in the resurrection at all, Jesus proved from the Torah (the only part of the Bible they accepted) that God taught the resurrection by his use of the present tense verb when referring to dead people – "I AM THE GOD OF ABRAHAM," though he was long dead.

Third, the Pharisees used <u>theological nuance</u> against him. Because they believed in the sacredness of the whole law (613 commandments), they asked Jesus to pick the greatest one, meaning that the others would be less important. Again, his response was brilliant, proving their nearsightedness and narrow-mindedness. "Love God with your entire being" and "love your neighbor as yourself" summarize everything else in the law and the prophets. Not only are these individual commandments (like they asked), they are summary commands as well.

Following this barrage against him, Jesus responded with a short "stumper" of his own. The religious leaders knew that Messiah was to be the son of David (vs. 42), but they missed that he would be more than that. Jesus asked how, then, the great King David could call Messiah his "Lord" if he were just his son. They had no answer, and that stopped the public examination of the Lamb of God (vs. 46).

Chapter twenty-three contains Jesus' final public statement, immediately following the debates of chapters 21 and 22. This statement came in three parts. The first was a warning directed to the crowds against the teachings of "THE EXPERTS IN THE LAW AND THE PHARISEES" (vs. 2). The crowd had just witnessed their examination of Jesus and his teaching and observed how he responded and shut down the religious leaders. Jesus warned them that these false shepherds loved their positions but led people away from God rather than toward him (vs. 2-12).

The second part of Jesus' statement was directed toward the religious leaders themselves, who had just heard Jesus tell people to not follow them. In this section Jesus pronounced seven "WOES" on these religious leaders[7], because they had missed the Messiah and led people away from him. He excoriated them for keeping people out of the kingdom (vs. 13, 15) and twisting the Scriptures for their own gain (vs. 16-22), for focusing on the letter of the law but not the spirit (vs. 23-24) and putting on religious pretentions which were nothing but hypocrisy (vs. 25-28). Finally, he charged them with the murder of the saints and prophets (vs. 29-36). Even though they did not "pull the trigger" themselves, their attitudes and actions were the same as those who committed the murders. Additionally, Jesus foretold that they would indeed become murderers when they would slay his yet-to-come prophets (including the apostles).

The third part of his final public statement was both a cry and a prophecy (vs. 37-39). As Jesus wept over the holy city which had rejected him and would kill him in less than 48 hours, he prophesied that he would not return until Israel turned back to him and recognized him for who he truly is. This will finally happen at the end of the Tribulation, when Satan's plan to wipe out the Jewish nation will be proven impossible.

Chapters twenty-four and twenty-five contain the last of Jesus' major teachings, called the Olivet Discourse. As Jesus and the apostles left Jerusalem

---

7 Most Greek manuscripts, including the most significant ones, do not include verse 14, which some Bibles include as an eighth "woe".

on Wednesday evening, the men were pointing out how nicely the Temple remodel was coming along. Almost in passing, Jesus mentioned that the entire structure would be destroyed (vs. 1-2). This, naturally, lead to the apostles' questions: *When will this happen and how will we know it's time?* (vs. 3) In chapter 24, Jesus ignored their first question, *when*, but gave some details on the signs of his return.

First, they must know that many things "MUST HAPPEN" that will cause alarm but are not necessarily signs of his coming. These include an increase in natural disasters, regional and world wars, and false Messiahs (vs. 5-8) – things every generation has noticed since then. There will also be an increase in persecution against those who follow Jesus (vs. 9-14). While we can see these things happening even today, this will grow much worse in the end times, and Jesus said that these are not yet the signs of his return.

However, Jesus then gave a series of specific signs people in that day can watch for. The first sign will be "THE ABOMINATION OF DESOLATION" that Daniel had prophesied (vs. 15; Daniel 9:27).[8] Jesus warned the Jews to literally run for their lives when this happens (vs. 16-21), because this will set the stage for a series of persecutions and catastrophic events (vs. 22-28). The second major sign, occurring just before Jesus' return, will be the darkening of the celestial bodies (vs. 29), as prophesied by Isaiah and Joel. The third sign will be "THE SIGN OF THE SON OF MAN" (vs. 30). Whether this is a symbol or Jesus himself, the next thing the survivors will see will be "THE SON OF MAN ARRIVING ON THE CLOUDS OF HEAVEN" (vs. 30). His first act will be one of judging people on the earth (vs. 31-51).

There is much discussion regarding whether any or all the Olivet Discourse relates to the Church. Except for the generic events and persecutions Jesus mentioned in vs. 4-12 (which have happened in various degrees

---

8 Those who believe that Daniel's prophecy was completely fulfilled by Antiochus IV Epiphanes in the second century B.C. cannot explain why Jesus said it was still to come. Those who believe that the destruction of Jerusalem and the Temple in A.D. 70 are the fulfillment cannot explain what the "ABOMINATION OF DESOLATION" could refer to. A literal interpretation of Daniel 9 and 11 and Matthew 24 (along with Revelation) can lead only to the conclusion that this prophecy is still unfulfilled.

throughout the history of the Church), the clear detail and signs that Jesus gave are all related to the nation of Israel, not the Church. Some hold that the gatherings mentioned in verses 31 and 36-44 must refer to the Rapture of the Church. However, the clearest passage detailing the Rapture (1 Thessalonians 4:13-18) does not match up with the details Jesus gave here. In this case (as will be proved in chapter 25), the people gathered in this passage are taken away to various judgments on this earth; they do not "MEET THE LORD IN THE AIR" (1 Thessalonians 4:17) and return to heaven with him.

Chapter twenty-five continues the Olivet Discourse from chapter 24, specifically focusing on the judgments mentioned in 24:31, 36-51 that Jesus will commence following his return. To illustrate this, Jesus told the disciples two parables. The first was about ten virgins who were awaiting the return of the Bride and Groom (vs. 1-13). Those who insist on making this parable refer to the Rapture of the Church miss one crucial point. It is true that the Rapture will follow the pattern of a Jewish wedding ceremony, in that the groom would go to the bride's home to collect her and take her back to his home. This could happen at any moment, so the bride and her maidens were to always be watching for him to come. However, this arrival takes place in order for the groom to take his bride to the wedding. After the wedding, the couple would go away to consummate their union. The party could not happen until after their return. In the same parable, Luke 12:35-36 pointed out that they will be "WAITING FOR THEIR MASTER TO COME BACK FROM THE WEDDING CELEBRATION" not "come back for the wedding celebration." These virgins, then, must represent Israel waiting for Messiah to return and establish his new home in the Kingdom.

The second parable, frequently applied to the Church and the Judgment Seat of Christ (1 Corinthians 3:11-15; 2 Corinthians 5:10), is one of reward and judgment for those who will or will not serve God during Jesus' absence (vs. 14-30). Two points must be noted. First, the reward for faithful service will be entrance into the kingdom (vs. 21, 23). Application to the Church would mean that serving God is the basis of salvation and entrance to heaven, a teaching completely foreign to the salvation by grace found in the Scriptures. Second, the punishment for unfaithful service will be judgment in "THE OUTER DARKNESS" (vs. 30). Application to the Church would mean that not serving God means damnation, with no regard to one's faith. Again, this is contrary to the clear teaching of Scripture on salvation and condemnation.

Following the two parables, Jesus clarified <u>when</u> this judgment will take place, <u>who</u> will be judged, the <u>basis</u> for judgment, and the <u>results</u> of the judgment. It will take place "WHEN THE SON OF MAN COMES IN HIS GLORY... [AND SITS] ON HIS GLORIOUS THRONE" (vs. 31). This must be after the signs prophesied in 24:15-31. It will be "ALL THE NATIONS" (πάντα τὰ ἔθνη, *panta ta ethne*), a reference to Gentiles (not the Church), who will stand before him for judgment (vs. 32). They will be judged based on how they treated "THE LEAST OF THESE BROTHERS AND SISTERS OF MINE" (vs. 40, 45), a reference to the Jewish people during the time of Tribulation, not poor people generally. Finally, those who will treat them well will "INHERIT THE KINGDOM" and "ETERNAL LIFE" (vs. 34, 46), whereas those who do not treat them well will be sent "INTO THE ETERNAL FIRE" and "ETERNAL PUNISHMENT" (vs. 41, 46).

Those who apply this passage to the Church, insisting on a mission of social programs in the name of Jesus, badly miss the context and ignore the outcome of their interpretation. If this applied to the Church, salvation and damnation would be based solely on our social ministries, not the gospel. Under this interpretation, churches and Christians who boldly and clearly preach the gospel of Jesus are still condemned to eternal hell if they do not help the homeless, feed the hungry, and engage in prison ministry. While these things are good, they are not the primary mission of the Church and are certainly not the basis for salvation. They will, however, be the basis on which Gentiles who survive the Tribulation will or will not gain entrance to Jesus' kingdom.

Chapter twenty-six sets the stage for the rest of the book, including the climax of Jesus' ministry and mission. On Wednesday evening, following the Olivet Discourse, Jesus told his apostles again what was to come, this time with the actual timeline, even while the plans were taking place (vs. 1-5). That evening he had a meal with friends outside the Jerusalem city limits, when a woman poured expensive perfumed oil on his head. Though the apostles "BECAME INDIGNANT" about the perceived waste, Jesus saw it as the burial preparations he would not actually receive following his death (vs. 6-13; see Luke 23:56 – 24:1).

Between Jesus' final teachings and prophecy of his death, Judas Iscariot finally had enough. The "Messiah" he had invested the past several years into was apparently not who Judas thought he would be, and he thought Jesus should be revealed for the charlatan Judas thought he was. Knowing the religious leaders wanted to arrest Jesus, Judas knew he could find the perfect opportunity to make it happen (vs. 14-16).

On Thursday, Jesus had the apostles prepare for the Passover he would eat with them that evening. During the meal, Jesus revealed that it would be one of their own group who would betray him (vs. 17-25). Naturally, this disturbed the men, leading Peter at one point to claim his undying devotion to Jesus. Jesus responded with the famous prophecy of Peter's three denials (vs. 31-35). It was during the Passover meal that Jesus once again prophesied his death, using the elements of the bread and wine to represent his body and blood which he would give for all the people. He also mentioned that his death was necessary to fulfill the new covenant promised through the prophet Jeremiah (vs. 26-30).

Taking the eleven apostles (minus Judas) to Gethsemane, Jesus spent several hours there in prayer, submitting himself to the Father and preparing himself for the "CUP" of anguish he was about to endure (vs. 36-46). Knowing that Judas would lead the others to him there, Jesus willingly went to meet them (vs. 45-46). True to his word, Judas led Jesus' enemies directly to him, where they arrested him, as foretold by the prophets. Though some of the apostles tried to defend him, Jesus stopped them all and placed himself in the hands of those who would kill him. Shaken and terrified, every single one of his friends ran for their lives (vs. 47-56).

The final section of the chapter (vs. 57-68) briefly describes the mock trials Jesus suffered before the Sanhedrin, who used false testimony to find something against him. Finally, they condemned him to death for blasphemy, when he quoted from Psalm 110:1 and Daniel 7:13 claiming to be the Son of Man, who is God himself (vs. 63-65). While this was happening, Peter was outside fulfilling Jesus' prophecy of his denials (vs. 69-75).

Chapter twenty-seven opens early Friday morning, with the Jewish leaders bringing Jesus to Pilate. While Rome allowed the Jews to rule themselves for the most part, they could execute someone only for profaning the temple grounds. Other than for that reason, only Rome could execute people. So, although they had found Jesus guilty and wanted the death penalty, they needed Pilate to allow it (vs. 1-2).

In an interesting plot twist, Matthew revealed that Judas never intended for it to go this far. He wanted Jesus exposed as a false Messiah, but he did not understand the depth of hatred the Jewish leaders had for him. When he confronted them about it, and they did not budge, he threw his "finder's fee" back at them and committed suicide in regret for his actions. The leaders ended up buying the field where Judas killed himself, under his name, to be used "AS A BURIAL PLACE FOR FOREIGNERS" (vs. 3-10).

Matthew did not include all the events that happened Friday; others can be seen in the other gospels. In his plan to present Jesus as the true Messiah, Matthew included only those interviews with Pilate that reflected Jesus' true identity and his absolute perfection in preparation for what was about to happen. Like Isaiah 53:7 promised, Jesus stood silent before his accusers (vs. 11-14) and was condemned in the place of rebels (vs. 15-23; Isaiah 53:12). Turned over to the Roman crucifixion squad, Jesus was beaten and tortured, both physically and verbally (vs. 24-31; Isaiah 53:5). Finally, he was crucified alongside two criminals while passersby mocked and derided him (vs. 32-44; Isaiah 53:3-4, 12).

Though Jesus hung on the cross for six hours (9:00 a.m. to 3:00 p.m.), three of them were in supernatural darkness, while God placed humanity's sin on him (vs. 45-50; Isaiah 53:4-6, 10-11). After a final few statements, Jesus breathed his last, giving up his life for us (vs. 50). At that moment, two things took place showing the significance of Jesus' death. First, the curtain in the Temple separating the people from the Most Holy Place of God's presence was ripped, signifying that the way to God was now open (vs. 51). Second, graves were opened, showing that death no longer held power over mankind. Significantly, following Jesus' resurrection, "MANY SAINTS WHO HAD DIED WERE RAISED" (vs. 52-53).

Still fulfilling prophecy, Jesus was buried in a rich man's tomb (vs. 57-61; Isaiah 53:9). To prevent Jesus' followers from stealing his body and claiming the resurrection he had prophesied so many times, on Saturday morning the Jewish leaders requested that Pilate seal and place a guard at the tomb. This, they were sure, would end the Jesus nonsense for good (vs. 62-66).

Chapter twenty-eight, of course, is the greatest chapter in Matthew's account. Early Sunday morning, when the women went to the tomb to finish the burial preparation on Jesus' body, they found the grave open and empty and an angel with the great news of his resurrection, just as he had promised them (vs. 1-7). As if that were not enough, on their way to tell the disciples of their finding, they saw Jesus himself, who gave instructions that they were to meet him in Galilee (vs. 9-10).

Only Matthew includes the short account of how the Jewish leaders reacted to the resurrection (vs. 11-15), proving that they tried to cover up the true story, because they continued to reject Jesus as Messiah.

The final verses contain what has come to be known as the Great Commission, some of Jesus' final commands to the apostles (vs. 16-20). Because of his death and resurrection, "ALL AUTHORITY" has been granted to Jesus to build his Church, so he commissioned the apostles to "MAKE DISCIPLES OF ALL NATIONS." They were to do this by "BAPTIZING THEM" and "TEACHING THEM TO OBEY" Jesus' teachings. Knowing that hard times would come, he left them with the promise of his continued presence (via the Holy Spirit, John 14-16) throughout the entire coming age.

PASSION WEEK

In A.D. 33, Passover was Saturday, April 4, making it a "high Sabbath" (John 19:31).

Jesus died on Friday, April 3, the "day of preparation" when the Passover lambs were sacrificed (Matthew 27:62; Mark 15:42; Luke 23:54; John 19:31).

Therefore, the Last Supper, betrayal, and arrest were on Thursday evening, April 2.

Jewish days are calculated from 6:00pm to 6:00pm. Thus, Passover (and Sabbath) began Friday at 6:00pm.

Sunday

	Matthew	Mark	Luke	John
Healing of blind men in Jericho	20:29-34	10:46-52	18:35-43	
Meal with Zacchaeus in Jericho			19:1-10	
Parable of 10 minas			19:11-27	
Dinner in Bethany, anointed by Mary		14:3-9		12:1-11
Spent the night in Bethany/Mount of Olives			21:37	

Monday

	Matthew	Mark	Luke	John
Triumphal Entry	21:1-11	11:1-10	19:28-40	12:12-19
Went to the Temple to look and teach		11:11	21:37	
Spent the night in Bethany/Mount of Olives		11:11	21:37	

Tuesday

Cursed the fig tree	21:18-22	11:12-14		
Cleansed the Temple	21:12-13	11:15-18	19:45-45	
Teaching and healing	21:14-16		19:47; 21:37	
Spent the night in Bethany/Mount of Olives	21:17			

Wednesday

Jesus' authority challenged (priests, scribes, elders)	21:23-27	11:27-33	20:1-8	
Parables about authority (Jesus)	21:28 – 22:14	12:1-12	20:9-19	
Challenge: taxes (Pharisees)	22:15-22	12:13-17	20:20-26	
Challenge: marriage, resurrection (Sadducees)	22:23-33	12:18-27	20:27-40	
Challenge: greatest commandment (Pharisees)	22:34-40	12:28-34		
Challenge: Messiah's identity (Jesus)	22:41-46	12:35-37	20:41-44	
Woes and Warnings (Jesus)	23:1-36	12:38-40	20:45-47	
Widow's offering (Jesus)		12:41-44	21:1-4	
Olivet Discourse (Jesus)	24-25	13	21:5-36	
Judas' 1st meeting with chief priests	26:14-16	14:10-11	22:1-6	
Spent the night in Bethany/Mount of Olives			21:37	

Thursday

	Matthew	Mark	Luke	John
Preparation for the meal	26:17-19	14:12-16	22:7-13	
Meal (includes foot washing)	26:20-25	14:17-21	22:14-16	13:1-30
New Covenant announced	26:26-29	14:22-25	22:14-20	
Upper Room & Garden Discourse	26:31-35	14:27-31	22:21-38	13:31 – 16:33
Garden prayer	26:36-46	14:32-42	22:39-46	17:1 – 18:3

Late Th/Early Fri

	Matthew	Mark	Luke	John
Betrayal & Arrest (Thurs evening)	26:47-56	14:43-52	22:47-53	18:4-11
Trials before High Priest & Sanhedrin (overnight)	26:57-75	14:53-72	22:54-71	18:12-27
Judas' 2nd meeting with chief priests and suicide	27:3-10			
1st appearance before Pilate	27:1-2	15:1-5	23:1-5	18:28-32

Friday, 6:00am-6:00pm

	Matthew	Mark	Luke	John
Appearance before Herod, 1st beating and mocking			23:6-12	
2nd appearance before Pilate; Barabbas released	27:11-23	15:6-15	23:13-25	19:4-16
Scourging	27:24-31	15:16-20		
Crucifixion (9:00a-3:00p); death at 3:00p	27:32-56	15:21-41	23:26-49	19:16-37
Burial (3:00p-6:00p)	27:57-61	15:42-47	23:50-56	19:38-42

Saturday

Tomb sealed and guarded	27:62-66	

Sunday

Resurrection (pre-dawn)	28:1-10	16:1-8	24:1-12	20:1-9

Mark

The shortest of the four gospels by far, Mark has gained prominence in recent days, especially from modern higher critics. Beginning in the early 1800s, liberal scholars started to insist that Mark was written first (the Church historically acknowledged that Matthew held that distinction), around 60 A.D., and that Matthew and Luke both borrowed from Mark and other sources for their accounts. This position is so popular that it is generally assumed and unquestioned in many works. Part of the reason for this preference is Mark's emphasis on Jesus' actions rather than his theology – something liberal scholarship very much tends to stress and avoid, respectively.

It is true that Jesus' actions are the highlight of Mark. Much less time is given to his background and his teachings compared to the other gospels. Mark presents Jesus as a man of action, constantly on the move from one event to the next. Mark's use of εὐθύς (*euthus*, "immediately") is regularly noted in commentaries, as Jesus went "immediately" to his next place or miracle. (Mark contains 41 of the New Testament's 51 occurrences of the word, and it appears in all but three of his 16 chapters.)

Several of the Early Church Fathers (including Papias, Ignatius, and Eusebius) linked Mark with Peter, noting that Mark had become Peter's disciple and that he had recorded many of Peter's teachings and memories, albeit not necessarily in chronological order. This would certainly account for the personal influences found throughout the book, yet the sporadic nature of the selection of events. It also may explain why Mark alone would include the angel's command that the women should "TELL HIS DISCIPLES, EVEN PETER" (16:7) that Jesus had been raised.

It seems that Mark was writing to a Roman audience, who did not understand certain Jewish terms and traditions, so he had to explain them (see 3:17; 5:41; 7:3, 11, 19, 34; 15:22, 42). Additionally, Mark pointed out that Simon, who carried Jesus' cross, "WAS THE FATHER OF ALEXANDER AND RUFUS" (15:21). Later, in Romans 16:13, Paul greeted a Rufus in Rome. These are the only two occurrences of the name.

Chapter one entirely skips Jesus' early life. Instead, Mark introduced John the Baptizer as the promised messenger who would "PREPARE THE WAY FOR THE LORD" (vs. 3) and moved directly to the account of Jesus' baptism.

Mark's introductory note is interesting. He intended to not let Jesus' background overshadow his mission. This was common in Roman culture. The families and background of servants was unimportant; they just needed to do their jobs. By not including Jesus' family history, Mark put the emphasis on his identity as tied to his mission: "THE BEGINNING OF THE GOSPEL OF JESUS CHRIST, THE SON OF GOD."

Notice the lack of detail in Mark's account of Jesus baptism and temptation (vs. 9-12; four verses) compared to Matthew's (16 verses) and Luke's (15 verses). Mark's point was clear: John announced him, Satan tested him, then he went to work.

The rest of chapter one covers the same amount of time as Matthew 4-8. In these 32 verses, Jesus began his preaching ministry, began to call his disciples, and performed three individual miracles (casting out a demon, curing a fever, curing leprosy) and many others (vs. 34). Yet, in doing all of that, Mark recorded only about seven sentences of Jesus' actual speech.

Again, for Mark and his readers, Jesus' actions really did speak louder than his words. Mark's presentation also pointed out that, even early on, Jesus did not necessarily seek publicity and notoriety. Though that certainly came, he silenced the demons (vs. 25, 34), spent time alone (vs. 35), and preferred the rural villages (vs. 38, 45).

Chapter two continues the record of Jesus' early ministry and includes more teaching than chapter one. Jesus had chosen Capernaum as his ministry headquarters. After spending time in the rural villages, he returned there for some larger urban ministry. It was here, in the cities, that animosity first grew against him. In a demonstration of his deity, Jesus announced forgiveness on a paralytic (vs. 3-5). When the religious leaders pushed back against what they knew that meant (only God can forgive, vs. 7), Jesus used the healing miracle to authenticate his ability to forgive. This surprised the crowd of people, who turned to God in praise.

Building his group of followers, Jesus invited Levi (Matthew), a tax collector, to follow him, resulting in a dinner party at Levi's house. Naturally, Levi's friends were also tax collectors, and the religious leaders (whom Jesus had just embarrassed in the previous miracle) used the opportunity to begin their slander campaign against him. Jesus' response was that it was those very people who needed him the most (vs. 17).

The criticism by the religious leaders against Jesus continued, as Mark showed in the last two accounts. First, they questioned his loyalty to their tradition, because Jesus and his disciples did not fast when John's disciples and the Pharisees did (vs. 18). His response was that fasting often indicated mourning, something that was unnecessary in his presence. Truth is greater than preferred tradition. Second, they questioned his obedience to the Law, because Jesus' disciples picked wheat on a Sabbath day. He responded that the Law was never intended to keep hungry people from eating, and precedent, in fact, allowed for it. He further insisted that he knew God's intent when the Sabbath law was made, another declaration of his deity in the face of their interpretation of the Law. Truth is greater than personal theology.

Chapter three concludes the first half of Jesus' ministry and sets the reader up for the rest of the work Jesus would do leading to his death. Following the backdrop of picking wheat on the Sabbath, Jesus chose to heal a man on the Sabbath in a synagogue (vs. 1-6). The religious leaders had decided to use this as a litmus test, of sorts, to finally determine what they thought of Jesus. Knowing how hard their hearts were (vs. 5), Jesus healed the man, driving them to begin their plans to have him killed (vs. 6).

After continuing to preach and heal people (vs. 7-12), Jesus decided to expand his ministry. From the thousands of people who were following him, he chose only twelve "so THAT THEY WOULD BE WITH HIM" and multiply his ministry (vs. 14). Though Mark specifically noted only that they would "PREACH AND . . . CAST OUT DEMONS" (vs. 15), the other writers include other miracles as well. These twelve, including Judas Iscariot, would be his "APOSTLES."

Sometime after that (Mark does not say how long), Jesus returned "HOME" (probably to Capernaum, 2:1) and was greeted with full rejection from the religious leaders, not just the local ones but from Jerusalem as well (vs. 22). By calling him a pawn of Satan, they demonstrated they had taken sides against him and his ministry. Jesus responded that this attitude was unforgiveable, even into eternity (vs. 28-29). When his family tried to "rescue" him from the shame and disgrace they thought he was bringing on himself and them by engaging with the religious leaders in this way, Jesus began to drive home the point that spiritual family is more important than religious connections or standing or bloodlines. Those who do God's will are Jesus' closest family (vs. 31-35).

Chapter four contains one of the longest sections in Mark that is dedicated to Jesus' teaching, apart from Passion Week. Even then, except for the last few verses, chapter four contains just four parables and the explanation of the purpose of Jesus' parables. The purpose, first mentioned in Isaiah 6:9-10, was so that believers would receive new truths, while unbelievers would not be able to understand them, keeping them from heaping additional judgment upon themselves for rejecting it. From this point on, Jesus spoke in parables to the crowds but explained them to the disciples (vs. 10-12, 33-34).

First is the parable of the sower and the seed (vs. 1-9, 13-20). One of the few parables that Jesus explained in detail, he illustrated how the word is spread out to people, like seed is scattered in a field. People respond differently, depending on their life circumstances. From some, Satan steals it away immediately (see 2 Corinthians 4:4). Others receive it but quickly turn away because of personal persecution or other priorities. Some do receive the word, let it grow in them, and produce a varied harvest for God.

Second is the parable of the lamp (vs. 21-25), which illustrates that the things we have from God are not to be hidden away but rather used. Some rewards and blessings may be directly tied to the service people perform in obedience to God.

The third and fourth parables refer to the kingdom of God. In one, the kingdom is like sown seed, growing regularly, without the farmer understanding how (vs. 26-29). In the other, the kingdom is like a mustard seed. Even though it starts small, it grows into an enormous tree, offering refuge for all the birds around it (vs. 30-32).

The single non-parable in this chapter recounts one of many times Jesus demonstrated his authority over creation. When the disciples were stuck in a terrifying storm on the Sea of Galilee, they woke him from a nap in the back of the boat (vs. 35-41). Their fear for their safety caused them to doubt his care for them. When he calmed the storm, their fear changed to awe as they began to realize even more what his claims really meant.

Chapter five contains three events, all remarkable miracles that continued to prove Jesus' divine authority. The first took place in Gentile territory, outside of Israel, on the other side of the Sea of Galilee. When Jesus and his disciples reached the other side, they were immediately approached by a demon-possessed man, outcast from his community to live in the local graveyard (vs. 1-5).[9]

Upon seeing Jesus, the demon (through the man) immediately acknowledged his deity, falling before Jesus and begging to not be judged by him, because Jesus had ordered him out of the man (vs. 6-13). Verse 10 notes that the demon begged Jesus repeatedly to spare him, not just once. Mark gave a detail that does not show up in any other story: Jesus asked the demon his name. No explanation is given for this detail. However, the answer was astounding. There was not just one demon in him but thousands! A Roman legion could include up to 6,000 soldiers. Instead of premature banishment to the abyss, they asked that Jesus send them into a nearby herd of pigs, which he granted. The demons immediately destroyed the entire herd by running them over the cliff into the lake. When the people from the surrounding area heard what happened and saw the man in his right mind listening to Jesus, they were afraid and sent Jesus away (vs. 14-20). Jesus told the man to stay there as a witness to the power of God.

The second event occurred back in Israel. Jairus was a ruler in a local synagogue whose daughter was gravely ill (vs. 21-24). On their way to see the girl, an unexpected third event took place. A woman with a constant hemorrhage for twelve years approached Jesus (vs. 25-34), believing he could heal her. Apparently, more out of respect for his time rather than unbelief, she intended to touch him, be healed, and return home. However, Jesus knew that someone had been healed, so he stopped, turned to her, and blessed her.

Moving again toward Jairus' house, word came that the girl had died

---

9 The description of what the demon did to him is provides striking insight into the type of destruction the Enemy produces.

(vs. 35-43). Due to the change of circumstances and the growing rejection of his claims, Jesus limited the number of people who saw this miracle to only Jairus and his wife and Peter, James, and John. Once alone, Jesus took the girl's hand and called her back to life. To keep the story circulating that she had just fallen asleep (much like Jesus' perspective on Lazarus in John 11:11-13), Jesus ordered strict silence on the matter, and, in a touch of practicality, told the parents to feed their daughter.

Chapter six is the second-longest chapter in Mark, surpassed only by chapter fourteen, which records the night of Jesus betrayal and arrest. Having returned to Nazareth, Jesus preached in the synagogue on the Sabbath as was his custom (vs. 1-6). However, validating the adage, "Familiarity breeds contempt," his hometown neighbors rejected him, primarily because they had watched him grow up. This led Jesus to state what has become another proverbial saying: "A prophet is without honor in his own country." Mark made the interesting point that Jesus was in fact hindered from doing miracles here because of their unbelief.

Matthew recorded Jesus' sending of the twelve to preach, heal, and cast out demons earlier in the chronology than Mark did (vs. 7-13; Matthew 10). However, it is possible, and even likely, that he did this on more than one occasion. Jesus' powerful ministry caught the attention of Herod (vs. 14-29). It is somewhat humorous that God recorded Herod's superstitions; he thought John the Baptizer had been resurrected and was haunting him. This led to Mark recording the reason for John's death – he had repeatedly spoken out against Herod's illicit marriage to Herodias (his brother's wife), until she had had enough. Not unlike a politician today caught with a "hot mic," Herodias caught Herod making a drunken promise for anything her daughter wanted. Herodias had her request John's head, literally, on a silver platter.

Jesus knew the importance of rest after a period of intensive ministry, so when the Twelve returned from their latest itinerant tour, Jesus took them away for a break. However, the crowds would not stay away, so Jesus continued to teach them (vs. 30-34). After a long day of teaching, when the crowds did not leave on their own, Jesus tasked the disciples with feeding the crowd (vs. 35-44). By this time, they should have known to trust him for everything. Instead, they complained that it was impossible, so Jesus performed his greatest miracle (save the resurrection itself) – feeding possibly as many as 20,000 people with five small loaves of bread and two fish, with twelve full baskets left over.

Following this massive meal, Jesus personally sent the crowd away and sent the disciples across the lake, while he went up the mountain to pray, which was probably his intention when he took the disciples there for their retreat originally (vs. 45-52). As the Twelve fought against a supernatural storm, Jesus walked across the top of the water. Only Mark contains the humorous note that Jesus intended to walk right past them. Instead, he got into the boat with them, stopped the storm, and went to the other side with them. There he continued to heal those who sought him out (vs. 53-56).

Chapter seven puts a focus on ministry that Jesus did outside of Israel. Although much of his early ministry was dedicated to the Jewish people, Jesus did not neglect the Gentiles. In a sense, it could be said that the continued rejection that he received from the Jews drove him to Gentile ministry.

The first half of the chapter (vs. 1-23) reveals another encounter between Jesus and the religious leaders. What is significant is that, even though Jesus was still in Galilee, these religious leaders had come from Jerusalem, proving that the animosity against Jesus was expanding (vs. 1). The issue they had this time was that Jesus and his disciples did "NOT LIVE ACCORDING TO THE TRADITION OF THE ELDERS" (vs. 5). Although this was not part of the Mosaic Law from God, these traditions had been elevated by the religious leaders to nearly the same level as the Law. In their minds, to violate these traditions was a rejection of their authority as interpreters of the Law.

Jesus' response was two-fold. To the religious leaders, he called them out on their own hypocrisy, pointing out that they followed their traditions even when they directly contradicted God's given law (vs. 8-13). Following this, he also spoke to the crowds, warning them that true defilement came from their hearts, not necessarily what they touched or ate (vs. 14-15). He clarified this to his disciples when they were alone (vs. 17-23). For Jesus, the spiritual drives the physical, not the other way around.

Fresh from this attack by the religious leaders, Jesus moved outside of Israel into Tyre, where a woman approached him and asked him to heal her demon-possessed daughter (vs. 24-30). This led to a conversation in which Jesus seems harsh or rude to us. Rather, he was pushing her to see if her faith was in him or in his power. Her answer proved what he was looking for, and he healed her daughter immediately from a distance. Leaving Tyre, Jesus remained in Gentile territory, where some people brought him a deaf and mute man, whom Jesus healed (vs. 31-37).

A special note in chapter seven regards the several words and phrases that Mark felt the need to explain (vs. 3-4, 11, 19, 34). This points to an audience that was not familiar with Hebrew customs and language. See the introduction for more information on his intended readers.

Chapter eight is another compendium of several events, much like the first few chapters. Immediately following the miracles in Gentile territory in chapter seven, Jesus did another one. Much like the feeding of the five thousand Jews in chapter six, Jesus provided lunch for four thousand this time (vs. 1-10). He had hoped his disciples would remember his power from before and believe in him, but they still doubted his ability to feed that many people. Although the events are similar, and some may confuse them, the location, number of people, and amount of initial food are different from the previous feeding. Additionally, when Jesus confronted the disciples about their unbelief, he referred to the two feedings as separate events (vs. 14-21).

The disciples were not the only ones who still did not believe. Mark included a short account of some Pharisees who claimed they would not believe without another sign (vs. 11-12). Even though Mark did not often include certain details, he did note that Jesus was becoming exasperated with the constant unbelief. In this case, he sighed "DEEPLY IN HIS SPIRIT" when he refused to do any more "TRICKS" for their amusement. This confrontation led to yet another trip across the lake (vs. 13).

Firmly back in Israel, Jesus was approached by people with a blind man. In a similar way to the deaf/mute in 7:33, Jesus chose to heal this man privately instead of in the middle of the crowd (vs. 22-25). For a reason that is never given, Jesus healed this man in two steps rather than just one, the way he normally did. After the first step, the man could see shapes but could not make out the detail. Only after the second step was he healed completely.

Jesus, then, took the disciples to a remote area for a period of intense teaching. He needed to begin preparing them for what was to come with respect to his death and resurrection (vs. 31). Before he did this, though, he wanted to be sure his disciples were clear on his identity and mission (vs. 27-30), so he asked them who people thought he was. Following their responses, he asked for their opinion. Famously, Peter replied, "YOU ARE THE CHRIST." This apparently caused Peter to think that he had a new level of relationship with Jesus, because when Jesus spoke of his impending death, Peter attempted to rebuke him (vs. 32). Instead, Jesus had to rebuke Peter for acting like the devil himself – saying all the right words without the core belief supporting them (vs. 33). If Jesus really was the Christ, Peter was standing against God.

The final section focuses on Jesus' call for more followers (vs. 34-38). More than just walking around with him, a true follower must be willing to give up anything which interferes with Jesus as his top priority.

Chapter nine begins with one of the few cases in which Mark notes a specific time. In this case, it was "SIX DAYS LATER," after Jesus' teaching on truly following him, that he allowed Peter, James, and John to see something they would never forget (vs. 2-13). Although John's brother, James, never wrote any recorded Scripture, seeing Jesus radiating his divine glory in the Transfiguration most certainly affected these three men in a significant way. Both Peter and John later wrote of their experience as a transformational event (2 Peter 1:16-18; John 1:14; 1 John 1:1-4). They witnessed Jesus talking with Moses and Elijah (how did they recognize them?), which must have been exciting. Most importantly, though, they heard the voice of God himself. It was one thing for Peter to declare, "You are the Christ"; it was another matter completely to hear the Father say, "THIS IS MY SON!"

While Jesus and the other three were on the mountain, a man had approached the remaining nine disciples with his demon-possessed son, hoping they could heal him, but they could not (vs. 14-29). Mark is the only of the Synoptic writers to mention that this had caused the disciples to get into an argument with "EXPERTS IN THE LAW" (vs. 14). It is easy to speculate that the religious leaders had used this as an example to prove that Jesus and his disciples were not as powerful as they claimed. When Jesus came, he chided the man for his faltering belief, but he compassionately healed the boy immediately. When the disciples asked about their inability to do it, Jesus told them that only prayer could drive out this kind of demon. This provides a little insight into the hierarchy of the demons and a reminder that God's work requires God's power.

After this Jesus told the disciples again that he would be killed and resurrected, but they did not understand (vs. 30-32). Instead, the recent events of Peter's declaration of faith, the Transfiguration, and the inability of the nine to cast out the demon led the disciples into a quiet argument about who was the greatest among them (vs. 33-37). When Jesus called them out on it, he reminded them that being great comes with humility and service and, most importantly, our connection to Jesus. In response, John pointed out that some people were using Jesus' name for their own ministry instead of his (vs. 38-41). Jesus noted that one cannot serve in Jesus' name without genuineness for long. Paul once noted that he did not care why Jesus was being preached, as long as it was the true gospel message (Philippians 1:12-18). However, those who lead people away from Christ, especially young people, will receive harsh judgment (vs. 42-50).

Chapter ten contains a series of final encounters and teachings that Mark considered important leading up to Jesus' entry into Jerusalem. Although Mark recorded that Jesus was teaching the crowds, he did not say what the topic was. However, since the Pharisees asked, "Is it lawful for a man to divorce his wife?", it is possible that Jesus was teaching about marriage (vs. 1-12). Jesus countered their trap with the simple teaching of Scripture, that divorce was a divine concession, but God's plan is always a permanent union between a man and woman. Adultery was the only legitimate grounds for divorce Jesus gave that still fit within the Mosaic Law.

Later, a man came to Jesus; Mark is the only writer to note that he was running (vs. 17-22). Although he was very careful to obey the Law, he knew that there must be something more. His question about eternal life was not about salvation in the Christian sense; he wanted to be sure that he was good enough to enter Messiah's kingdom (see Matthew 5:20). Knowing the man's heart, Jesus revealed that his money was his god, and that he would not part with it, even to get into the kingdom. Rather than seeing wealth as an automatic indication of God's favor, Jesus noted that it is difficult for the wealthy to enter God's kingdom, because money and God require exclusive allegiance (Matthew 6:24). Peter must have thought that they would receive special reward for giving up their possessions to follow Jesus (vs. 28-31), but if that was the basic expectation, what would they gain? Jesus assured him that they would gain far more following him than they could ever give up.

Following another prophecy of his own death and resurrection (vs.

32-34), James and John approached Jesus to make a specific request about their kingdom inheritance; namely, they wanted the positions of power right next to him (vs. 35-45). Although this angered the other disciples, Jesus was more concerned with their lack of understanding of the gravity of the situation. Promising him they could handle anything they faced, they did not expect Jesus' answer. Yes, they would face great suffering, but he could not promise them anything in the kingdom beyond what he had told them previously (Matthew 19:28). This led to yet another discussion on the link between greatness and service.

As his final miracle, literally on his way to present himself in Jerusalem, Jesus healed a blind beggar identified as Bartimaeus (vs. 46-52). He had obviously been waiting for Jesus to come that way again and would not accept the crowd's rejection until he could meet Jesus personally. When Jesus demanded that they let him come, Bartimaeus' request was simple: "RABBI, LET ME SEE AGAIN." This simple faith was enough for Jesus. He healed him immediately, and Bartimaeus followed Jesus into Jerusalem.

Chapter eleven begins the final section of Mark's writing, with the last six chapters being devoted to Jesus' Passion Week. To fulfill Zechariah 9:9, Jesus had two disciples procure an unbroken colt that he would ride into Jerusalem to present himself to Israel as her rightful King Messiah (vs. 1-11). The crowd following him from Jericho (10:52) and Bethany (vs. 1; the home of Lazarus, John 11:1) created a little parade, putting coats and branches on the road for him, shouting "HOSANNA!" (Psalm 118:25-26) to announce his arrival.

Mark recorded several more events from Monday and Tuesday of that week – Jesus' actions in chapter eleven and his teachings in chapter twelve. Jesus stayed outside of Jerusalem in Bethany each evening, away from the jurisdiction of the Jewish leaders. Leaving Bethany one morning, Jesus cursed a fig tree for not having even the early fruit (vs. 12-14). The next day he used that as an illustration for the disciples that they should "HAVE FAITH IN GOD," because he delights to answer the prayers of those who believe.

Jesus also used his first day in the Temple to clean it a second time (vs. 15-19; see John 2:14-22). This riled the anger of the "CHIEF PRIESTS AND EXPERTS IN THE LAW," who began to plan his assassination without stirring up the crowds who loved to hear him. When they tried to confront him verbally, demanding to know who authorized Jesus to teach and preach, he twisted it around back on them, asking who they thought authorized John the Baptizer. Because there was no answer that would please the crowd, they simply refused, opening the way for Jesus to do the same.

Chapter twelve contains six separate teachings that Jesus gave in the Temple. Most of these were in response to direct challenges from the religious leaders. In the parable of the tenants (vs. 1-12), Jesus revealed that the religious leaders were nothing more than tenants that God had allowed to work with his people. However, whenever he sent his own men (the prophets), they beat or killed them. Finally, the landowner sent his own son, whom they also killed, another of Jesus' clear claims of deity and predictions of his own death at their hands.

The Pharisees tried to trap Jesus into either supporting or publicly rebelling against the Roman government by asking him about the required taxes to Rome (vs. 13-17). He responded with the famous saying, "GIVE TO CAESAR THE THINGS THAT ARE CAESAR'S, AND TO GOD THE THINGS THAT ARE GOD'S." Not only did this shut down their trick question, it certainly included the poignant implication that they were more focused on Rome's will than God's.

With the Pharisees stopped for the moment, the Sadducees tried their hand against Jesus (vs. 18-27). Creating a hypothetical situation in which a woman legitimately married seven brothers in succession, according to the levirate law to provide an heir for one's brother, they asked which one of the seven would be her husband in the afterlife. Jesus started by telling them that relationships in the afterlife, including marriage, are not like this life, demonstrating that he personally knew about it. He also took the opportunity to correct their theology about the resurrection. They did not even believe in an afterlife (vs. 28), but Jesus reminded them that God "IS NOT GOD OF THE DEAD BUT OF THE LIVING."

After this an expert in the law tried to catch Jesus by asking him the greatest commandment of the entire Law (vs. 28-34). Jesus again showed his superior understanding and authority by demonstrating how God structured the Law in a hierarchical fashion, with two laws summarizing the rest. Who could argue that anything was more important than loving God with one's entire being? In this case, the man was open to Jesus' teaching, causing Jesus to note how close he was to true faith.

With all the questions stopped (vs. 34), Jesus made two final comments to the crowds. First, he proved from Scripture that even David knew that the Messiah, the son of David, would be greater than himself (vs. 35-37). Second, he warned the crowds about the hypocrites who taught them the law (vs. 38-40). Although they looked good on the outside, they were concerned only with themselves, and they would be punished by God. As a kind of summary of his final teachings over the recent days, Jesus pointed his disciples to a widow who gave almost nothing into the offering box (vs. 41-44). No matter how anyone else viewed it, Jesus saw that she gave everything to God, compared to the small percentages the other gave. This, he noted, was exactly the kind of heart God wants – someone who will obey God no matter the personal cost.

Chapter thirteen contains Mark's version of the Olivet Discourse, Jesus' response to the disciples' question about the end times. The discussion was precipitated by the disciples' admiration of the Temple grounds (vs. 1-4). Jesus responded that the whole thing would be torn down, so they asked when it would happen and how they would know it was coming.

Interestingly, Jesus began his response with the warning to not be tricked when several people would claim to have revelation from God or even that they themselves were Messiah. Jesus also noted that wars and natural disasters are not signs of his return (vs. 5-8). Instead, Jesus turned to prophecy that was already given. While there would certainly be time of persecution before then, the key event to watch for will be the "ABOMINA-TION OF DESOLATION" that Daniel prophesied (vs. 9-23). Mark's note, "LET THE READER UNDERSTAND," in verse fourteen shows that he was not going to comment on or explain this teaching as he had done previously in this book. It is up to the reader to study this and understand it. Jesus promised that those days will be filled with unprecedented persecution of the Jews, so much so that all would be killed if God were not controlling the situation.

The actual sign of his coming will be visible in the sky to all the earth at the moment of his return (vs. 24-27). When he comes, it will be in power and glory and judgment. Jesus promised that the generation which will see these signs will see the coming itself. This should be a warning to all those who teach that these signs have been going on for centuries, because Jesus said they would come quickly, in one generation. Jesus said that Israel should not allow herself to "FALL ASLEEP" waiting for his return (vs. 32-37). When those signs begin, they need to understand them and prepare themselves to meet him.

Chapter fourteen is the longest chapter in Mark and primarily covers Jesus' Passover evening with his disciples. In verses 3-9 Mark recorded the incident when Jesus was anointed with expensive oil. John notes that it was his friend, Mary, who did it before Jesus' entry into Jerusalem (John 12:1-8). Mark placed it here to show the connection with Judas finally being fed up enough with Jesus to betray him (vs. 10-11).

Verses 12-21 tell of Jesus' final Passover meal. Jesus' foreknowledge of the details of that night is shown in a simple, yet powerful, way – the man, the jar of water, the large room. Whatever was going to happen that night, Jesus made sure his disciples knew that he was in control of the whole event. That control continued throughout the evening as Jesus declared that he was about to be betrayed, that the culprit was sitting at the table with him, and that he knew who it was.

After the Passover meal, Jesus declared that his blood was the blood that would fulfill the covenant, when it was "POURED OUT FOR MANY" (vs. 22-31). Leaving the Upper Room, Jesus made three more predictions: first, that they would all scatter when he was struck down; second, that he would meet them in Galilee after rising again; and third, that Peter would deny him three times.

Coming "TO A PLACE CALLED GETHSEMANE" Jesus asked the Eleven to wait for him while he prayed, but that they should remain alert (vs. 32-42). After some time, possibly a full "HOUR," Jesus returned to find them sleeping and chided them. This time he told them that they, too, should pray, but they fell asleep again. After the third time of the same thing, it was time to go. Judas arrived with a mob of Temple soldiers, backed with the authority of the religious leaders (vs. 43-52). When they tried to arrest Jesus, there was a brief struggle. Mark did not name Peter as the aggressor, possibly out of respect for Peter as his mentor. Just as Jesus had said, "ALL THE DISCIPLES LEFT HIM AND FLED." Only Mark notes the young man who, when they tried to arrest him, "RAN OFF NAKED, LEAVING HIS LINEN CLOTH BEHIND." Many scholars think this was a reference to Mark himself, acknowledging his own cowardice as well.

For the rest of the night Jesus was tried in the Jewish court (vs. 53-65). The fact that "THEY DID NOT FIND ANYTHING" proving him guilty of death did not stop them. They were willing to convict him on false testimony that even the witnesses could not agree on. Finally, the high priest asked Jesus the one question he would not ignore: "ARE YOU THE CHRIST, THE SON OF

THE BLESSED ONE?" Jesus answered with the very name of God himself, "I AM," and then quoted from both Psalm 110 and Daniel 7, two of the clearest Messianic passages in the Hebrew text. That was all they needed to condemn him to death for blasphemy. During the trial, Peter was in the courtyard outside of the very building in which Jesus was being tried (vs. 66-72). As Jesus claimed his true identity, Peter denied any association with Jesus, even swearing that he had never met him. Then the rooster crowed.

Chapter fifteen begins "EARLY IN THE MORNING" on Friday (vs. 1-5). The Jewish leaders had done all they could do. Rome allowed them to carry out any kind of punishment they wanted against their own people, except for the death penalty. Only the Roman governor could do that. Because of the Passover that day and the Sabbath the next, they had no time to lose. Right after daybreak, they took Jesus to Pilate to have him executed.

Pilate had made it a policy to release one prisoner at Passover (vs. 6-20), and he had in custody Barabbas, a revolutionary and murderer. He thought the people would certainly rather have Jesus released than Barabbas, so that was the choice he gave them. Pilate also had personal issues with the Jewish leaders, so he thought he could use this to take a jab at them (vs. 10). He did not expect that they would be able to incite the whole crowd to push against Jesus. Even though Pilate could find nothing wrong with him, he capitulated to their demands, released Barabbas, and handed Jesus over to the crucifixion guard. After a torturous flogging, the soldiers took Jesus inside where they continued to beat and mock him, placing a robe on his shredded back that they would later rip off again.

On the route to the crucifixion site, they pressed into service a traveler named Simon to carry Jesus' cross (vs. 21-32). As noted in the introduction, only Mark records the names of Simon's sons, Alexander and Rufus. Rufus is later addressed by name by Paul in Romans 16:13. Reaching Golgotha, they offered Jesus a numbing agent, which he refused, then nailed him to the cross and hoisted him up. In fulfillment of Psalm 22:18, they threw dice to divide his personal effects. Mark noted that "IT WAS NINE O'CLOCK IN THE MORNING WHEN THEY CRUCIFIED HIM," meaning that everything that happened with Pilate (and Herod; Luke 23:6-12) took place in a matter of only about three hours that morning. For three hours Jesus hung there, exposed and suffocating, while people walked by, shaking their heads and mocking, along with the mercenaries who were being crucified at the same time.

At noon, a supernatural darkness covered everything and lasted for three more hours (vs. 33-41). Mark recorded only one of Jesus' famous last statements, the quote from Psalm 22:1, "MY GOD, MY GOD, WHY HAVE YOU FORSAKEN ME?" Thinking he would hang there for a while longer yet, they offered him sour wine again, but it was time. He cried a final loud word and died. At that moment, the curtain in the temple hiding the Most Holy Place was torn from the top to the bottom, a feat humanly impossible. Having watched all the events of the day, the centurion in charge realized that Jesus was completely different from anyone he had crucified before. Mark noted that several women who followed Jesus were watching from a distance, but he did not mention any of the other disciples.

With the beginning of Sabbath only hours away (vs. 42-47), there was not much time to take care of the body. Joseph of Arimathea, who was a member of the council who had just condemned Jesus, asked Pilate for Jesus' body in order to bury it. With permission, they took down the body, wrapped it quickly, and put it in Joseph's own tomb, closing it with a large stone.

Chapter sixteen requires some examination. Due to a series of variants between Greek manuscripts, this chapter could end with verse eight, verse eight plus a closing tag, or include all twenty verses. Most conservative scholarship agrees that verses 9-20 were not included in Mark's original writing. This causes concern for some, though, because, while the first eight verses do record Jesus' resurrection and the angelic appearance, none of the detail from the other gospels is included, and verse eight ends in fear, not what the resurrection was meant to convey.

However, that is not to say that the other verses are not authentic. The writing style does not match the rest of Mark, but it is possible that Mark wrote the ending later. This would account for some manuscripts having the ending. However, another explanation is possible as well. It may be that someone, with or without Mark's approval, compiled a few "good" events to finish the story with a happier ending.

Although the final verses were almost certainly not written at the same time as the rest of the book, and it is impossible to know for sure if they are authentic, a quick look over them reveals nothing that contradicts the rest of Scripture. Verses 9-11 record the unbelief of the disciples upon receiving word of Jesus' resurrection, as attested in the other gospels. Verses 12-14 match Luke's account (24:13-43) of Jesus' appearance on the road to Emmaus and his subsequent appearance to the Eleven. The commission in verse 15 is comparable to Matthew 28:19. Verses 19-20 record his ascension and the disciples' obedience in preaching the gospel.

Only verses 16-18 are specifically unaccounted for, and they have caused a great deal of debate over the centuries. However, if we approach them in their context, without the need to build entire doctrines out of them, they still do not contradict clear Scripture. In verse 16 it sounds as if baptism is necessary for salvation along with belief. However, even the verse itself singles out faith alone in the second half. Additionally, the apostles preached the importance of baptism alongside salvation (though not *for* salvation) throughout the early years of the Church, especially to the Jewish people. A comparison of Acts 2:38-41 with Mark 16:16 could show Peter's influence on the later addition.

Even verses 17-18 do not contradict other revealed Scripture. The fact that we do not have record of Jesus saying these things elsewhere does not mean that he did not. In fact, in the Upper Room he told the Eleven that they would continue to perform miracles (John 14:12), and throughout the Apostolic Age of the Church, some people did do miracles under the direction of the apostles. Although these verses should not be used to say that these miracles would continue indefinitely, it is true that they did happen for several decades.

The final point of note in this chapter is the singular mention of one apostle, Peter (vs. 7). Mark alone records the angel saying, "Go, TELL HIS DISCIPLES, EVEN PETER." It is impossible to know if the women told him this privately, but Peter certainly held dearly the knowledge that Jesus called him back by name. That the Holy Spirit allowed Peter's apprentice, Mark, to record this forever was an act of extraordinary grace.

Luke

The third gospel was written by "Luke the physician" (Colossians 4:14). It is the first volume of the two-part history he wrote for Theophilus (Luke 1:1-4; Acts 1:1-2), who was likely a Roman official or possibly even Luke's publishing underwriter. Luke stated his goal was to provide a clear, well-researched (although not necessarily strictly chronological) account of Jesus ministry (Luke) and the beginning of the Church (Acts).

Whether it was intentional or not, Luke's account places a heavy emphasis on Jesus' *humanity*. From the otherwise unknown details of Jesus' birth and boyhood to specific names, dates, and locations, Luke provides a unique view of the finiteness of the infinite, yet incarnate, Son of God. Several parables and miracles exclusive to Luke offer insight into Jesus' humanity – especially his compassion toward fellow humans. The parables of the prodigal son and the Good Samaritan, the raising of the widow's dead son, and Jesus' meal with Zacchaeus all reveal a man full of great love and sympathy. **In Luke, we are invited to embrace God in the flesh.**

Chapter one introduces a series of pairs: two birth announcements, two mothers, two sons, two hymns of praise. The differences, though, are as important as the similarities: two adults long past child-bearing years and an unmarried, virgin teenage girl; one announcement received with skepticism, the other in pure faith.

In addition to Jesus' humanity, Luke pointed to the purpose of his coming immediately – Jesus was to be Israel's long-awaited Messiah-Deliverer. Gabriel told Zechariah that his son, John, would fulfill Malachi's prophecy of Messiah's predecessor, pointing people to Jesus (Malachi 3:1; 4:5-6). He told Mary that Jesus would fulfill God's promise to David that his royal dynasty would never end (2 Samuel 7:8-16). One day Jesus will sit on David's throne in Jerusalem forever (Luke 1:31-33). In their songs of praise, both Mary and Zechariah focused on the deliverance of Israel as promised throughout the Hebrew Scriptures. Allusions to several psalms are prominent throughout their songs.

Chapter two is bookended with two well-known (but unique to Luke) stories of Jesus' early life – his birth in Bethlehem and his visit to the Temple at twelve years old. Unlike Matthew, Luke went into great detail from the human perspective of Jesus' birth. The 70-mile trip from Nazareth to Bethlehem was at the demand of the human emperor, Caesar Augustus. Based on historical records, this was probably in the winter of 5 B.C. or spring of 4 B.C.[10] Rather than an "inn" in the Western sense, Joseph and Mary probably stayed in the courtyard stable of an extended relative (since their families both traced back to Bethlehem). The use of the manger or feeding trough was a result of the flood of people crowding the little village. Once the crowds moved back to their respective homes, there was nothing to keep the new little family from moving into the house (see the notes on Matthew 2). Although prompted by the angelic announcement, the shepherds' visit set the stage for Jesus' association with people of all classes and statuses. (Shepherds were often treated with contempt as low-class workers.)

---

10 Harold Hoehner gives a thorough treatment of the dates for John's and Jesus' births, ministries, and deaths in his book, *Chronological Aspects of the Life of Christ* (Zondervan, 1977). All dates offered here are based on Hoehner's research and conclusions.

The rest of chapter two continues the emphasis on the requirements placed on Jesus, the human. As a doctor, Luke was especially interested in the fact that Jesus was circumcised on the eighth day, in perfect accordance with the Law of Moses. Luke alone recorded that Mary obeyed the law of purification for forty days after Jesus' birth. Tying directly back to the deliverance theme of chapter one, Luke also recorded two special people who were blessed to have seen the young Messiah. While in the Temple for Mary's purification sacrifice, Simeon and Anna approached the young family, pronouncing blessings on them and praise to God for the arrival of Israel's Deliverer.

Luke concluded the detail of Jesus' early life showing two acts of submission to his human parents. Moses' law required that all Jewish men visit Jerusalem at specific times of the year. Luke pointed out that when Jesus was twelve years old, he accompanied his parents to Jerusalem for Passover. If he had already undergone the manhood ritual of the time, Jesus would have been required to attend the feast. Thus, he was obedient to the law from the very beginning. After losing track of him for three days, his parents were naturally upset that he had not stayed with them, although he had been safe with the rabbis in the Temple. In true rabbinic fashion, Jesus was asking pointed questions; in essence, he showed himself as their teacher, especially when they had no response to his probing. Luke pointed out that Jesus voluntarily submitted himself to his parents' authority and obediently returned home with them (2:51). The chapter concludes with a statement that Jesus grew physically like any other boy his age, but that he also grew in wisdom and favor with God and people.

Chapter three continues Luke's parallel between John and Jesus. In the first two chapters, we find their angelic announcements, followed by their births, circumcisions and namings, and a brief account of their boyhoods. John's story always came first, then Jesus'. Now, in chapter three, we find the beginning of their respective ministries. Again, Luke continued his pattern telling of John first, then Jesus.

Unlike the other writers, Luke offered a couple of broad time frames to identify the beginning of their ministries. John began before Jesus since Jesus had John baptize him and went into the wilderness for forty days (chapter four) before officially beginning to preach. Thus, Luke dated John's ministry (3:1-3) but only mentioned Jesus' approximate age (3:23). Luke used the timelines of six rulers to narrow down the year: Tiberius Caesar, Pontius Pilate, Herod, Philip, Lysanias, and Annas/Caiaphas (3:1-2), though only "THE FIFTEENTH YEAR OF TIBERIUS CAESAR" is precise. John began to minister at some point in A.D. 29 and baptized Jesus later that year, probably during the summer or fall, when Jesus would have been 32 years old. "ABOUT 30 YEARS OLD" (3:23) is an accurate approximation, not an exact age, as many have understood it.[11]

As Malachi prophesied (4:5-6) and Gabriel promised (Luke 1:16-17), John's message had one main theme: *Messiah is coming so prepare your hearts.* Baptism was (and still is) a frequently-used method to identify oneself with a prophet's or teacher's message, so John baptized many people who repented of their sin because of Messiah's imminent arrival. It is interesting that one of the natural results of their clean hearts was the desire to do good works. John did not suggest or teach good works in place of repentance for sin but as further proof of repentance. Baptism is a single event, but good works are to be a believer's lifestyle.

Luke ended this section with what seems to be an unimportant afterthought. Matthew began his story with Jesus' heritage. Why would Luke tuck it away after his baptism? There are at least two reasons. First, whereas Matthew focused on Jesus' Jewish and royal line (promoting his connection to Abraham and David), Luke focused on his human line, which came solely

---

11 Jesus' first Passover after his baptism, recorded in John 2:12-25, would have been in the spring of A.D. 30, following his 33rd birthday.

through Mary. Although Mary is not named here, this is her family tree. Joseph became "THE SON OF HELI" (or "Eli") by marrying Heli's daughter; Joseph's biological father was Jacob (Matthew 1:16). Second, Luke traced Jesus' line all the way back to Adam, the direct creation of God, to encompass the entire human race. This emphasizes that Jesus was *more than just Jewish*. Jesus' temptations, ministry, and sufferings would all affect him to the core of his humanity, and his work would be for all humans, not just the Jews. As we will see, Gentiles will receive much more attention in Luke than the other gospels, and Jesus' full humanity – especially his weaknesses and sympathies – will be on full display. Luke placed the genealogy precisely at this point to remind us that Jesus was as human as everyone he came to save.

Chapter four picks up Luke's narrative following Jesus' human genealogy. As in Matthew 4, Luke 4 notes that, immediately after his baptism, the Holy Spirit led Jesus into the wilderness to be tempted by Satan himself. Whereas Matthew's account almost makes it seem as if Jesus suffered three temptations after 40 days of fasting, Luke clarified that Satan barraged Jesus throughout those 40 days, culminating with the big three temptations that are detailed. Jesus responded to each temptation by quoting the Hebrew Scriptures (all from Deuteronomy). Decades later Paul wrote that it is the spoken Word of God that serves as "THE SWORD OF THE SPIRIT" for us, too (Ephesians 6:17).[12] In our spiritual battles, it is imperative we can quote Scripture. At the end of Jesus' temptations, Luke noted that the devil was not done; he just waited for a better opportunity to strike again (4:13). He would certainly continue his attack throughout Jesus' ministry, an encouraging thought to we who suffer temptation every day as well.

The Holy Spirit is more prominent in Luke than the other Gospels. He has already been mentioned nine times by 4:13. This points to Luke's

---

12 The Greek term for "word" here is ῥῆμα (*rhema*), which refers specifically to spoken words as opposed to written words.

emphasis on Jesus' humanity. Jesus lived his life in total submission to the Holy Spirit's leading and ministered in the Spirit's power, just as the New Testament calls Christians to do. Following his temptation, Jesus moved back to his home region "IN THE POWER OF THE SPIRIT" (4:14) and began his itinerant preaching and teaching. One Sabbath morning he attended synagogue in Nazareth, as normal, and read from Isaiah 61:1-2a, publicly claiming to be the Spirit-anointed Messiah. In response to the disbelief and condescension from his fellow Nazarenes, Jesus cited two great stories from the Jewish Scriptures, both about the salvation of Gentiles. Those listening were greatly offended and tried to throw Jesus off a cliff. His life was miraculously spared.

From that point, Jesus' headquartered his Galilean ministry in Capernaum on the Sea of Galilee. From this central location, he announced the coming of his Messianic Kingdom and proved his claim with the miracles that the prophets said Messiah would do. (Naturally, Doctor Luke was particularly interested in the *healing* miracles.) Jesus spent a year in the northern part of Israel and the surrounding Gentile regions, offering himself as their promised Deliverer.

Chapter five continues Luke's account of Jesus' first year, in Galilee, with a specific focus on four types of ministry – calling, healing, forgiving, and teaching. In each of these, we find a profound sense of Jesus' compassion. First, Luke recorded Jesus' calling of some of his early disciples (vs. 1-11). Using a boat to give him some space (and possibly amplify his voice with the water), Jesus was teaching the crowds on the Capernaum beaches. Knowing that the fishermen had caught nothing overnight, he miraculously provided them with a large haul. This miracle served to provide for them financially and to prove his identity to them (vs. 8). They became convinced that he was worth following.

Second, Jesus healed a man "WHO WAS COVERED WITH LEPROSY" (a doctor's notation). The preliminary discussion was about Jesus' willingness to do so, which he was. The man's natural response was to show and tell everyone he knew, but Jesus required that he follow the Mosaic Law, because he was still considered unclean until certified by a priest that he was not. Verse 16 adds another aspect to Jesus' humanity. In addition to showing Jesus' total reliance upon the Holy Spirit, Luke emphasized that Jesus also depended on prayer to fulfill his ministry.

Third, in what is usually considered a healing miracle, Jesus used the opportunity to <u>forgive</u> a man's sins. The healing itself was a secondary act meant to demonstrate who Jesus was. Miracles always supported the message (vs. 26). Finally, Luke recorded a specific <u>teaching</u> moment, which showed Jesus' human compassion for the most marginalized. Even as a doctor, Luke knew that Jesus was concerned for more than just people's physical health, and Jesus' statement he was the physician for the spiritually sick (vs. 31-32) must have been special to Luke. When confronted by the religious legalists, who condemned him for his disciples' actions, Jesus used the opportunity to identify himself as the long-awaited one (using a bridegroom as an example). He also used a short parable to point out that did not come to offer simple additions to their old way but rather to offer a new and better way. However, he already knew that many would reject him because they were comfortable with their old way of life (vs. 39). What a great reminder to follow Jesus, even when it becomes uncomfortable for us.

Chapter six naturally divides into two distinct sections. In the first (vs. 1-16), we find two shifts in Jesus' ministry method. To this point, Luke has portrayed Jesus in terms of his compassion, kindness, and teaching authority, who let his message and miracles speak for themselves. It is noteworthy, then, that in the first two events of chapter six, Jesus became intentionally controversial, specifically about the man-made laws governing the Sabbath. What God had designed to be a benefit to the Jewish people had become a burden. Without reservation, Jesus promoted the spirit of the original law by allowing his disciples to enjoy God's provision (vs.1-5) and by healing a man's hand (vs. 6-11). Both acts of kindness and compassion were condemned, as he knew they would be.

The second shift in Jesus' ministry had to do with manpower. Jesus had such a large following by this time that he was no longer able to do all the ministry himself; simply put, he needed help. After spending all night alone in prayer (once again demonstrating his complete dependence on both the Father and the Spirit), he selected from among his hundreds or thousands of followers twelve men whom he could authorize and empower to multiply his ministry. These he commissioned as his "APOSTLES" (vs. 13).[13]

The second major division of this chapter is often called the "Sermon on the Plain." It is very similar to, but should not be confused with, the "Sermon on the Mount" for a couple of reasons, not the least of which was their respective locations. Matthew 5:1-2 states that "HE WENT UP THE MOUNTAIN...SAT DOWN...[AND] BEGAN TO TEACH" his many disciples, whereas Luke 6:17 states that "HE CAME DOWN" from a mountain to "A LEVEL PLACE" where he spoke to "A VAST MULTITUDE." Another difference is in the timing. Luke placed this teaching immediately following the selection of the Twelve, while Matthew has his long before then. A third difference is in the content. While there are certainly obvious similarities, Luke's version is much shorter and tends to emphasize more immediate human needs than general spiritual needs. For instance, compare Matthew's "BLESSED ARE THE POOR IN SPIRIT" (5:3) and "BLESSED ARE THOSE WHO HUNGER AND THIRST FOR RIGHTEOUSNESS" (5:6) with Luke's "BLESSED ARE YOU WHO ARE POOR" (6:20) and "BLESSED ARE YOU WHO HUNGER NOW" (6:21). Matthew recalled that Jesus commanded them to "BE PERFECT" like the Father (5:48), whereas Luke noted the command was to "BE MERCIFUL" like him (6:36).

What should we do with these differences? Do they prove the Bible

---

13 The Greek word ἀπόστολος (*apostolos*) is more than a simple messenger. An "apostle" was an envoy or ambassador, carrying his sender's full authority to both deliver and enforce the message.

contradicts itself as some want to believe? Do we chalk them up to human error or bad memories, proving that the Bible is neither inspired by God nor perfect? I suggest that a much better option is to realize that these differences support the fact that Jesus was an itinerant preacher who taught the same themes repeatedly at different times, in different locations, and to different audiences, always adjusting the length and content as each situation demanded, rather than simply reciting a "one size fits all" sermon that he kept in his pocket for every occasion. This accurately reflects his humanity and everyday life while maintaining the truth of Biblical inerrancy.

Chapter seven continues Jesus' ministry in Galilee during the early part of his ministry (approximately the first year). This selection includes four incidents, each of which demonstrates Jesus' compassion on those around him. First, like Matthew, Luke recorded Jesus' healing of a centurion's servant (vs. 1-10). The healing at a distance would especially interest Doctor Luke, but the focus on Gentiles is also important. Based on the Roman commander's statement, Jesus marveled at the man's simple faith, a faith that was noticeably missing among the Jewish people.

The second event is unique to Luke, the touching story of a widow's only son who died, leaving her alone (vs. 11-17). Luke never mentioned the cause of death, only that Jesus "SAW HER [AND] HE HAD COMPASSION FOR HER" (vs. 13). He brought the young man back to life, bringing joy to both the widow and the community.

The third event was a conversation between John the Baptizer and Jesus (vs. 18-35). Although Luke did not mention it, Matthew records that this happened after John was imprisoned (Matthew 11:2). Given the circumstances, he asked if Jesus was really who John thought he was. Jesus' response was not to scold John for his disbelief or condescendingly teach him; he simply said, "What have you seen that would prove I'm not? Go with what you know to be true." Jesus, then, used the opportunity to explain to the crowd who John truly was – the prophet who would announce the Messiah (Malachi 3:1) – and scolded them for demonizing John and not believing him.

Finally, Luke gave the account of the woman who anointed Jesus' feet (vs. 36-50). All four gospels give a similar account with varying details. In Luke, the woman was called "A SINNER" (vs. 37), the owner of the home was a Pharisee named Simon (vs. 36, 44), and it happened while Jesus was ministering in Galilee (northern Israel). Jesus' response was to forgive the woman's sins. The other three gospels (Matthew 26:6; Mark 14:3; John 12:1) place the event in Bethany (southern Israel), a week before his crucifixion. Simon (a common name) was a leper, not a Pharisee. They did not call the woman a sinner, and Jesus did not forgive her sins. Instead, Jesus considered this a preview of preparing his body for burial. As we have noted before, similar details should cause us to read carefully, not assume the events are the same and that the differences are contradictions in the text.

Chapters eight and nine conclude Jesus' ministry in Galilee with a series of events before he headed toward Jerusalem. No chapters in Luke contain as many distinct events as these two. The focus is not meant to be on the events themselves, so some of them are very short, lacking detail. Rather, Luke's focus was on Jesus' view of these events. Notice the recurring theme of Jesus' compassion: for women (vs. 1-3), for true followers (vs. 19-21), for his disciples (vs. 22-25), for the demon-possessed man (vs. 26-39), for Jairus and his daughter (vs. 40-42, 49-56), and for the sick woman (vs. 43-48). Luke could not include more evidence of Jesus' compassion into a single chapter than he did in chapter eight.

The only other section that this chapter includes is a single parable, revealing a chronological clue not found elsewhere. Matthew 13 records that Jesus used parables as an intentional method of hiding the truth from unbelievers after they had begun rejecting him. Luke's inclusion of the first parable at this point seems to show that, although the rejection had started, it took some time to spread, and Jesus continued his preaching, teaching, and healing ministry while his rejection grew. Eventually, he ministered in Israel using parables almost exclusively and doing miracles for only those individuals who believed. He eventually limited his large group ministry to Gentile crowds outside of Israel.

Chapter nine is a brief survey of a dozen, mostly unrelated, events. Luke's sixty-verse fly-over took Matthew nine chapters (see Matthew 10-18), although the order is different between the two writers. Considering that these are some of the most "famous" or "popular" events in the Gospels – sending out the Twelve, the feeding of the five thousand (the only miracle recorded in all four gospels), Peter's confession of the Christ, the Transfiguration, etc. – it seems that Luke did not want to skip them but did not consider giving much detail as highly important to his purpose.

The key to Luke 9 is really verse 51: "Now WHEN THE DAYS DREW NEAR FOR HIM TO BE TAKEN UP, JESUS SET OUT RESOLUTELY TO GO TO JERUSALEM." It is the turning point in the book. This follows two declarations proving that Jesus knew why he was going there – to "SUFFER MANY THINGS AND BE REJECTED...AND BE KILLED, AND ON THE THIRD DAY BE RAISED" (vs. 22) and "TO BE BETRAYED INTO THE HANDS OF MEN" (vs. 44). The two events following verse 51 fit this theme. First, Jesus was rejected by the Samaritans, who had once gladly welcomed him (John 4:39-41). Second, those who might have once answered the call to "FOLLOW ME" began to offer excuses instead (vs. 57-62).

Truly following Jesus is a lifelong process of leaving behind anything that we currently love more than him. Biblical discipleship is all about Jesus, learning to know him better and love him more. The closer Jesus got to Jerusalem, the smaller the crowds became.

Chapter ten contains three events that are unique to Luke. Each of them provides an example of Jesus' compassion for people, especially regarding our relationship with him. The first event shows Jesus sending out 72 people[14], apparently in addition to the 12 apostles (vs. 1-24). The instructions Jesus gave this group are similar to those he gave to the Twelve in Luke 9:1-6 and Matthew 10. Aside from the number of people (12 versus 72), the major difference seems to be the purpose of the two commissions. In Matthew 10, it seems that Jesus was multiplying his ministry by using the Twelve as official apostles. He clearly limited their ministry to Israel only (Matthew 10:5-6). In Luke 10, Jesus had the 72 going "AHEAD OF HIM...INTO EVERY TOWN AND PLACE WHERE HE HIMSELF WAS ABOUT TO GO" (vs. 1). It seems that they were mainly <u>preparing</u> for his ministry rather than <u>extending</u> his ministry. With no clear exclusion, the 72 might also have gone through Samaria and Gentile regions, since Jesus would be going there (17:11-19).

The conversation between Jesus and his new messengers contains two key elements. First is the famous "WOE" that Jesus put on the cities of Chorazin, Bethsaida, and Capernaum in which Jesus demonstrated his omniscience in telling what would have happened had the people of those cities repented (vs. 13-15). This reveals that God's knowledge is not limited to the real but also includes the possible. He knows 1) the consequences of the choices we make, 2) the consequences of the choices we do not make, and 3) which choices we will make. This does not mean that God causes all these things or choices but that his infinite knowledge is not limited by our choices.[15]

The second key element of Jesus' instructions was that they were to carry the gospel of the kingdom (vs. 9). Since Jesus had not yet died and

---

14   There seems to be equal evidence in the ancient manuscripts for either 72 or 70 here, with godly scholars on both sides of the discussion. Textual criticism does not overwhelmingly support either side, so it becomes a matter of interpretation. Neither translation changes the meaning of the text.

15   "Open Theism" teaches that God knows the consequences of what *could* happen depending on our future choices but he does not know what we will choose; therefore, he knows only the possible future but does not know anything in the future with certainty. Predictive prophecy shows that theory is untrue, since God claims to know the outcome of future events, often exhibiting that knowledge with great detail.

rose again, they could not preach the gospel of the cross. Instead, they were preparing the way for Messiah to come into the cities, so their message was that Messiah had come to offer his kingdom, and the people needed to repent and follow him.

The second event in this chapter is the well-known parable of the Good Samaritan (vs. 24-37). Jesus' told this story in response to a religious leader's question of what God expected from his people. When he did not like Jesus' response (love God and love your neighbor), the leader needed to justify his own lack of obedience (vs. 29), so he asked Jesus, "WHO IS MY NEIGHBOR?" In his parable, Jesus demonstrated that was the wrong question. In verse 36, Jesus asked, "WHICH OF THESE THREE MEN DO YOU THINK BECAME A NEIGHBOR TO THE MAN WHO FELL INTO THE HANDS OF THE ROBBERS?" Instead of asking, "Who is my neighbor?" ("Who do I have to love?"), we should ask, "To whom can I be a neighbor?" ("How can I love?")

The third event occurred at the home of Martha (vs. 38-42). In John 11 we discover that Martha and Mary had a brother named Lazarus and that Jesus loved the three of them dearly. The timing and setting of this gathering is unknown. Jesus' response of "MARTHA, MARTHA" when she complained to him about Mary's lack of assistance in preparing the meal is the tender response of a close friend. Jesus was far more concerned about the spiritual health of his friends than whether he received a big meal. Mary had "CHOSEN THE BEST PART" of that visit (vs. 42).

Chapter eleven opens with the disciples' request that Jesus would teach them to pray, "JUST AS JOHN TAUGHT HIS DISCIPLES." The Lord's response is a short version of the prayer found in Matthew 6:9-13 (vs. 1-4), followed by the teaching on prayer found also in Matthew 7:7-11 (vs. 9-13) and an example of persistence in prayer not found elsewhere (vs. 5-8). Some copies of Luke have the longer version of the prayer to match Matthew, but this was probably not original to Luke. Copyists likely added the longer sections to bring Luke in line with Matthew. Matthew includes the prayer within the longer teaching called the "Sermon on the Mount," which Jesus probably taught repeatedly in smaller portions, rather than as a specific answer to the disciples' request.

Most of the chapter brings together the two events that occurred when the Jewish religious leaders formally rejected Jesus as Israel's Messiah. Matthew recorded both the Galilee (chapter 12) and Jerusalem (chapter 22) rejections, but Luke did not make that distinction. Since both groups of Pharisees condemned Jesus in similar ways, it is possible that Jesus responded to both in similar ways as well, calling out their blasphemy regarding his casting out demons, pointing to his death and resurrection as "THE SIGN OF JONAH," and pronouncing his woes upon them and their hypocrisy. Although many of the common people still wanted to believe in him, they had seen many false Messiahs come and go, and they thought they could trust their religious leaders to steer them correctly. Unfortunately, this time they were wrong. The closer Jesus got to Jerusalem, the more opposition he faced from the religious leaders and common people alike.

Chapter twelve contains a series of teachings that Jesus gave over several months as he moved toward Jerusalem. He directed most of these toward his disciples (vs. 1); some, however, were general principles which applied to the crowds at large. Jesus' recurring topic at this time was keeping the proper focus. The first teaching was a warning and encouragement to his disciples to focus on God and his plan (vs. 1-12). Nothing can be hidden from him, and no matter what happened to them, God would always be faithful to fulfill in them what he promised. The second teaching was a parable Jesus gave in response to a question from a landowner (vs. 13-21). Headed toward Jerusalem, Jesus insisted that earthly matters are of secondary importance to eternal matters, and he refused to get bogged down in temporary issues, encouraging us to do the same.

The third teaching is a favorite reprise from the Sermon on the Mount (vs. 22-34). Because of God's faithfulness, Jesus' followers need not worry about storing up things on earth. Not only will God provide for our physical needs, but he has also prepared eternal possessions and rewards for us as well. For now, Jesus said, whatever has our attention has our hearts, and that should be God, not possessions. The fourth teaching was an encouragement to use the possessions and time that we have faithfully in God's service (vs. 35-48). Our possessions are on loan from God, and he expects us to use them for his purposes, not our own. For those who do, there will be a reward; for those who do not, there will be punishment of some kind.

The fifth teaching was mostly an aside but contains an important principle for today as well (vs. 49-53). Jesus noted that his teachings and the lifestyle that he demanded would cause division between his followers and the rest of the world, even within families. If the lifestyle of Christians does not make unbelievers uncomfortable in some way, it reveals that the believers are not being Christ-like. For now, Christ is the great divider, not the great uniter. Believers and unbelievers should be markedly different.

The final teaching was an indictment on the immediate listeners (vs. 54-59). They could read the weather and adjust their lives accordingly, but they refused to embrace the Messiah right in front of them, even though the Hebrew prophets gave so much information about him. The parable about settling out of court is a nod to the truth that people need to settle with Christ in this life. Once they stand before the Judge (God), it will be too late.

Chapter thirteen contains four distinct sections. The first section was a parable Jesus gave in response to some people who tried to get him to speak on a political matter (vs. 1-9). Instead of taking the bait, Jesus used a couple of current events to point out two timeless prinicples: 1) physical suffering and death are not necessarily linked to one's spiritual condition and 2) judgment is coming for those who do not repent.

In the second section, Jesus healed a woman on the Sabbath day, in the synagogue, to the horror of the religious leaders (vs. 10-21). When they chided him for doing work on the Sabbath, he responded by condemning their misunderstanding of God's intent and by telling two short parables. These parables indicated that the kingdom of God, which the Jews greatly anticipated, has both an internal and external component. The internal side will change a person from the inside, while the external side will ultimately provide rest and relief for all kinds of peoples, not just the Jewish people, in the Messianic Kingdom.

The third section provides another example of Jesus' teaching that entrance into his kingdom will not be based solely on ethnicity (vs. 22-30). On the one hand, Jews must come into relationship with the King, not just be in proximity to him (vs. 26-27). On the other hand, Jesus will welcome people "FROM EAST AND WEST, AND FROM NORTH AND SOUTH," who will sit alongside "ABRAHAM, ISAAC, JACOB, AND ALL THE PROPHETS IN THE KINGDOM OF GOD" (vs. 28-29).

The fourth section is reminiscent of Nehemiah (vs. 31-35). When he faced opposition to his work, Nehemiah said, "I AM ENGAGED IN AN IMPORTANT WORK, AND I AM UNABLE TO COME DOWN" (Nehemiah 6:3). Similarly, when Jesus was warned that Herod might try to kill him, he responded, "LOOK, I AM CASTING OUT DEMONS AND PERFORMING HEALINGS TODAY AND TOMORROW, AND ON THE THIRD DAY I WILL COMPLETE MY WORK" (vs. 32). In other words, "I'm busy, and his threats are not going to throw off my schedule!" (It is worth noting that it was a group of Pharisees who tried to save his life.) Although Jesus was ignoring Herod's idle threats, he was fully aware of the serious nature of Israel's ultimate rejection, and he wept over what he knew was in store for them until they will one day finally accept him.

Chapter fourteen is actually only two stories, though it may seem like more. The first four sections (vs. 1-6, 7-11, 12-14, and 15-24) all took place at the same event – a Sabbath dinner at a leading Pharisee's house (see vs. 1, 7, 12, 15). First, the religious leaders allowed a sick man to sit right next to Jesus. When Jesus challenged their continued resistance toward his healing on the Sabbath, they were unable to respond, humiliating themselves. Second, Jesus spoke to the crowd at large, giving what might be mistaken as public relations or business advice. Instead of choosing the best seat for oneself at public gatherings, when you may be asked to move, choose a less public seat, and you may be publicly asked to move forward. Rather than simple business advice, though, Jesus was teaching that God honors humility in every aspect of life. Third, continuing the theme of personal humility, Jesus advised the dinner host to invite people who could not repay him for his kindness, because God will reward that kind of attitude toward others. Fourth, Jesus told the parable of the great banquet. Understanding God to be the banquet host (vs. 15), Jesus not-so-subtly told all the rich people around him that one's station in life does not guarantee a seat in God's coming kingdom. In fact, God would open it up to anyone and everyone, which he did by crucifying Jesus for all people. The gospel message is available to all and must be shared with all, especially after those who initially received the offer rejected it.

The second part of the chapter seems connected to the first, but it is unlikely that "LARGE CROWDS" were at the Sabbath dinner with Jesus (vs. 25). Instead, Luke placed this teaching here to connect it with Jesus' parable but not necessarily with the event itself. Although Jesus invites everyone into his kingdom, it is not something we should take lightly. In fact, truly following Jesus means to bear the shame and ridicule ("CROSS") that comes with being associated with him. It also requires loving him more than even our family members. Many will not follow Jesus for fear of what their parents or family will say; Jesus said that is not good enough. While we are not necessarily called to "burn bridges" with our loved ones, there may be a time that we are called to make a choice between them and Jesus, and Jesus demands our full allegiance. Still, he wants this to be an intentional choice, not an emotional one. "Think it through," he said. "See if you are willing to do whatever I ask. Ultimately, nothing else can be more important to you than I am."

Chapter fifteen is probably one of the most well-known chapters in Luke, yet it is also frequently misunderstood. The key to the whole chapter is found in the first three verses. The Jewish religious leaders were unhappy that Jesus spent time with sinners, "so JESUS TOLD THEM THIS PARABLE," not three parables. The entire chapter is the same parable told in three different ways. In this parable:

God is the shepherd, the woman[16], and the father

The "sinners" are the lost sheep, the lost coin, and the lost son

The "non-sinners" are the other sheep, the other coins, and the other son

Notice in these scenarios that the lost items/son were already a part of the group/family but became lost. Something happened so that they had become separated from the group – the sheep left the pasture, the coin left the pouch, and the son left the house. Jesus gave this parable to demonstrate to the religious leaders that those "SINNERS" were still Jews who were born into the promises God made to Israel. However, when he came and offered the Kingdom, not all of them had accepted him, making them "lost" yet still sheep, coins, and sons. Ironically, the religious leaders considered themselves to be "in," yet many of them were more lost than the sinners they despised because they were not only rejecting Jesus themselves but leading others away from him, too.

This parable is often used today to portray God as looking for unbelievers

---

16 The fact that God the Father is portrayed by a woman concerns some people, but it should not for at least three reasons. First, God is spirit and neither male nor female, so portraying himself as one or the other does not affect the reality of who he is. Second, although God typically used male pronouns to refer to himself throughout Scripture, he used other imagery as well, including a mother bird (Deuteronomy 32:11; Matthew 23:37). Third, both males and females are created in God's image, meaning that we both carry his likeness, which is essentially non-human and non-physical, yet he has characteristics usually associated with one gender or the other. In short, to see God portrayed as a woman in a fictional story does not assail against his person or his character, but instead gives a different, fuller perspective on who he is.

to be saved. While it is true and can be proven from other Scripture that God does indeed want people to be saved, unbelievers are not a part of the family from which they could leave. A more accurate principle from this chapter that applies to Christians is that God does not stop "looking" and "waiting" for those who are already part of the family but have wandered away. Sometimes we call these "backslidden Christians." For those who have not wandered off, we must continue to do the Father's work cheerfully and celebrate when our wandering brothers and sisters come back, because this makes the Father exceptionally glad (Galatians 6:1; James 5:19-20; 1 John 5:16; Jude 22-23).

Chapter sixteen contains two of Jesus' well-known parables with a teaching between them. The first parable was directed toward his disciples (vs. 1) but was overheard by some local Pharisees (vs. 14). In his parable, Jesus taught of an asset manager who was fired by his master for mismanaging the owner's wealth (vs. 1-9). So he would not lose everything, the manager approached the owner's debtors with a "discounted rate" to get their help. This rate may have been part or all the commission or even illegal interest he had added to their debt. By cutting their bills drastically, he won their friendship. Although the owner did not approve of the manager's initial bad management, he had to commend his quick thinking.

Jesus pointed out that, compared to unbelievers, believers are often foolish in their financial matters, and that should not be one of our characteristics (vs. 8-9). He taught that our faithfulness or lack thereof is the same, no matter if we have much wealth or a little (vs. 10-12). However, we must not get caught in the trap of serving wealth rather than serving God, because the two are mutually exclusive (vs. 13). The Pharisees who overheard this thought it was absurd. Wealth is a sign of God's blessing, isn't it? Jesus responded that their lives showed that they were not serving God. They justified their wrong priorities (vs. 15), ignored the Messiah's offer (vs. 16-17), and did not honor marriage (vs. 18).

The second parable is the famous story of the rich man and Lazarus (vs. 19-31). The point is not, as some have tried to make it, that rich people automatically go to hell while poor people are spiritual and go to heaven. Helping the poor was one of the commands under the Jewish law, so the rich man's refusal to do so showed his attitude toward God's law. In this parable, Jesus made four very important points.

First, the afterlife is real and eternal. Not only did the rich man and Lazarus recognize each other from this life, but they also recognized Abraham, who had been dead for 2,000 years.

Second, the pain or pleasure experienced in the afterlife is real. The rich man was "IN ANGUISH" (vs. 24), while Lazarus was "COMFORTED" from his sores (vs. 25). Even after death, the rich man felt the punishing fire and requested water to quench his thirst.

Third, perspective in the afterlife is different. At some level, the rich man remembered his brothers. Though we do not know the relationship he had with them in life, he was infinitely concerned about them now, asking Abraham to have Lazarus warn them for him. It seems he thought they were as greedy as he was and were also headed to eternal torment. Notice also that the rich man, when asking on behalf of his brothers, never asked for his own release. There is the implication that he knew there was no way out.

Fourth, the Scriptures are the final word. Abraham's response was significant. He said that even a resurrection would not be enough to convince people of the truth if they already ignored what God had given in the Scriptures. This is what Paul wrote in Romans 1, that people suppress the truth by their unrighteousness, refusing to believe in Jesus even though God proved who he was by raising him from the dead. A person who rejects the Scriptures has rejected all of God's revelation.

Chapter seventeen is a compendium of several topics ranging from forgiveness, faith, and duty at the beginning to end times prophecy at the end.

Luke did not intend to offer a timeline of these events; rather, he wanted to include them before approaching Passion Week in chapter 19.

In verses 1-4, Jesus taught that there is no limit to forgiving one's brother when he repents. However, contrary to much modern Christian thinking, Jesus also insisted that sin should be rebuked and that causing a brother to stumble into sin is a serious offense. All these are repeated throughout the apostolic letters and must be heeded even today. Verses 5-6 offer a short statement on how much we could accomplish if done in faith. On the other hand, from the perspective of being God's servants, verses 7-10 imply that it does not take a lot of faith to obey God's clear commands. As much as serving God can be a joy, and he has certainly promised rewards for those who serve faithfully, there is a sense that we are to obey simply because we should, even when it is not glamorous or joyful. **Faithful service, at its core, is about God, not us.**

Throughout this gospel, we have seen that Doctor Luke loved the healing miracles, emphasized Jesus' compassion, and pointed out when Jesus included non-Jews in his ministry. The account in verses 11-19 includes all three. On his way to Jerusalem to offer himself to die, Jesus stopped to heal a group of lepers near Samaria. Although he healed ten lepers that day, only one – a Samaritan – turned around to thank Jesus for getting his life back. The fact that only "THIS FOREIGNER" praised God for healing caught Jesus' attention and prompted him to say that his faith had delivered the man. This refers to both physical and spiritual deliverance.

In the final section, Jesus gave a short teaching prompted by a question about when the kingdom would come (vs. 20-37). Many modern teachers have taken verse 21 to mean that the kingdom is only a spiritual reality which resides within believers. However, the Pharisees believed the Messiah would bring the kingdom with him when he came. Because Jesus had already spent a few years identifying himself as the Messiah and offering his kingdom, their question was basically, "If you know so much, tell us when the Messiah will come and bring his kingdom." His response was to point to himself again: "I'm here, but you have rejected me."

The teaching on the coming kingdom was not to the unbelieving Pharisees but "TO THE DISCIPLES" (vs. 22). Jesus taught that a physical kingdom was still to come, and because specific signs would precede it, they should not allow themselves to be led astray by false prophets or false messiahs. Only after the Tribulation judgments on Israel and the unbelieving world will Jesus return to establish his kingdom. Matthew, Paul, John (in the Revelation), and the Hebrew prophets contain much more detail than Luke on this topic.

Chapter eighteen is the final chapter before Luke began his account of the Passion story. The chapter begins with two parables not included in the other Gospels. The explanation of the first parable (vs. 1-8) is in verse one: we "SHOULD ALWAYS PRAY AND NOT LOSE HEART." To illustrate this, Jesus told of a widow who kept pestering a judge to provide her justice, until he finally relented. If an unrighteous judge will finally relent toward a woman he did not care about, how much more will God give justice to those he loves if they would only ask?

The second parable (vs. 9-14) is the famous story of the Pharisee and the tax collector. In this story, the Pharisee stood before God proud of his long list of good deeds. He saw himself as better than others, and he expected that God did, too. The tax collector, on the other hand, knew how God viewed him and begged for mercy because of his sin. Jesus said that this man was "JUSTIFIED" (declared righteous) before God because of his humility. A wonderful reminder for Christians is that God cannot be any more merciful toward us than he was at the cross. We do not have to beg for mercy for sin, only confess it and live out his forgiveness.

The next two teachings were also recorded by the other gospel writers with varying levels of detail. In verses 15-17 Jesus insisted that even little children were worth his time. With his continued talk of death, it seems the disciples began to act more like bodyguards than apostles and ministry partners. When they tried to stop parents from bringing their children, Jesus had to correct their thinking in this regard. Young children, Jesus said, are a great example of the innocent and humble attitude God wants us to keep before him, like the tax collector of the previous parable.

The encounter with the rich young ruler and the following teaching in verses 18-30 is found in Matthew and Mark as well. Matthew noted that he was young (19:20), while Mark wrote that he ran urgently to Jesus (10:17). His concern was whether he was doing enough of the right things to get into Messiah's kingdom. When Jesus asked him about how well he kept God's law, he was happy to say that he did so "WHOLEHEARTEDLY...SINCE MY YOUTH." However, Jesus knew that actions do not always accurately reflect the heart. Even though the man did all the right things, he still loved his wealth more than God. Jesus told him that God wanted his heart and that his money was holding him back. It was true; he walked away from Jesus "VERY SAD, BECAUSE HE WAS EXTREMELY WEALTHY." The principle is not that a person must sell everything and give it away to the poor for salvation. Instead, Jesus told his followers, only full trust in God alone can bring someone to the Messiah/Savior. Because it was assumed that wealth automatically meant God's blessing, this was confusing to them. Jesus responded that submitting everything to God would result in reward in this life and heaven, far greater than money could ever buy.

After another prediction of his death and resurrection (vs. 31-34), Jesus came to Jericho, where he healed a blind beggar, another example of his compassion (vs. 35-43). In this case, the man had expressed his faith in Jesus as the Messiah by calling him the "SON OF DAVID" instead of just "Rabbi" or "Teacher." The man believed that Jesus was the one sent from God, and he placed his life into Jesus' hands. The result was that the people praised God for Jesus and his works.

Chapter nineteen contains two final events before Jesus' Triumphal Entry, and both are unique to Luke. The first is the famous story of Zacchaeus (vs. 1-10). Although he was a hated tax collector, he was interested in seeing and hearing Jesus. When Jesus came to Jericho, he invited himself to Zacchaeus' house. Even before they reached the house, Zacchaeus had a change of heart about the money he had stolen over the years and promised to repay it multiple times over. Jesus said that Zacchaeus had received salvation because his faith was shown in his actions.

Immediately afterward, Jesus told a parable to the crowd (vs. 11-27). Luke noted that "THEY THOUGHT THAT THE KINGDOM OF GOD WAS GOING TO APPEAR IMMEDIATELY" (vs. 11). This is one of a few subtle hints in Scripture that Jesus' return would not necessarily be soon. The parable of the ten minas is like other parables that Jesus told, but it has some differences as well, so we should not try to interpret it to mean the same as the others. Jesus was the nobleman who came to receive a kingdom but was rejected (vs. 14). While he was gone, he expected his followers ("SERVANTS") to invest his resources in his business (vs. 13), and they would report to him upon his return, "AFTER RECEIVING THE KINGDOM."[17] The principle of serving God with one's resources is a common theme in the New Testament epistles. It is important to note that this parable does not teach that those who squandered their resources lost their positions or salvation, but they did lose their reward or inheritance in the kingdom. It was only those who rejected him that he had killed.

Like the other gospel writers, Luke included the account of Jesus' entry into Jerusalem (vs. 28-48). As Zechariah prophesied, Jesus rode into the city on a donkey to officially present himself as the Messiah-King (Zechariah

---

17 In Jesus' story, the kingdom did not exist while the nobleman was gone. This shows that Jesus' kingdom is not yet in existence during the Church Age. It will not be established until after Jesus returns at the Second Coming, before the Millennium.

9:9), while his followers made a loud procession for him.[18] This concerned the Pharisees because they thought the commotion would disturb the preparations for Passover later that week. Jesus responded that someone would praise him at his entrance, even if it had to be the rocks. Luke closed this section only briefly mentioning Jesus' cleansing of the Temple and teaching there daily. He did, however, include a record of Jesus weeping over Jerusalem that none of the other Gospel writers include. Matthew mentioned one later in the week that is different than what Luke recorded here (Matthew 23:37-39).

Chapter twenty continues Jesus' public teaching in Jerusalem during Passion Week. On Tuesday, Jesus' teaching authority was challenged by the religious leaders (vs. 1-8). As had happened so many times before, they attempted to catch him in his own words, but instead, he spun it around on them, and they were unable to answer him. Ironically, he proved his authority by showing that he did not answer to them.

In verses 9-19, Jesus told a parable about tenants leasing a vineyard. Unlike many of his other parables, even the religious leaders understood the meaning of this one and wanted to arrest him because of it. The "SLAVES" sent by the owner were the Hebrew prophets who the Jews murdered throughout the centuries (vs. 10-12). The "SON" was Jesus, who used this parable to prophesy his own death at their hands (vs. 15).

The religious leaders needed to get the populace on their side against Jesus, so they attempted to trick him again in a way assuring he would either infuriate the crowd or show himself treasonous to Rome. When they asked him about paying taxes, he replied with his famous statement, "GIVE TO CAESAR THE THINGS THAT ARE CAESAR'S, AND TO GOD THE THINGS THAT ARE GOD'S" (vs. 25).

Seeing that the Pharisees were unable to trap him, the Sadducees

---

18   Sometimes we hear that the crowd in Jerusalem was welcoming Jesus into the city. This was not the case. Instead, he had a large group of followers come with him from Jericho who were making the noise that caught the attention of those in the capital.

made their attempt (vs. 27-40). They fabricated a story about a woman who legitimately married seven brothers but was unable to bear any of them a son. Their question: "IN THE RESURRECTION, THEREFORE, WHOSE WIFE WILL THE WOMAN BE?" Ironically, the Sadducees did not even believe in the resurrection, so their deceit was obvious. Still, Jesus used the opportunity to make a statement about the afterlife, namely, that marriage as we know it will not last into the eternal state. He followed that with a statement proving that their disbelief in the resurrection was against the teachings of Moses, so they were even contradicting themselves![19] This silenced them for good (vs. 40). He finished with a warning to the crowd that they should not listen to the religious leaders, because they were full of pride and under God's judgment (vs. 46-47).

Chapter twenty-one contains one small event followed by Jesus' teaching about the end times. Sunday School teachers often teach verses 1-4 as if they were linked to the previous section on pride. However, neither Luke nor Mark (12:41-44) indicates that Jesus was looking at the givers' hearts. When he noticed the people bringing their offerings to the Temple, he mentioned only that the widow gave a much higher percentage than the others, because she gave everything she had.

The rest of the chapter contains Luke's version of the Olivet Discourse. It is slightly shorter than Mark's version but much shorter than Matthew's, which includes the parables of the ten virgins and the talents and the judgment of the sheep and goats (chapter 25). The key point in all three of these accounts is that this discourse was Jesus' response to the disciples' question about the signs indicating when Jerusalem would fall (vs. 5-7). However, instead of answering that question directly, Jesus took the opportunity to provide insight into the end times more generally. Although the

---

19 The Sadducees accepted only the five books of Moses in their Bibles, so Jesus always quoted only Moses to them.

description Jesus gave in verses 20-24 was fulfilled in A.D. 70 when Rome destroyed Jerusalem and the Temple, the following verses (25-28) have never yet happened. These will be the signs of his return (detailed more fully in Revelation), and nothing can stop that (vs. 29-33).

Jesus ended his teaching with a command that they (specifically the Jewish people) should not let themselves be lulled into complacency by his delayed arrival. Instead, they should continually watch for their Messiah's return (vs. 34-36).

Chapter twenty-two details the events of Thursday into the early hours of Friday morning. The first few verses (1-6) probably happened on Wednesday, because Luke seems to make a distinction between verses one and seven. When Jesus did not make the power move against Rome that Judas expected and wanted, Judas must have considered him a fraud and made plans to have him arrested.

The Passover was on Friday that year[20], so Jesus had Peter and John (mentioned by name only here) make the preparations on Thursday (vs. 7-13). At 6:00 that evening it would have been Friday (the days run evening to evening), so Jesus did eat the Passover with his disciples on Friday, not Thursday night. During the meal, he stated that his body would be given for them, and eating the Passover in the future was to be done in his remembrance as the ultimate Passover sacrifice.[21] After supper he did the same with the wine, linking it to his blood which would institute the new covenant (vs. 14-20). Jesus then mentioned that one of the Twelve would betray him.[22] Their genuine surprise and investigation devolved into an argument about

---

20 Harold Hoehner does a fantastic job detailing this in his *Chronological Aspects of the Life of Christ* (Zondervan, 1977).

21 There is never a command for Jewish Christians to stop celebrating the Passover. Though God did not place that command on Gentile Christians, Passover still holds great significance to the Jewish people, especially those who have come into relationship with their Messiah.

22 Judas Iscariot was still there during the Passover meal. The fact that he was not a true believer in Jesus did not change his ethnic status as a son of Israel.

their personal greatness (vs. 21-30).

Within the prophecy that Peter would deny Jesus, only Luke included the conversation where Jesus mentioned that Satan wanted to scatter the disciples (vs. 31-38). In another often- overlooked prophecy, Jesus declared that Peter would return first, and he commissioned Peter to help restore the others.[23] Luke noted that Jesus "CUSTOMARILY ... [WENT] TO THE MOUNT OF OLIVES"; this is why Judas knew he would find him there (vs. 39). During Jesus' torturous prayer, only the doctor recorded the physical effects that it had on him: "HIS SWEAT WAS LIKE DROPS OF BLOOD FALLING TO THE GROUND" (vs. 44). Likewise, Luke made special mention that the disciples did not sleep because of apathy; they were "EXHAUSTED FROM GRIEF" (vs. 45).

As he expected, Judas found them (vs. 47-53). When the disciples attempted to put up a fight, Jesus would not allow it, to the point that he healed a wound on one of Judas' men. (All three other Gospel writers include the skirmish, but only Luke mentioned the healing.) The final section of the chapter records the juxtaposition of Peter denying that he even knew Jesus while Jesus was being beaten and abused in place of Peter and the rest of us (vs. 54-71). After his unjust beating, Jesus stood trial before the Jewish Council and was condemned for blasphemy.

Chapter twenty-three finishes the crucifixion story through 6:00 Friday evening, the beginning of the Sabbath (vs. 56). Because Rome did not allow the Jews to put anyone to death on their own, condemning Jesus to death for blasphemy required the permission of the local Roman governor, Pontius Pilate, before they could execute Jesus (vs. 1-5). However, Rome was a pluralistic society, and they knew that Pilate did not care what Jesus believed and taught, so they needed a crime that he would notice; they chose treason against the Roman Empire.

---

23 Jesus switched from the plural pronoun ("YOU ALL") in verse 31 about all the disciples to the singu-
    lar pronoun ("YOU" Peter) in verse 32.

As a part of his detailed investigative report, Luke alone mentioned that Jesus had a separate hearing before Herod, who had gone to Jerusalem for Passover (vs. 6-12). This incident would have been interesting to Luke's Roman addressee, who would likely have not been able to figure out how two ruthless rulers like Pilate and Herod could ever get along. With Jesus back in his custody, Pilate tried everything he could to keep peace with Rome and still assuage the Jewish religious leaders, but they would not have it (vs. 13-25). They demanded Jesus' death, and Pilate finally gave in.

As they led him away, several things took place. First, Simon of Cyrene was forced to carry Jesus' cross (vs. 26). Second, in response to some women who wept for him, Jesus' told them that the judgment coming on Israel would be just as ruthless (vs. 27-31). This probably referred both to the Roman invasion in A.D. 70 and the Tribulation. Third, although Matthew briefly mentioned the criminals crucified with Jesus, only Luke told of the salvation of one of them, continuing his theme of Jesus' compassion for all people (vs. 32-43). Additionally, in verse 32, Luke stated that "TWO OTHER CRIMINALS WERE ALSO LED AWAY TO BE EXECUTED WITH HIM," identifying Jesus as one of three criminals, which was both the legal and popular opinion. Fourth, though Luke did not record most of the events at the cross or Jesus' famous last words, he did record those of the centurion who clearly understood Jesus' innocence (vs. 44-49). Finally, Jesus was removed from the cross and buried in a tomb owned by "A MEMBER OF THE COUNCIL" (vs. 50) who obviously had not been swayed by the mob. This took place just as "THE SABBATH WAS BEGINNING," or just before 6:00pm on Friday (vs. 54). The women went home to prepare the embalming spices that they would bring back early Sunday to finish a proper burial. Luke's note that "ON THE SABBATH THEY RESTED" is a vast understatement of a day which contained a wealth of emotion.

Chapter twenty-four begins with the resurrection, with basically the same detail that the other Gospel writers included (vs. 1-12). However, the rest of the chapter is unique to Luke. As two of Jesus' followers slowly walked back home to Emmaus on Sunday, "ABOUT SEVEN MILES FROM JERUSALEM," (11 km) Jesus appeared to them, but they were unable to recognize him (vs. 13-32). It must have been interesting for him to listen to their perspective on the events of the previous couple of days. Sadly, even though they heard of his resurrection (vs. 22-23), they did not believe that he was truly the Messiah, only "A PROPHET" (vs. 19) who they "HAD HOPED...[WOULD] REDEEM ISRAEL" (vs. 21). He scolded them for their lack of belief and worked his way through the Scriptures showing them how all these things were prophesied and required to take place (vs. 25-27). What a shock when their eyes were finally opened as he began to eat a meal with them in their home, then immediately disappeared. They finally had the proof they needed, more than the information from the women which they apparently had not believed (vs. 30-32).

While they regrouped with the Eleven to tell their story, Jesus appeared again (vs. 33-43). Peter had already seen him (vs. 34), so this was getting to be a regular occurrence, yet they still had a hard time believing it (vs. 37). Graciously, Jesus appeared to all of them and offered them several physical proofs, including eating "IN FRONT OF THEM."[24]

As he had done with the two en route to Emmaus, Jesus taught them from the Scriptures how they should have expected him to "SUFFER AND . . . RISE FROM THE DEAD ON THE THIRD DAY" (vs. 46).[25] Not only that but they, who were "WITNESSES OF THESE THINGS" (vs. 48), would be his spokesmen proclaiming "REPENTANCE FOR THE FORGIVENESS OF SINS...TO ALL NATIONS, BEGINNING IN JERUSALEM" (vs. 47), exactly where Acts picks up. Luke ends with a brief account of Jesus' ascension that Luke would expand upon in volume two, the Acts (vs. 50-53).

---

24 This gives an implication about the ability, if not need, to consume food in our glorified bodies.

25 Verse 44 is a wonderful statement in which Jesus gave his acknowledgment and approval of the Hebrew Scriptures (only the 39 books in the Protestant Old Testament) as inspired and authoritative.

John

John wrote his account of Jesus' ministry much later than the others, by approximately 30-50 years, during the early A.D. 90s. By this time, the other three (Matthew, Mark, and Luke) had been widely circulated, and their stories were probably well-known. This may partially explain why John's record was so different than theirs.

Only in John do we read of the activities of the pre-incarnate Son of God (1:1-3). Only in John do we read of a Temple cleansing at the beginning of his ministry (2:12-22). Only in John do we hear Jesus make his seven great "I am" statements.[26] Only in John do we find the Upper Room Discourse and its unprecedented Church-Age teachings (chapters 14-16). Only in John do we hear Jesus pour out his heart in Gethsemane (chapter 17). And only in John do we watch him gently restore Peter following his resurrection (chapter 21). All these, along with many other unrecorded miracles, the Holy Spirit preserved for us through John's pen as the first generation of Christians began to die off.

John's writing style and language are often simple, something beginning Greek language students thoroughly enjoy. Throughout his gospel and letters, he used common themes such as light and darkness and truth and error. His

---

26 Bread of life (6:35); Door (10:7); Light of the World (8:12; 9:5); Good Shepherd (10:11, 14); Resurrection and the Life (11:25); Way, Truth, and Life (14:6); Vine (15:1, 5)

writing is simple to understand yet complex in its depth and richness. A child can grasp its message while a scholar meditates on its intricacies.

Unlike the other writers, John's emphasis was not on Jesus' humanity or his activities or even his suffering. John had one sole purpose: **to present Jesus to the world as the eternal Son of God**, proven by his bold miracles and even bolder teachings. After providing one account after another John came near the end of his book and presented this simple challenge to his readers:

"Now Jesus performed many other miraculous signs in the presence of the disciples, which are not recorded in this book. But these are recorded so that you may believe that Jesus is the Christ, the Son of God, and that by believing you may have life in his name" (20:30-31)

Beyond anything else, John insisted on telling the story of God in the flesh, who came not to condemn the world but to save it (3:17). Everything Jesus did and said pushed him a little closer to that day when he would accomplish the work given him by the Father to bring him glory (17:4).

Chapter one immediately broke from the tradition of the Synoptics[27] from the first verse. Because his focus was on Jesus' deity, rather than beginning with Jesus' human birth John went all the way to eternity past, borrowing the language of Genesis 1:1 to state Jesus' preexistence. "In the beginning... the Word was fully God." Although groups such as the Jehovah Witness interpret this to mean that he was a created, god-like being, John's precise use of the Greek language requires a reading that attributes deity to Jesus from the very start. Additionally, John revealed that not only did "God create the heavens and the earth" (Genesis 1:1) but Jesus, the Eternal Son,

---

27 The word *synoptic* means "to see together." In the Bible, it refers to the first three Gospels (Matthew, Mark, and Luke), which often record the same events, albeit from different perspectives.

was the active creator of all things (vs. 2-5).

To accomplish the Father's work (17:4), the Eternal Word "BECAME FLESH AND TOOK UP RESIDENCE AMONG US" (vs. 14). Though that necessarily hid his eternal glory, John claimed to have seen it, though he never revealed when (John did not record the Transfiguration, Matthew 17:1-8). Ultimately, Jesus did the one thing that no one else could ever do: he revealed God to man (vs. 18).

John is more like Mark than Matthew or Luke in the sense that he skipped Jesus' formative years, choosing to jump directly to John the Baptizer[28] and Jesus' introduction to ministry. The apostle John likely wrote from Ephesus, where John the Baptizer at one time had a following (Acts 19:1-7), which may explain his careful point that John "WAS NOT THE LIGHT, BUT HE CAME TO TESTIFY ABOUT THE LIGHT" (vs. 8). The Baptizer also made clear that he was not the promised Messiah, instead, quoting Isaiah that he was simply the forerunner of the Christ (vs. 19-28). When Jesus came to have John baptize him, he boldly pointed to Jesus as "THE LAMB OF GOD WHO TAKES AWAY THE SIN OF THE WORLD!" (vs. 29) Where he gained this specific revelation is unknown, but it seems that he had instructed his own disciples to follow the Messiah when they saw him because two of them left John to follow Jesus (vs. 35-39). Interestingly, although all four gospels include the voice from heaven at Jesus' baptism, John seemed to hint that only Jesus and the Baptizer heard it (vs. 32-34).

Although the second disciple who left the Baptizer for Jesus was not named, the first was "ANDREW, THE BROTHER OF SIMON PETER" (vs. 40). The rest of chapter one indicates the word-of-mouth that helped build Jesus' initial following: Andrew, the unnamed disciple (possibly John himself), Peter, Philip, and Nathanael (vs. 41-51). This time spent with Jesus early on explains their "quick" response to drop everything and follow him full-time

---

28 It is important to distinguish between John the apostle, who wrote this gospel, and the Baptizer, who was the forerunner of Jesus.

later as shown in the Synoptics.

Chapter two records the first of several miracles found only in John. Contrary to *pseudepigraphical*[29] writings like the Gospel of Thomas, which claim that Jesus did miracles even throughout his childhood, John stated that this wedding in Cana was "THE FIRST OF HIS MIRACULOUS SIGNS" and how "HE REVEALED HIS GLORY" (vs. 11). John did not provide enough detail about the event for us to figure out everything, but for some reason, Mary got involved when the groom ran out of wine, assuming that Jesus should do something about it (vs. 1-11). Because he had not done miracles before, it is unlikely that she expected one. In fact, Jesus' response was essentially, "That's none of our business!" However, he did get involved, turning about 150 gallons of water into wine.[30] It is important to note that only the servants who had drawn the water and Jesus' disciples were aware of what had happened. Jesus did not make it into a public show. This level of personal interaction is characteristic of John's gospel.

Whereas the Synoptics all record the Temple cleansing during Passion Week (Matthew 21:12; Mark 11:15; Luke 19:45), only John recorded this one at the beginning of Jesus' ministry (vs. 12-22). Some say that it was the same event as the Passion Week cleansing rather than a separate event, because John did not include the second one, and they think it unlikely that Jesus would have done it twice. However, there are two reasons to see this as a separate incident. First, verses 12-13 are dated in such a way that this had to happen shortly after the wedding in Cana, which itself was said to have taken place "ON THE THIRD DAY" after Jesus' conversation with Nathanael (vs. 1). To push this incident to the end of Jesus' ministry requires moving the previous

---

29 *Pseudepigraphical* means "false writings." These are books attributed to the apostles (Thomas, Judas, Peter, etc.) but contain information that contradicts the Scriptures, and they were never considered legitimate or canonical by the Early Church.

30 Much has been written about what type of wine he made, especially regarding its alcohol content. Suffice it to say that the *sommelier* thought it was "very good" and should have been set out first, before the guests were drunk.

passages as well, which could not be if Cana was his first miracle. Second, verse 23 shows Jesus doing more miracles and people believing in him after this cleansing, exactly the opposite of what happened during Passion Week. At that time, he did no miracles, and people turned against him. It is best to understand that Jesus cleansed the Temple twice, like bookends of his public ministry.

Chapter three contains the first, and possibly the most famous, of several personal conversations Jesus had that John recorded. Many people have speculated that Nicodemus approached Jesus at night because he was afraid of the other Pharisees or other people, but the text does not offer that picture. In fact, Nicodemus himself admitted, "WE KNOW THAT YOU ARE A TEACHER WHO HAS COME FROM GOD" (vs. 2). His position as "THE TEACHER OF ISRAEL" (vs. 10) possibly required that he "vetted" up-and-coming rabbis who did not come through the official channels so that he could verify their teachings. Since every rabbi had a "yoke" or set of teachings that he placed on his followers so they could enter "THE KINGDOM OF GOD" (vs. 3; see Matthew 11:28-30), it would have been natural for Nicodemus to try to determine what Jesus was teaching the masses.

Jesus, of course, had a spiritual message rather than a religious, works-based one. "BORN AGAIN" can legitimately be translated *"born from above,"* making it a play on words. Nicodemus heard "BORN AGAIN" and thought biology, whereas Jesus meant "born from above" by the Spirit (vs. 4-8). Because the Hebrew Scriptures had already taught this truth (Ezekiel 11:19-20; 36:26-27), this should not have been news to Nicodemus, and Jesus chided him for not understanding it. He followed it with a reference to Moses and the bronze serpent which foreshadowed the method of salvation (Numbers 21:4-9).

There is a debate over whether Jesus' speech stopped at verse 15 or whether he continued through verse 21. It seems that the dialogue ended with verse 15, at which point John wrote an explanation of what Jesus meant in verses 13-15. There are at least three reasons to take this approach. First, the "FOR" at the beginning of verse 16 is explanatory and does not require that it continues the dialogue. Second, it would be uncharacteristic for Jesus to switch from "SON OF MAN" (twice in verses 13-14) to "SON OF GOD" (three times in verses 16-21), without a transition for Nicodemus. However, since the purpose of the book was to present Jesus as the Son of God, and John had already done so multiple times, it is a fitting follow-up to Jesus' own words. Third, the topic changes rapidly between verses 15 and 16, and there is no other example of this in Jesus' interactions in John. Rather, John explained that Jesus was indeed "LIFTED UP" to make salvation available to the whole world but effective only for those who believe. This personal faith or belief is the sole determining factor in a person's eternal judgment and the basis for how a person lives in this life.

The chapter concludes with a "territorial dispute" between Jesus' disciples and those of John the Baptizer (vs. 22-30). John's disciples had become incensed that Jesus' disciples were baptizing more people than they were. John quickly and carefully reminded them that his whole mission was to point people to Jesus, as he had often told them, humbly stating, "HE MUST BECOME MORE IMPORTANT WHILE I BECOME LESS IMPORTANT" (vs. 30). The writer, then, summarized again the practical doctrine leading to the Baptizer's conclusion that all believers should embrace (vs. 31-36).

Chapter four records a second famous personal conversation with Jesus. He had been spending time near Jerusalem but decided to leave because he was drawing too much attention from the Pharisees. Verse four makes a significant statement: "HE HAD TO PASS THROUGH SAMARIA." Geographically, this was not true. Jews frequently traveled around Samaria specifically so they would <u>not</u> go through it. If Jesus "had to" it was only because of his mission.

In this case, his mission was to talk to a woman who had gone to draw water during the wrong time of day, far away from the city (vs. 4-26). In a manner shockingly uncharacteristic of any Jewish man, Jesus spoke to her, asking for a drink of water. This led to a conversation about living water, which leaves no thirst at all. As with Nicodemus, the woman could think only physically, whereas Jesus was speaking spiritually. To prove himself as a prophet, he pointed out that he knew both her personal history and present status, even though they had only just met. This convinced her that he was a true prophet and caused her to ask a theological question about worship style and location that she must have wondered for some time.[31] Again, as with Nicodemus, Jesus' skirted the actual question and moved straight to the point: "GOD IS SPIRIT, AND THE PEOPLE WHO WORSHIP HIM MUST WORSHIP IN SPIRIT AND TRUTH" (vs. 24). Apparently discouraged, she sighed that eventually Messiah would come and straighten it all out. At this, Jesus did what he did not even do for Nicodemus: he revealed his identity to her – "I . . . AM HE."

Returning to town, she tried to get people to go outside to meet Jesus. Because of her well-known status around town, the best she could do is plant the thought in their heads. The NET Bible accurately translates her attempt: "SURELY HE CAN'T BE THE MESSIAH, CAN HE?" (vs. 29) While she was in town, Jesus took the opportunity to teach his disciples about true ministry, even in a "questionable" context (vs. 31-38). When the villagers finally did come, they met Jesus, believed in him, and invited him to stay for two days before he moved on to Galilee (vs. 39-42). Back in Cana, he healed an official's sick son from a distance at the pleading of the father (vs. 46-54).

John noted that this was "HIS SECOND MIRACULOUS SIGN" in Galilee (vs. 54). This is significant for two reasons. First, it helps fit John into the chronology of the Synoptics. None of them record Jesus spending much time in Jerusalem or Judea this early in his ministry, so this southern ministry

---

31   It is both ironic and sad that worship styles and locations still cause so many debates today. While there are certainly guidelines set out in Scripture, Jesus showed that getting the message correct is the more important priority.

is unique to John and took place before the ministry in the other gospels. Second, John was clearly referring to the first two Galilee miracles, because he already said that Jesus had done miraculous signs "IN JERUSALEM AT THE FEAST OF THE PASSOVER" (2:23). Both the first and second miracles in Galilee were in Cana (2:11), before Jesus began healing the crowds (see Matthew 4:23).

Chapter five skips the early Galilean ministry that the Synoptics record, bringing Jesus back to Jerusalem for "A JEWISH FEAST" (vs. 1). There is considerable debate over which feast this was because identifying it would help with the chronology and timeline. Since John specifically mentions three Passovers (2:13, 23; 6:4; 12:1) and does not call this one a Passover, one could conclude that it may not have been. However, he also explicitly named the "FEAST OF TABERNACLES" (7:2) and "THE FEAST OF THE DEDICATION" (10:22), so the generic reference to "A JEWISH FEAST" makes it impossible to identify with certainty.[32]

Regardless of the exact feast, Jesus did attend in Jerusalem. While he was there, he performed a unique healing. Whereas the Synoptics show Jesus working with the vast crowds, healing hundreds and thousands at a time, John's focus was much more personal. Sometimes it is easy to forget that Jesus did not heal crowds, he healed people, and John emphasized the personal touch of the Savior. In this case, Jesus seems to have walked past and stepped over "A GREAT NUMBER OF SICK, BLIND, LAME, AND PARALYZED PEOPLE" to reach one man so that he could heal him (vs. 3-9). What a wonderful visual for a reader who has lost hope![33] At issue for the religious leaders was not

---

32 Given the placement of this event within the context of chapter six and allowing for the extended Galilean ministry of the Synoptics, there is good reason to see this as the Passover two years into Jesus' ministry.

33 There is a textual issue regarding whether verse four should be included or not. For sake of brevity we will only say that it is not found in the earliest Greek manuscripts and some of the manuscripts that do include it also have a symbol noting that they thought it was inauthentic. Nearly all conservative scholars reject its inclusion. However, whether it was original or not does not affect the meaning of the passage in any way.

that Jesus healed the man but that he did so on "A Sabbath" (vs. 9, 16). This is the first time John plainly showed the growing opposition between Jesus and the Pharisees (although 4:1 hints at it). When they approached the man to rebuke him for carrying his mat on the Sabbath, he replied that Jesus had healed him and told him to do so (vs. 10-15).

Verses 16-18 show the attitude of the religious leaders toward Jesus, including their early plans (still at least one year out from the crucifixion) to kill him. The rest of the chapter contains Jesus' first recorded defense of himself to them. In verses 19-30 Jesus insisted 1) that he worked and spoke only on the agenda of the Father, 2) that the Father had assigned to him the right to judge and save, and 3) that he was the Father's personal representative. Further, in verses 31-47, he insisted that he had the two or three witnesses that the Law required to prove him as authentic. These were John the Baptizer, his own deeds and miracles, and the Scriptures. Jesus' final question is just as appropriate today as it was then: "If you will not believe the Scriptures, how will you believe my own words?" (vs. 47, paraphrased)

Chapter six records the only miracle (except the resurrection itself) that appears in all four gospels – the feeding of five thousand men – yet it was only John who gave us the great follow-up teaching. The miracle itself adds no detail not found elsewhere: a multitude of probably 10,000-20,000 people stayed with Jesus all day, being healed and listening to his message; Jesus multiplied "five barley loaves and two fish" to feed them all to satisfaction; and there were twelve full baskets of leftovers (vs. 1-15). After the meal, the people attempted to make Jesus their king by force. John also recorded the follow-up miracle (vs. 16-24). Having sent the people away and the disciples back across the lake, Jesus prayed for a while, then walked across the violent sea, met the disciples, calmed the storm, and miraculously transported the boat to the other side.[34]

---

34 John did not record Peter walking on the water, but neither Matthew nor Mark recorded that the

It is at this point that John alone includes a major discourse (vs. 25-58), including the first of his seven "I am" declarations – "I AM THE BREAD OF LIFE." Jesus' teaching was his direct response to the crowd's question when they found him: "WHAT MUST WE DO TO ACCOMPLISH THE DEEDS GOD REQUIRES?" Jesus' simple response was the same then as it is today: "BELIEVE IN THE ONE HE HAS SENT" (vs. 28-29). Rather than responding in belief, they immediately asked for more signs (it was time for breakfast, after all), which Jesus refused. Instead, as with Nicodemus and the Samaritan woman, he changed the topic from physical bread to spiritual nourishment, which was available only through himself.

Their first negative reaction came from their own <u>experience</u>; they knew his family and background (vs. 41-42). Although the previous day they had wondered if he was "THE PROPHET" (vs. 14), now they demonstrated they were not interested in his word from God; they just wanted to be fed. Their second negative reaction came from their <u>unbelief</u>; they could not differentiate the spiritual from the physical, so Jesus' requirement to "EAT THE FLESH OF THE SON OF MAN AND DRINK HIS BLOOD" (vs. 53) was nonsensical and abhorrent to them. Jesus clarified that what he had said was spiritual, but they would not believe (vs. 63). In what is probably the worst verse in the entire Bible, "MANY OF HIS DISCIPLES QUIT FOLLOWING HIM AND DID NOT ACCOMPANY HIM ANY LONGER" (vs. 66).

The chapter ends with Jesus challenging the twelve apostles directly if they would leave as well. Peter's response should be the believer's mantra, no matter what we face in this life: "LORD, TO WHOM WOULD WE GO? YOU HAVE THE WORDS OF ETERNAL LIFE" (vs. 68).

Chapter seven through the first half of chapter ten all occurred at the same "FEAST OF TABERNACLES" (vs. 2), so they comprise a series of consecutive

---

boat "IMMEDIATELY . . . CAME TO THE LAND WHERE THEY HAD BEEN HEADING" (vs. 21), mentioning only that they got there.

events. Again, John noted that "THE JEWISH LEADERS WANTED TO KILL" Jesus, so he planned to attend the feast somewhat in hiding (vs. 10).

"WHEN THE FEAST WAS HALF OVER," Jesus did make himself known and "BEGAN TO TEACH ... IN THE TEMPLE COURTS" (vs. 14). However, there was still backlash from his healing of the lame man on the Sabbath (vs. 21-23; 5:1-9).[35] As expected, the two responses in Jerusalem were the same as from those in Galilee; their experience and unbelief prevented them from accepting Jesus' claim that he was from heaven, sent to and for humanity (vs. 25-36). Even so, many people did believe in him, further dividing the crowd and upsetting the stability the religious leaders had tried so hard to maintain.

A few days later, "ON THE LAST DAY OF THE FEAST," Jesus again took a public platform (vs. 37-49). Offering one of his clearest public invitations in John, Jesus called the people to come to him and find the living water promised by the prophets. John added the explanatory note in verse 39 that Jesus was prophesying about the Holy Spirit, who "HAD NOT YET BEEN GIVEN, BECAUSE JESUS WAS NOT YET GLORIFIED," a key truth in dispensational theology. Again, the crowd was divided, but the religious leaders' plan to arrest him at that time was thwarted. Nicodemus appeared the second of three times here, defending Jesus' rights as a Jewish citizen, but he was strong-armed out of the way by the others (vs. 50-52).

Chapter eight begins with a disputed passage. Scholars are divided about the authenticity of the passage about the woman caught in adultery (7:53–8:11). Many Bible translation committees choose to bracket and footnote the story rather than completely remove it, although they do not believe it is originally part of John. Whether the event itself genuinely occurred or not (and there is no reason to think that it did not), the language, style, and

---

35 This connection between chapters five and seven is sometimes argued to prove that the chapter five feast could not have been Passover. Since the Feast of Tabernacles was in the fall and Passover in the spring, it seems too long between them for this kind of response.

placement do not fit this narrative, which naturally resumes in vs. 12.[36] The great truth of the meeting is that Jesus showed the religious leaders their own sinfulness[37], while at the same time forgiving the woman of hers. It is essential to note his final words to her were "DO NOT SIN ANY MORE." He did not excuse her sin, but he did forgive it, knowing that they had probably entrapped her just to make a point.

Jesus responded to the retaliation against him from chapter seven with his second famous "I am" statement – "I AM THE LIGHT OF THE WORLD" (vs. 12). Since he was likely standing in the Temple (7:37), the reference may have been to the large candlesticks erected for the feast. Again, the Pharisees rejected Jesus' testimony about himself, so he responded with one more additional witness than he gave in chapter five – God himself as Jesus' Father (vs. 12-20). He continued stating some of the same things again, this time also prophesying his death, but still, they did not understand (vs. 21-30).

However, many people had already believed him, and many more did now, so he addressed them directly with spiritual teaching. The result was more negative reactions from the religious leaders (vs. 31-59). First, they questioned his teaching. Then, they attacked his personal background. Finally, they charged him with being demon-possessed. Each time Jesus responded with more truth against their lies. In a final statement, he plainly declared his deity by claiming that Abraham was glad to see him arrive, because "BEFORE ABRAHAM CAME INTO EXISTENCE, I AM!" (invoking the Old Testament personal name of God). At this, the mob tried to kill him, but he escaped from the Temple.

---

36 Some writers think that the story is genuine but should be included elsewhere, because the narrative flows naturally from 7:52 to 8:12 if not "interrupted" by the account.

37 Also debated is exactly what Jesus wrote in the dirt. Since the account does not say, it is impossible to be certain, but one view with a great deal of possibility was that he wrote the Ten Commandments, covering any sin the accusers may have committed, including adultery (the seventh commandment). Of special note is that he wrote "ON THE GROUND WITH HIS FINGER" (vs. 6). Compare this to the Ten Commandments which were "WRITTEN BY THE FINGER OF GOD" (Exodus 31:18).

Chapter nine continues the John 7-10 narrative. On his way out of the Temple, escaping the blood-thirsty mob, Jesus stopped to heal a blind man, because he is "THE LIGHT OF THE WORLD" (vs. 5, spoken the same day as 8:12). The disciples' question about the reason for the man's blindness betrayed their commonly-held belief that all sickness was a punishment for sin (vs. 1-7), the opposite of the belief that wealth signified God's favor. Instead, Jesus declared that sometimes things are simply given as a platform from which God will glorify himself. Although we do not like sickness and suffering, this perspective is essential to keep our proper focus in the middle of suffering.[38]

The rest of the chapter demonstrates the circus that happened because of the hatred the Pharisees had for Jesus. (Not only was it the last day of the feast, but it was also a Sabbath day again, vs. 14). Rather than celebrating with the man, who had been blind from birth, they interrogated him about his healing – going so far as to accuse him of only pretending to be blind (vs. 18)! They also interrogated his parents (vs. 18-23) and threatened to excommunicate them and their son from the synagogue if he did not renounce Jesus, whom he still had never yet seen (vs. 24-34). The detail John provided would have made the story slapstick funny if it were not so sad.

Jesus found the man, who believed in him immediately because of the healing and the treatment of the Pharisees against him (vs. 35-39). Speaking spiritually again, Jesus declared that he came specifically to help blind people see. Some Pharisees must have followed the man, because they overheard the conversation and asked Jesus if they were blind, which he affirmed (vs. 40-41).

Chapter ten finishes the story of the Feast of Tabernacles, then jumps ahead a couple of months. In verses 1-21, Jesus added two new "I am"

---

38 This is not to say that all sickness or suffering is God-given. All creation groans under the curse of sin (Romans 8:18-22), and sickness is part of that natural groaning. However, as in the case of this man, God does sometimes cause or allow certain events or situations specifically so he can step in and reveal himself again.

statements. First, he told a parable about a sheepfold and its gatekeeper (vs. 1-10). The gatekeeper alone decided who could enter and exit the sheepfold, prompting Jesus to claim, "I AM THE DOOR FOR THE SHEEP" (vs. 7). His purpose in coming was the exact opposite of the enemy. Instead of offering only death and destruction, Jesus offers life and abundance.

Shifting the parable a little bit, Jesus declared that he was not only the door, he was also "THE GOOD SHEPHERD" (vs. 11-13). This designation separated him from those who were only hired to watch the sheep, whose only goal was their own safety and salary, and who run at the first sign of trouble. This was a direct reference to the Pharisees, based on Ezekiel 34, where God condemned the false shepherds who mistreated his "sheep," the nation of Israel. Once again Jesus prophesied his death, this time including his resurrection, stating that he was personally in control of its occurrence (vs. 14-18). With each of these several interactions during the feast, the division in the crowd grew wider, with the favorite accusation that Jesus was demon-possessed (vs. 19-21).

Verse 22 moves forward about three months to "THE FEAST OF THE DEDICATION" in winter (more commonly known as "Hanukkah"). Jesus was back in Jerusalem in the Temple area, where the religious leaders approached him again, looking for something for which they could condemn him. This time they <u>wanted</u> him to claim to be Messiah (vs. 22-30). Instead, he once again claimed full deity, rather than being just a great prophet. When they intended to kill him again, he stopped them and asked for their reasoning (vs. 31-39). They responded that he had blasphemed by claiming to be equal with God, but he deftly argued that it was not blasphemy if it were true. This infuriated them, and they tried to grab him again but to no avail. He left Israel for a short while, staying on the other side of the Jordan River, where many people came to believe in him (vs. 40-42).

Chapter eleven is not specifically dated, but it took place during the four months between the feast of the Dedication and the following Passover (12:1). Jesus was still "hiding out" on the other side of the Jordan River when he received word that his dear friend Lazarus was deathly ill (vs. 1-16). Rather than going to see him right away, Jesus decided to wait for two days, declaring to his disciples, "THIS SICKNESS WILL NOT LEAD TO DEATH, BUT TO GOD'S GLORY." Although Lazarus did die in the intervening days, that is not where the sickness ended, proving again that the Father was in control of the obedient Jesus, even in events far removed from his location. After those two days, Jesus intended to visit his friends, but his disciples tried to stop him because of the death threats he received the last time he was there. After a few back and forth comments, and seeing that Jesus was not going to be swayed, the disciples agreed to go, with Thomas woefully stating, "LET US GO TOO, SO THAT WE MAY DIE WITH HIM" (vs. 16).

The rest of the chapter can be divided into three sections, all responses to Jesus' arrival: Martha's and Mary's response (vs. 17-37); Lazarus' response (vs. 38-44); and the people's response (vs. 45-53). Martha's and Mary's response was based in grief and their incredulity that Jesus did not come to them right away. They believed that, if he had come, he could have prevented Lazarus from dying (vs. 21, 32). In their grief, they limited his power to only the living. This set up his fifth great declaration – "I AM THE RESURRECTION AND THE LIFE" (vs. 25) – and his greatest question, relevant for all people and all time – "DO YOU BELIEVE THIS?" (vs. 26)[39]

Going to the tomb, Jesus ordered that the people remove the stone from the mouth of the cave. After a quick run-in with Martha again, Jesus offered a prayer of thanks that God always heard him and called for Lazarus to come out of his grave. We must not overlook the fact that only Lazarus, the dead man, responded immediately and obediently to the Savior that day; everyone else argued with him or questioned him. With new life, Lazarus

---

39 This is a wonderful passage for funerals of believers and unbelievers alike. Jesus' claim followed by Jesus' question puts the focus on the individual's relationship with him, nothing else.

came out of the tomb, "TO GOD'S GLORY" as Jesus had said.

The crowd responded to this miracle variously, as did the crowds in Jerusalem. Some believed in Jesus (vs. 45). Others relayed the story to the religious leaders (vs. 46). In council together with the priests and Pharisees, Caiaphas (unknowingly) made his great prophetic statement that he intended to have Jesus die "FOR THE PEOPLE" (vs. 50). John clarified that Jesus indeed would die, not just for Israel but for all people (vs. 51-52; 1 John 2:2). From this point on, Jesus stayed away from Jerusalem for the next few months leading up to Passover as he prepared himself for what was to come (vs. 54-57).

Chapter twelve records the final pieces of Jesus' public ministry. The Passion Week that the Synoptics unpacked in multiple chapters each, John limited to this one chapter, because his focus would be on Jesus' time with his disciples, which the other writers mostly panned.

It was also John who helped solidify the chronology of the Passion Week. With the Passover on Friday that year,[40] "SIX DAYS BEFORE" (vs. 1, probably inclusive, since they would not have traveled far on the Sabbath) would have been Sunday, meaning that Jesus' "Palm Sunday" entry into Jerusalem "THE NEXT DAY" (vs. 12) would have actually been on Monday. This fits best with the other details given in the Synoptics.

It was in Bethany, the hometown of Lazarus, that Martha and Mary entertained Jesus and his disciples. During this meal, Mary anointed Jesus' feet, which he accepted as his burial anointing (vs. 1-8). Word got out that Jesus was there, so the religious leaders planned to get both Jesus and Lazarus, because so many people were still coming to believe in Jesus because of Lazarus' resurrection (vs. 9-11).

While they were making their secret plans, Jesus made his move first.

---

40 Harold Hoehner's *Chronological Aspects of the Life of Christ* (Zondervan, 1977) is indispensable for those studying the timeline of Jesus' life and death.

In fulfillment of Zechariah 9:9 he rode a donkey's colt into Jerusalem, with his disciples and other believers leading the way from Bethany, celebrating his arrival and telling the others about him. Yet Jesus did not use this time for public aggrandizement (vs. 20-36). Rather than meeting with a lot of people, Jesus declared his purpose for being there – to die and rise again. The Father responded with a voice from heaven, but the crowd heard only thunder. Once again Jesus' plain teaching – this time about his death – was rejected. "ALTHOUGH JESUS HAD PERFORMED SO MANY MIRACULOUS SIGNS BEFORE THEM, THEY STILL REFUSED TO BELIEVE IN HIM" (vs. 37), and even many who did believe still refused to acknowledge him publicly, because "THEY LOVED PRAISE FROM MEN MORE THAN PRAISE FROM GOD" (vs. 43).

In his final public statement, Jesus called one more time for people to come to him and believe in him for eternal life. Those who did not would face God's judgment (vs. 44-50).

Chapters thirteen through seventeen have almost no parallel in the Synoptics. Except for the Passover meal itself and Jesus' prophecy that Peter would deny him (vs. 21-38), the rest of this exceptional section is found only in John.

At some point during the Passover meal, Jesus prepared himself to wash the feet of his disciples, including Judas Iscariot (vs. 1-17). John noted that this came from the proper perspective of who Jesus was and his role in God's eternal plan (vs. 3). Based on Jesus' interaction with Peter, it seems clear that this was a symbolic gesture, not something that is required to be repeated throughout the Church Age. Jesus told Peter, "IF I DO NOT WASH YOU, YOU HAVE NO SHARE IN ME" (vs. 8), yet he acknowledged that Peter had already been cleansed. As he had done so frequently, Jesus was speaking of spiritual matters while using a physical illustration. In this, we find the seeds of the principle John later developed that a believer (someone already cleansed) still needs "maintenance cleaning" through confession of sin (1 John 1:5-10).

Additionally, this represented a humility in service toward one another that Jesus did expect them to continue (vs. 12-17).

In verses 21-30 Jesus foretold his betrayal by Judas. Here again, John helped clarify how Jesus could speak so plainly yet the disciples did not understand. It appears that John quietly asked Jesus who the betrayer would be.[41] Jesus' response, then, was to John, not to the entire room, so when he spoke to Judas, no one understood or reacted against him, including Peter.

Only after Judas left do we find the beginning of new teachings, just for the faithful Eleven, especially over the next three chapters. The first was that the disciples should learn to love one another with Christ's own love, as a major display of their faith to an unbelieving world (vs. 31-38). Probably in an attempt to show that he was ready for the task, Peter swore that he would always follow Jesus, only to hear that he would actually deny him.

Chapter fourteen is the first of three chapters called the "Upper Room Discourse," although only chapter fourteen took place in the upper room (vs. 31). In this time of extended teaching, it is essential to note three keys for proper interpretation. First, only the eleven believing apostles were present, since Judas had already left. Second, the entire teaching assumes their saving faith. Jesus had already told them that they were clean (13:10) and reaffirmed that in 15:3. Spiritual growth or maturity, not salvation or belief, is the defining issue throughout. Third, much of this teaching referred to things that were still future for the apostles. A comparison of what was future to them at this point with what was present in their later writings (along with Paul's) proves that this teaching was the first detailed information revealed about the coming Church Age.

After the promise that he would go away then return for them, Jesus offered his sixth declaration: "I AM THE WAY, AND THE TRUTH, AND THE

---

41 Since John asked at Peter's request, who would draw his sword later that evening (18:10), it is not a stretch to think that Peter was ready to take care of the betrayer right then.

LIFE. NO ONE COMES TO THE FATHER EXCEPT THROUGH ME" (vs. 6). It would be essential that they understood this truth in their upcoming evangelistic ministry and the persecution they would suffer. However, in a demonstration of continued misunderstanding, Philip asked if they could see the Father, prompting Jesus again to state his full deity and role within the Godhead (vs. 8-14).

The first new future Jesus promised would be the coming of the Holy Spirit (vs. 15-31). His coming would accomplish three things. First, he would replace Jesus as the apostles' personal connection to God while Jesus was away. This would be through an indwelling presence rather than a physical presence as when Jesus had been with them. Second, he would cause them to remember everything that Jesus had taught them for their later ministry (both for teaching and writing).[42] Third, he would bring God's peace upon them during what would prove to be a tumultuous time. Believers throughout the Church Age have continued to share in some of these blessings.

Chapter fifteen occurred while Jesus and the apostles were on the move from the upper room to Gethsemane. Whether Jesus was pointing to the sculpted vine on the Temple wall or a physical grapevine in a vineyard along the way, he used the illustration of the vine and branches as the basis of his final "I am" declaration and a significant teaching for believers of this dispensation (vs. 1-16).

"I AM THE TRUE VINE AND MY FATHER IS THE GARDENER...YOU ARE THE BRANCHES" (vs. 1, 5). Because of the mention that branches have the possibility of being burned (vs. 6), many have taken this passage to mean that believers can lose their salvation. Again, it is important to remember that one must read salvation into the passage to reach this conclusion, because

---

42 Although the Holy Spirit does have an enlightening ministry toward Christians (1 Corinthians 2:9-16), this promise more specifically refers to how the Spirit would inspire the Scriptures through the apostles and how they would speak under persecution. See Matthew 10:19-20 for an earlier version of this promise to the twelve apostles.

salvation is not a topic found anywhere in the text of the Upper Room Discourse. Rather the entire passage is about spiritual maturity and service, how branches are to bear fruit for the Gardener. The mention of burning is incidental in the middle of the teaching on staying connected to Jesus, his words, and his love. This connection is exhibited and strengthened by willful obedience to him.

It is a wonderful truth to remember that the branch is not ultimately responsible for the vineyard. It is the Gardener who determines what fruit he wants, how much fruit is enough, and which branches will produce which types and amounts of fruit. It is the branches' job simply to submit to the care of the Gardner and produce what he desires and is cultivating in them (Philippians 2:12-13).

For those believers who insist on honoring the Father by obeying him and bearing much fruit for his use, Jesus promised that they would be hated by this world (vs. 17-27). This made sense to him because they hated and rejected him, and those who follow him would find the same response. However, this should not cause his followers to lose sight of their (our) mission. To help us stay on course, a fourth ministry of the indwelling Holy Spirit is that he supernaturally gave the same testimony about Jesus in this world that they would give.

Chapter sixteen concludes this discourse with final encouragements for the apostles. Jesus said that he specifically told them these things, rather than just letting them happen, "SO THAT YOU WILL NOT FALL AWAY" (vs. 1). No matter what situation they faced, they would have the indwelling Holy Spirit and the promise of the coming Savior himself. The Holy Spirit would go into the world before them, convicting people before the apostles preached the gospel. In this sense, it was even better than having Jesus with them (vs. 5-11).

Like creation and conscience (Romans 1), the Holy Spirit's conviction of the entire world will give no one an excuse before God. Since God "WANTS ALL PEOPLE TO BE SAVED AND TO COME TO A KNOWLEDGE OF THE TRUTH" (1 Timothy 2:4) and since Jesus "IS THE ATONING SACRIFICE FOR OUR SINS AND ... FOR THE WHOLE WORLD" (1 John 2:2), the message of the Holy Spirit in this world is for "ALL PEOPLE EVERYWHERE TO REPENT" (Acts 17:30), not just a select few.

Jesus also promised that the Holy Spirit would continue to teach them, since he would be speaking from God as did Jesus (vs. 12-16). There were things they just would not have been able to understand yet at that point. We can see this growing understanding throughout the stories and writings of the rest of the New Testament. The apostles were not exempt in having to work through their own spiritual growth process as we do today.

Throughout this discourse, the apostles had many questions. John did not record most of them in the previous chapters, but now that Jesus had approached the end, he acknowledged their questions and promised that they would understand everything in time (vs. 19-33).

One final change between their old way and the new way to come was the method of prayer (vs. 24-28). Jesus said that to that point they had not prayed in his name, but this was about to change. Now we pray to the Father in the name of (or with the authority and privilege of) Jesus himself. One last time he warned them of the trouble they were to face, but that they should not worry because he had already conquered the world (1 John 5:4-5).

Chapter seventeen is one of the greatest chapters in the entire Bible. Approaching Gethsemane after the Upper Room Discourse, Jesus spent time alone in prayer. Although the Synoptics record only that he prayed for God's will and that he had asked the apostles to join him from a distance, only John contains the actual prayer Jesus made. This is truly the "Lord's Prayer."

Jesus' prayer can be divided into three sections. In verses 1-5, Jesus began by connecting with the Father. He recognized that the eternal plan was always to glorify the Father; he stated that he had finished his work; and he asked that he be allowed to return to Heaven and reclaim the full glory he had set aside in his incarnation (see Philippians 2:5-8).

In verses 6-19, he prayed for his apostles who were sleeping a short distance away. He thanked the Father for the time he had spent with them, teaching them the Father's truth. He prayed for their safety from the Enemy in the coming days when he would no longer be with them, especially before the Holy Spirit indwelt them (nearly two months later). He asked that they would experience the supernatural joy that comes with being connected to the Father. He also prayed that they would stay consecrated to God through the Scriptures, something that all believers still need today.

Finally, in verses 20-26, Jesus prayed for all "THOSE WHO BELIEVE IN ME THROUGH THEIR TESTIMONY," i.e., all those who would come to faith after the apostles, including us today. He prayed specifically for our unity.[43] He also prayed that we would accomplish our mission of presenting the truth of Jesus to the world. He finished by praying for the day when we would all finally be together forever. What a wonderful thought to consider that the Savior prayed for me just hours before he faced the cross!

Chapters eighteen and nineteen cover approximately eighteen hours, from Jesus' arrest in the garden to his death and burial. Possibly trying to show the rushed way in which it happened, John only briefly mentioned a series of seven events that took place in fewer than twelve hours.

First, in an amazing display of sovereignty, Jesus took his apostles to meet with Judas (vs. 1-11). When Jesus identified himself, Judas' mob fell away in terror. He negotiated that they would take him and allow the apostles to go free. Peter, who had already said he would stand with Jesus, struck out

---

43   Many have taken this idea of unity to be Jesus' overarching message. Unfortunately, they attempt to do this at the expense of biblical doctrine and sometimes even salvation. Jesus does not want believers to be unified with the world, and the apostles later wrote that genuine Christian unity is based in the Scriptures and correct doctrine, not emotions or social programs.

with his sword, injuring the high priest's slave, but Jesus rebuked him.

Second, Jesus was put on trial and interrogated by the high priest himself (vs. 12-14, 19-24). Interestingly, John noted that they questioned him "ABOUT HIS DISCIPLES AND ABOUT HIS TEACHING" (vs. 19). His only response was that there were plenty of people who could answer those questions, because he taught in public. This was also the beginning of Jesus' physical torture, as an officer struck him in the face.

Meanwhile, while Jesus was being questioned, Peter was also being scrutinized (vs. 15-18, 25-27). Three times in a row someone recognized and identified him as being one of Jesus' followers. One person was even a relative of the man whose ear Peter had cut off. Each time he denied the association, then the rooster crowed as Jesus had said.

Fourth, Jesus was transferred to Pilate, the regional Roman governor, for questioning (vs. 28-32). Because the religious leaders insisted that they wanted Jesus executed (vs. 31), Pilate had to do an interview of his own.[44] Although he attempted to discover why they hated Jesus, he could not find any reason that Jesus deserved to die. He offered to pardon and release him, but they called for Barabbas' release instead.

Chapter nineteen continues the morning's events, skipping Jesus' short appearance before Herod (Luke 23:6-12). The fifth event in John's record, then, was Pilate's second interview with Jesus (vs. 1-16). Still unable to find any reason to execute him, Pilate had him beaten and humiliated instead, hoping that would satisfy the crowd, but it did not. It seems that he tried multiple times and methods to find a way by which he could release Jesus, but they refused his offers. Finally, the religious leaders threatened Pilate's political career by pitting him against Caesar if he released Jesus. At this Pilate gave them permission to crucify him.

---

44 Under Roman law, the Jews did not have the authority to execute anyone without the consent of the local Roman authority.

The sixth event was the crucifixion itself (vs. 17-27). This lasted for several hours, though John did not record the exact length or the period of darkness as found in the Synoptics. Jesus' opponents had one more run-in with Pilate, who wrote Jesus' criminal charge to be "JESUS THE NAZARENE, THE KING OF THE JEWS" (vs. 19). They naturally took offense at this, but Pilate was done being pushed around by them, and probably took some pleasure at their indignation and the fact that they could do nothing about it. While Jesus was on the cross, the prophecy was fulfilled about his robe being gambled away (Psalm 22:18). At the foot of the cross were some of the faithful women who had followed and supported Jesus, and John himself. Jesus charged John with taking care of Mary (probably because Joseph was dead by this time).

The final event of the day was Jesus' death (vs. 28-37). John recorded only two of Jesus' final statements – "I AM THIRSTY!" and "IT IS COMPLETED!" – before noting that Jesus gave up his own spirit. There is great irony in the religious leaders' insistence that the rituals of Passover and Sabbath be strictly observed while they violated several of them in their campaign against Jesus. However, because of their rush to get the bodies off the crosses and into their graves, the soldiers discovered that Jesus was already dead and did not break his legs, fulfilling another prophecy (Psalm 34:20). Instead, they punctured his side.

Joseph of Arimathea received permission from Pilate to bury Jesus' body, and he was accompanied by Nicodemus (his third appearance in John). They performed a quick burial and place the body in Joseph's own tomb before the beginning of the Sabbath at sunset (vs. 38-42).

Chapter twenty jumps ahead about 36 hours from sunset on Friday to sunrise on Sunday (vs. 1-9). Mary Magdalene (and other women, according to the other accounts) approached the tomb but found it open. She ran to tell Peter and John about it, and they came to find Jesus' body gone but the wrappings still in the tomb. When they went back home, Mary stayed there weeping at the shock of Jesus' body having apparently been stolen (vs. 10-18). In what can only be called an extreme measure of grace, Jesus appeared to her as the first to see him alive again. Not only did she get to announce the open tomb, she had the privilege to announce the resurrection as well.

Later that evening, while the apostles met in a locked room to discuss the day's events, Jesus appeared to them (vs. 19-23). Much has been written and debated about what Jesus meant when "HE BREATHED ON THEM AND SAID, 'RECEIVE THE HOLY SPIRIT'" (vs. 22). Comparing this passage with the permanent indwelling of the Holy Spirit in Acts 2, it seems that this was the point of their "salvation," where they were born again based on the resurrection, even though the Church had not yet begun. This temporary indwelling of the Spirit would be replaced by his permanent indwelling 50 days later. The statement about forgiving and retaining sins seems to look back to Jesus' only other recorded mentions of discipline in the Church context in Matthew 16:19 and 18:15-22.

Although there were several other appearances, John made special mention of one a week later, when Thomas was with the rest of the apostles (vs. 24-29). Apparently, he had refused to believe their report that Jesus was alive and said that he needed physical proof. At this, Jesus appeared and offered his hands and side as the proof Thomas needed. Immediately Thomas believed, but not without a minor rebuke from Jesus about his lack of faith.

The chapter ends with John's stated purpose of the book: that his readers would come to know Jesus as the true Messiah, the Son of God, and that they would believe in him for eternal life (vs. 30-31). Although Jesus certainly did and said much more than John recorded, nothing else is necessary to provide evidence of the truth of who he is and what he did.

Chapter twenty-one concludes John's gospel with a final appearance of Jesus not mentioned in the Synoptics. There is no indication given of how much time had passed between the chapter twenty appearances and this one (not more than forty days, Acts 1:3). However, Peter was unsure how to proceed or what was supposed to happen, so he went back to the thing he knew best: fishing (vs. 1-14). Early the next morning "JESUS STOOD ON THE BEACH" as they came back in with no catch. He told them to cast the net right where they were, and they brought in a whole load. (The fact that John counted out 153 fish is a bizarre detail that has stumped many commentators over the years.) At this, John told Peter that it was Jesus, and Peter jumped out of the boat and swam to shore. In what must have been a surreal moment for these seven apostles, Jesus invited them to have a private breakfast with him, featuring fish and bread over a charcoal fire. John noted that this was only the third time they had seen him as a group, although he had made other personal appearances.

Following breakfast, Jesus turned his attention to Peter, the one who had boldly declared his unwavering support then blatantly denied the Savior while he was being interrogated (vs. 15-19). In an amazing example of tough grace, Jesus restored Peter, one step at a time. The three calls have an obvious comparison to the three denials. Each time Jesus asked Peter to recant his denials, he also reinforced Peter's commissioning. He finished by foretelling the method of Peter's death – tied up and stretched out, which Church history shows to have been crucifixion.

Peter turned the conversation to John, asking how he would die (vs. 20-23). Jesus stated that was none of Peter's concern, and that John could live until Jesus' return if that was what Jesus wanted. John said that this was eventually blown out of context to mean that John would not die, which is not what Jesus said.

John concluded his writing with the famous reminder that it contains only a selection of Jesus' actual ministry (vs. 24-25). With a line reminiscent of great writers like C.S. Lewis, John thoughtfully mused, "IF EVERY ONE OF THEM WERE WRITTEN DOWN, I SUPPOSE THE WHOLE WORLD WOULD NOT HAVE ROOM FOR THE BOOKS THAT WOULD BE WRITTEN."

Acts

This second volume of the Luke-Acts set is entitled "The Acts of the Apostles." However, some prefer to call it "The Acts of the Holy Spirit," because, no matter how much recognition the apostles get, the Holy Spirit was the person and power behind them. In Acts alone, the Holy Spirit is referred to more than sixty times, at least twice the mentions he received in any other book of the Bible.

Acts is the story of the Church – what it is and how it began. Many favorite Sunday School stories appear in its pages as Luke introduced his reader, initially Theophilus, to both the good and the bad events the early Christians experienced. The book covers the first 30 years of Church history, from its inception in A.D. 33 through Paul's first Roman imprisonment, ending in A.D. 62.

There are at least three different ways to outline the book into its natural, broad divisions. The shortest outline is the simple division between Peter's work (chapters 1-12) and Paul's (chapters 13-28). Second, Acts 1:8 gives a threefold outline. Jesus told the apostles they would be his witnesses in Jerusalem (chapters 1-8), Judea and Samaria (chapters 9-12), and the furthest parts of the earth (chapters 13-28). Another outline, less obvious, reveals six key divisions using Luke's "progress reports" of the Church's growth in 6:7;

9:31; 12:24; 16:5; 19:20; and 28:31.

The major key to interpreting Acts is understanding that it is transitional in nature. Much of the book is *descriptive* (what the early Christians experienced or did) rather than *prescriptive* (what all Christians should experience or do). In fact, there are many things Luke recorded that we should not expect to be normative today, and recognizing those differences is an important component of correct interpretation.

Chapter one picks up immediately where Luke's gospel ended. It is obvious that Luke intended for this to be a second volume, as his introduction to Theophilus shows (vs. 1-2).[45] None of the gospels gives a full account of Jesus' work following his resurrection, but Luke noted in verse three that Jesus spent 40 days with the apostles, teaching them "ABOUT MATTERS CONCERNING THE KINGDOM OF GOD." One of these matters was the baptism of the Holy Spirit, which would occur shortly. Until that time (Jesus did not say how long), they were to wait in Jerusalem. However, after it happened, Jesus promised that they would "RECEIVE POWER," with the result that they would "BE...WITNESSES" (vs. 8). "My witnesses" means they would preach about Jesus, which makes sense because he had already told them that they would receive "THE SPIRIT OF TRUTH WHO GOES OUT FROM THE FATHER – HE WILL TESTIFY ABOUT ME, AND YOU ALSO WILL TESTIFY" (John 15:26-27).

Although they wanted to know more about the Messianic kingdom and its timing, Jesus would tell them no more. In what was apparently a surprise to them, Jesus ascended into heaven, slowly disappearing until they could no longer see him (vs. 9-11). As they searched the skies, two angels told them to obey Jesus' instructions to wait in Jerusalem. He would come back the same way he left – physically and visibly.

During the next ten days, they waited and prayed (vs. 12-14). At this

---

45 Based on the almost "hurried" ending in chapter 28, some people propose that Luke may have intended a third volume of Paul's later travels and additional Church history. What a great resource that would have been!

time, there were about 120 believers waiting for whatever was going to come next. Based on their interpretation of two psalms, they decided that Judas' position needed to be filled with a twelfth apostle (vs. 15-26). Rather than putting it to a popular vote, they took two steps. First, they nominated only those with specific qualifications – a man, who had accompanied them everywhere, and who had been part of the group since Jesus' baptism, which eliminated all but two candidates. Second, they placed these two men before God, praying and casting lots for direction. The lot fell to Matthias, "SO HE WAS COUNTED WITH THE ELEVEN APOSTLES."

Chapter two records the event that has set the tone for the past 2,000 years of human history. The apostles waited for ten days in Jerusalem for the baptism of the Holy Spirit that Jesus promised, until the Day of Pentecost (vs. 1-3). While the Twelve[46] were celebrating the Feast of Weeks together (Leviticus 23:15-22), the Holy Spirit entered the house where they had gathered, coming in the form of a singular flame of fire which divided itself and "CAME TO REST UPON EACH ONE OF THEM." This signified that his presence was not only general but individual.

Immediately the men (vs. 15) began praising God in other languages (vs. 4). Quoting the prophet Joel, Peter explained that this miracle was the manifestation of the Holy Spirit in them (vs. 14-21), which began to fulfill God's promise that the Spirit would come upon people again. We should note that this is the clearest passage in Scripture that describes what "tongues" are; they are human languages previously unknown[47] to the speaker. Additionally, it is important to observe that the preaching was done in the common language, not in the other languages. The other languages were used to give

---

46 Whether it was only the Twelve or the entire group of believers gathered on that day is debated, but the evidence seems to lean toward only the Twelve.

47 "Previously unknown" does not mean that the men learned these languages and were able to speak them fluently again. It means that, at the time of their speaking, they knew what they were saying, although they had not learned that language before.

praise to God, not the gospel message or new revelation or prophecy. This was the pattern in all three occurrences of speaking in tongues/languages in Acts (2:1-13; 10:44-48; 19:1-7).

After explaining how the Twelve could miraculously speak these other languages, Peter preached to the captivated crowd, highlighting two key points, each prefaced by "David said." First, Jesus was God's prophet, whom they publicly crucified, but he was resurrected (vs. 22-32). Second, Jesus was God's Messiah, and he ascended to heaven to wait until he can receive his kingdom (vs. 33-36). This was the crux of the matter: "GOD HAS MADE THIS JESUS WHOM YOU CRUCIFIED BOTH LORD AND CHRIST" (LORD = Jehovah, CHRIST = Messiah).

Under the conviction of the Holy Spirit, the crowd asked the apostles how they should respond to the message (vs. 37-41). Peter's reply was that they should repent – the same message given by John the Baptizer, Jesus, and the apostles over the previous several years. Upon repentance, they would gain forgiveness of their sins and the Holy Spirit as God's gift. Each one who believed should also be baptized as a public indication of this new belief.[48]

Out of the thousands in Jerusalem for Pentecost, "ABOUT THREE THOUSAND PEOPLE" joined the little band of Christians that day (vs. 41-47). Fully expecting that Jesus would return shortly, especially after that show of acceptance, they gathered together regularly, both in the Temple and in their homes. They began selling off their possessions and sharing what they had with each other, knowing they would not need anything in the Kingdom, because the prophets promised that Messiah would provide for them. They listened to the apostles teach, probably what they had learned from Jesus about the Kingdom (1:3). They were a happy, excited group, constantly sharing their joy with their neighbors. As a result, many others joined their group

---

48 Most English translations make it seem as if water baptism was required to be forgiven and receive the Holy Spirit. While it is a command in the sentence, the structure of the Greek language separates baptism from the rest of the sentence, not putting it on the same level as repentance but rather subsequent to repentance. Water baptism was the visible sign that these Jews – many of whom had possibly celebrated Jesus' death just weeks earlier – were now embracing him as the Messiah.

expecting to see Messiah again any day.

Chapter three offers just one example of what the end of chapter two looked like in reality. These new Jewish Christians did not change from their normal Jewish patterns. On one normal day, Peter and John went to the Temple for prayer and passed a certain lame beggar. When asked for alms (which was a normal act of obedience for Temple-goers), the apostles gave the man something much greater: his legs (vs. 1-7). The response was what we would expect – amazement from the crowds who recognized him as the lame man.

Peter used the opportunity to present the message of Jesus again. The purpose of that miracle (and the others recorded) was to point to the truth that Jesus of Nazareth was their Messiah. Just as Jesus had made the lame walk during his ministry, he was still doing it through these men, who were obviously commissioned with his power and authority. Even though the nation was guilty of crucifying him, Peter conceded that they did it out of ignorance (vs. 17). Although this did not remove their guilt, God had used their sin to fulfill his plan, and now he offered them another chance to accept his message: Jesus is God's Messiah; accept him in order to enter his kingdom.

Chapter four introduces the first major pushback since the crucifixion. Naturally, the religious leaders thought they had done away with Jesus for good. However, his followers were still preaching his message with results that made the leaders furious. As Peter and John were speaking to the crowd from chapter three, they were arrested and put in jail overnight. Luke noted that the people had already responded, though. The initial band of "ABOUT THREE THOUSAND PEOPLE" (2:41) had multiplied between five and ten times to "ABOUT FIVE THOUSAND MEN" (easily 15,000 - 30,000 people including families; vs. 1-4).

When Peter and John stood before the ruling council, it must have been surreal to know that Jesus stood there only months before. They certainly must have wondered if they would be crucified next, yet this did not stop them. Two years earlier Jesus had told them, "WHENEVER THEY HAND YOU OVER FOR TRIAL, DO NOT WORRY ABOUT HOW TO SPEAK OR WHAT TO SAY, FOR WHAT YOU SHOULD SAY WILL BE GIVEN TO YOU AT THAT TIME. FOR IT IS NOT YOU SPEAKING, BUT THE SPIRIT OF YOUR FATHER SPEAKING THROUGH YOU" (Matthew 10:19-20). On this day Peter was "FILLED WITH THE HOLY SPIRIT" and began to preach Jesus to the very ones who had dragged him to Pilate (vs. 8-12).

At that point, the religious leaders recognized four things: 1) these were not the same timid men who ran away a few months earlier when Jesus was arrested; 2) they were working under an influence that did not require formal training; 3) the man was undeniably healed; and 4) they had no legitimate case against the apostles. With the influence the apostles were gaining among the people, the leaders must have felt they were experiencing *déjà vu* (vs. 13-22). The only thing they could do was order the apostles to not preach Jesus again. When the apostles replied that was impossible because of the things they had experienced, the leaders could only double down on their insistence.

Upon being reunited, the church celebrated God's work in and through them. Amazingly, instead of praying for relief from what was certainly going to be growing persecution, they prayed specifically for boldness "TO SPEAK YOUR MESSAGE WITH GREAT COURAGE," which God granted them (vs. 23-31). The unity of the believers during this time was remarkable, especially compared to the petty divisions that would come very soon. They genuinely cared for one another, taking care of each other and submitting to the authority and wisdom of the apostles (vs. 32-37).

Chapters five and six demonstrate that, even in the early Church, sinful people are always the greatest hindrance to Christian ministry. In chapter five Luke recorded one such scandal. Some people apparently had made large donations to the community through the sale of private land (Barnabas, 4:36-37), resulting in public praise. A couple named Ananias and Sapphira desired the public recognition, but they wanted their money as well. So, they devised a plan to make a large donation, saying it was 100% of the sale proceeds, while keeping some of it for themselves. In a great act of power, the Holy Spirit gave Peter insight into what they had done and killed them immediately (vs. 1-10). This caused three results (vs. 11-16). First, the entire church was gripped with fear of sin. Second, those outside the church were afraid to get too close to the believers, maybe for fear they too would be "struck by lightning." Third, many came to faith in Jesus because of the power exhibited in that situation and the other miracles the apostles were doing. This was no mere show; God's power was visibly at work among the believers, and people crowded around them for healing the same way they had done to Jesus just three or four years earlier.

As more people joined this new movement, the religious leaders arrested the apostles again (vs. 17-26). This time they were miraculously released overnight, and they went back to the Temple the next day to preach. This caused confusion when the Sanhedrin ordered them from the jail to stand trial, because they were no longer there. Instead, they had to arrest the apostles again. This time Peter was blunt: "WE MUST OBEY GOD RATHER THAN PEOPLE" (vs. 29). Interestingly, it was a sage named Gamaliel (the apostle Paul's early mentor, Acts 22:3) who offered this warning: "If this is just a human thing, it will come to nothing, but if it truly is from God, we do not want to be on the wrong side of it" (vs. 34-39). Momentarily convinced, they released the apostles again, this time with a beating, and threatened them. However, this only drove the men harder to preach and honor Jesus.

Chapter six points out the second of the two major internal issues. Not only did personal pride and scandal attack the Church; they also had to deal with "church politics" and racial struggles. After some time had passed, the apostles were bombarded with complaints from the Greek-speaking Jews. They charged that their widows were being overlooked while the Hebrew-speaking widows were carefully cared for. The apostles knew this could greatly damage the Church, so they began to add structure to the church, namely a group of seven men who served under the apostles' direction to make sure all the widows were served.[49] As the church grew, the apostles needed to stay focused on the Word and prayer (vs. 1-6).

Verse seven contains the first of six "progress reports" Luke provided in Acts. Thus, we arrive at the first break, the church still growing yet unknowingly headed for her first major tragic blow.

One of the chosen seven men was Stephen, who is described as "A MAN FULL OF FAITH AND OF THE HOLY SPIRIT...FULL OF GRACE AND POWER" (vs. 5, 8). He was apparently a powerful preacher, and the Holy Spirit used him to perform many miracles alongside his preaching (vs. 9-14). This resulted in opposition against him personally. Even though he was not one of the Twelve, some foreign Jews (Asian, Egyptian, and Greek) had him arrested and produced false witnesses against him, much like they did against Jesus, accusing him of treason against God's Law. Luke included a wonderful little note that, as he stood before them, Stephen's face appeared angelic (vs. 15). What that means exactly is unclear, but they somehow knew that a messenger of God was standing before them.

Chapter seven is primarily the record of Stephen's defense statement to the Sanhedrin. The charge against him was speaking against the Temple and changing what Moses had given Israel (6:13-14), essentially going against God and his revelation. In his statement, Stephen recounted the history of

---

49 It is often assumed that these were the first "deacons," because that Greek word means "servant" or "minister." However, the ministry of some of these men far exceeded simply ministering to the church members. It is also worth noting that, even though the people may have found and nominated the Seven, they were officially commissioned and put into service by the Apostles, not the congregation.

God's dealings with Israel, reminding them of three key truths.

First, he reminded them that the Mosaic Law was not the totality of God's revelation (vs. 2-16). In fact, God spoke to Abraham long before he gave the Law, while Abraham was still a pagan serving idols. God made several promises to Abraham about his descendants, even though he did not yet have even one child. As he began to fulfill those promises, God protected the family for multiple generations, even in Egypt.

Second, he reminded them that Moses was not the flawless hero they made him out to be (vs. 17-29). Although God certainly used him, it was despite Moses' early actions and attitude, not because of them. He required time in the desert to grow his humility.

Third, he reminded them that when God finally did give the Law through Moses, the people rejected and disobeyed it (vs. 30-50). They immediately built an altar with Aaron and turned toward other gods throughout their history. When Solomon finally built that beautiful Temple they were so proud of, God himself reminded them that he "DOES NOT LIVE IN HOUSES MADE BY HUMAN HANDS."

Finally, after reminding them of all these things, Stephen turned their accusation back on them (vs. 51-53). "YOU ARE ALWAYS RESISTING THE HOLY SPIRIT, LIKE YOUR ANCESTORS DID!" At this, they immediately and unanimously moved to kill him (vs. 54-60). Seeing Jesus himself looking on, Stephen died with forgiveness on his lips, just as the Savior did.

Chapter eight introduces the key antagonist of the story. Luke mentioned that Saul was a co-conspirator at Stephen's murder, albeit not a full participant. The most zealous of his peers (Galatians 1:14), Saul used Stephen's "blasphemy" as the perfect impetus to begin an outright war with these Jewish traitors, who blatantly worshiped a criminal instead of God. He made it his personal mission to "DESTROY THE CHURCH" by any means necessary (vs. 1-3).

Like the Tower of Babel, however, God used this as the catalyst to scatter the early Christians and spread the gospel. For the first time, Samaritans were presented with the truth, and they accepted it in multitudes (vs. 4-8). The miracles Philip performed convinced even a local magician, Simon, that this message was truly from God (vs. 9-13). Peter and John arrived from Jerusalem to confirm what was happening, which they saw when the Holy Spirit came on the Samaritans (vs. 14-17). This impressed the magician who wanted that power as well, offering money to learn their "spell" (vs. 18-25). Some have questioned Simon's salvation because of this, but Peter's command that he should "REPENT OF THIS WICKEDNESS" and pray for forgiveness seems to indicate that his infant faith was genuine.

Luke recorded one more scenario of the gospel spreading beyond the Jewish people (vs. 26-40). Philip received a direct order through an angel to meet with a man on the road between Jerusalem and Gaza, whom he discovered to be an Ethiopian official. Philip caught up with him and got into his chariot, realizing that the man was reading from the prophet Isaiah without understanding it. Philip was able to start from that passage (Isaiah 53:7-8) and point him to Jesus. The Ethiopian believed, and Philip baptized him immediately. The Holy Spirit then "SNATCHED PHILIP AWAY" (the same verb used for the Rapture in 1 Thessalonians 4:17) and dropped him in Azotus, where he continued to preach the gospel.

There is a textual note to consider regarding verse 37. Only a handful of Greek manuscripts include this verse, and most of them were copied during the tenth to twelfth centuries (AD 900-1100). Because of their late date and scarcity, it is best to see this verse as a later addition to Acts. Those who argue that the gospel message is misrepresented without this verse are ignoring the facts that 1) Luke's purpose in this short passage was to show the rapid geographical spread of the gospel, not present the whole message and 2) the entire gospel message is found repeatedly in Acts and is not dependent on this one verse.

Chapter nine begins with "MEANWHILE," an ominous segue pitting God's great work through Philip with Satan's work through Saul. That was about to change. Securing warrants for all Jewish believers found in and around synagogues (their jurisdiction), Saul traveled to Damascus, more than 150 miles (240 km) north of Jerusalem, to arrest these Jews who had turned to worship Jesus (vs. 1-9). On the way, Jesus himself stopped Saul, and Saul was converted as well. However, the encounter blinded him, so he spent three days fasting and praying in darkness.

One of the disciples in Damascus Paul certainly would have arrested was Ananias. In a vision, God told him to go to Saul and lay hands on him so he could see again (vs. 10-12). Naturally, Ananias was reluctant, but God told him that Saul was God's man now, the one who would present the gospel to the Gentiles (vs. 13-16). Ananias obeyed. Saul regained his sight and immediately began preaching Christ, which caused him to have to run for his life (vs. 17-25). Paul included more detail in Galatians 1-2 than Luke does here, but eventually Saul made it back to Jerusalem to meet with the apostles, with Barnabas vouching for him (vs. 26-30).

During this time Peter also did some itinerant preaching, performing miracles as Jesus did, including healing a paralyzed man and raising a woman from the dead (vs. 32-43). This solidified the focus of the two men – Peter to the Jews and Paul to the Gentiles (Galatians 2:7-9).

Chapter ten records a major turning point in the history of the Church. To this point, the Church was still primarily Jewish, even after about ten years. When Luke gave his second progress report, he mentioned only the areas of "JUDEA, GALILEE, AND SAMARIA" (9:31). In this chapter, we find the first intentional gospel presentation to Gentiles. (The Ethiopian in chapter eight was probably a Jewish proselyte, someone who had converted to Judaism.)

God took two steps of preparation that made this transition from Jew to Gentile work smoothly. First, he chose a specific Gentile. Cornelius was "A

DEVOUT, GOD-FEARING MAN," a Gentile who had come to faith in the true God but did not fully convert to Judaism (vs. 2). God told Cornelius to send for the apostle Peter, who would come and preach to him (vs. 3-8, 30-33).

The second step was to prepare Peter for his new audience. Because he certainly would not violate God's laws of cleanliness except at God's command (vs. 28), God had to show Peter that the Mosaic Law was no longer in force. He did this using a vision (vs. 9-16). God told Peter to kill and eat both clean and unclean animals. He refused, based on his strict obedience to the Law. God's response was that when he called something clean, it was.[50] After seeing and hearing this three times, Peter was approached by Cornelius' men, who had come to call for him.

Putting the pieces together, Peter told Cornelius, "I NOW TRULY UNDERSTAND THAT GOD DOES NOT SHOW FAVORITISM IN DEALING WITH PEOPLE" (vs. 34-48), and he shared the gospel of Christ. Cornelius and his household responded in faith and were filled with the Holy Spirit. Interestingly, these Gentiles spoke in tongues though the Samaritans did not (8:17). Finally, they were baptized in water, but only *after* receiving the Holy Spirit (cf. Acts 2:38).

Chapter eleven records Peter's account of the events of chapter ten as he told them to the Jews back in Jerusalem, so verses 1-18 are essentially a repeat of the previous chapter. One specific point to note is Peter's choice of words in verses 15-16. Charismatics and non-charismatics often debate whether the events of chapter two count as "Spirit baptism," because those words are not there. However, here Peter identified the Spirit's coming on Cornelius the same "AS HE DID ON US AT THE BEGINNING.""THE BEGINNING" has to refer to Pentecost in chapter two, making that event the apostles'"Spirit baptism." The group concluded that this truly was the work of God, even among the Gentiles (exactly what Peter concluded in 10:34).

---

50 This was foremost in Peter's mind when he argued that they should not expect Gentiles to even attempt to obey the Law that the Jews could never obey (Acts 15:7-11). Slowly, he began to understand that the Mosaic Law had no hold or power over Christians of any ethnicity.

Luke took this opportunity to introduce the foundational Gentile church in Antioch, so he could transition to that story in chapter thirteen. Referencing the persecution he already mentioned in 8:1, Luke said that the scattered Jews preached only to other Jews (vs. 19-26). However, some proselytes began to expand that message to the Gentiles as well, with the result that "THE HAND OF THE LORD WAS WITH THEM, AND A GREAT NUMBER WHO BELIEVED TURNED TO THE LORD" (vs. 21). This caught the attention of the Jerusalem church, which responded by sending Barnabas to investigate. Recognizing the ministry possibilities there, Barnabas tracked down Saul to help him teach the people.[51] In reality, Antioch became the first Gentile church and Christian seminary. There was such a faithful response to the teaching that the name "Christian" was applied to them there.[52] Verses 27-30 record the prophecy of a severe famine that would hit the world. Thus began Saul's ongoing ministry of collecting funds from Gentile churches to support the believers in Israel.

Chapter twelve closes the first half of the book focusing on the Jews, Peter, and Jerusalem. Although the story comes back to Jerusalem periodically, the rest of Acts emphasizes the Gentiles, Paul, and "THE FARTHEST PARTS OF THE EARTH" (1:8). Sadly, but somewhat appropriately, this part of the story begins with the first martyr from among the apostles, James, the son of Zebedee and brother of John. Verse three is interesting: "WHEN [HEROD] SAW THAT THIS PLEASED THE JEWS, HE PROCEEDED TO ARREST PETER TOO." Even under the persecution that had started in chapter eight, Luke noted in 9:31 that the Church had mostly "EXPERIENCED PEACE." Apparently, that was no longer the case.

---

51   After leaving Damascus and some other events, Saul/Paul spent about ten years preaching in and around his home city of Tarsus (see Galatians 1:13-17). This probably formed the foundation of his work in southern Galatia.

52   Interestingly, the term "Christian" is very rare in Scripture, occurring only here, Acts 26:28, and 1 Peter 4:16.

The story of Peter's imprisonment is a Sunday School favorite. God sent an angel to release him (as he did in 5:17-21), but he had to wake Peter up first (vs. 4-11). Luke humorously noted that Peter obeyed the angel, even though he thought it was just another vision. Apparently, Peter was getting used to seeing visions! He was standing outside alone before he realized the truth.

The rest of the story is just as ironic. Peter's friends had gathered to pray, presumably for Peter and the future of the church (vs. 12-17). When he showed up outside the gathering, none of the adults believed that it was actually him at the gate; only the servant girl did. When they finally let him in, he told them what had happened then went somewhere else so they would not get into trouble as well. One of his instructions was particularly significant. He said, "TELL JAMES AND THE BROTHERS THESE THINGS" (vs. 17). Since "JAMES, THE BROTHER OF JOHN" had been executed (vs. 2), this was obviously a different James. However, since the first James (vs. 2) had to be identified, whereas the second did not (vs. 17), it is clear that the second James had already become highly influential in the Jerusalem church. He must have been "JAMES THE LORD'S BROTHER," who Paul wrote about in Galatians 1:19, who led the council in Acts 15, and who wrote the letter that carries his name.

The chapter concludes with two notes. First, God killed Herod. The backstory has to do with a quarrel between Herod and the people of Tyre and Sidon (vs. 20-23). Herod was an arrogant man, and when his supporters began to worship him as a god, the true God finally executed him. Second, Luke brought the story back to where he left off in 11:30. In fact, 11:30 and 12:25 could originally have been together if Luke added chapter twelve later.

Chapter thirteen records the first missionary tour from Antioch to other Gentile regions. It is important to note that the Holy Spirit specifically chose Barnabas and Saul for this mission (vs. 1-3), a nod back to Jesus' discussion with Ananias in 9:15. There are five significant points about their work shown in this chapter that would characterize the rest of Paul's ministry. First, they started "IN THE JEWISH SYNAGOGUES" wherever they went (vs. 5, 46). This was a theological issue for them (see Romans 1:16; John 4:22). Second, the Holy Spirit empowered them to perform miracles as a part of their ministry (vs. 6-12). This is the first time Luke associated miracles with either Barnabas or Saul. Third, Saul's message in the synagogues was similar to what he had heard Stephen say in chapter seven, a recounting of Israel's history of prophets sent by God, culminating with Jesus as the Messiah (vs. 16-41). Whereas Stephen emphasized their rejection of the prophets, Saul focused on Jesus as the one they had always anticipated. Fourth, their message was often received warmly by many God-fearing Gentiles but only a few Jews (vs. 42-45, 50). Twice Luke wrote that the Jews became jealous because of the Gentile response to Paul (13:45; 17:5). Later Paul told the Romans that was exactly part of God's plan (Romans 11:11). Fifth, the Jewish rejection of the gospel helped spur Paul on to his ultimate commission, preaching to the Gentiles (vs. 46-52).

It is also important to recognize that Saul used his Gentile name, Paul, as he ministered in Gentile lands.[53] Luke's note in verse nine that he was "ALSO KNOWN AS PAUL" seems to indicate that he probably went by both names in Antioch, depending on who he was with. However, since most of his work from this point on was in Gentile territory, Luke felt comfortable changing his usage to "Paul," as he would call himself in his messages and letters. During his regular trips to Jerusalem and the Temple, he most certainly would have gone by "Saul."

Their first stop was in Cyprus (vs. 4-12), where the Holy Spirit used Paul to identify and punish a sorcerer who was actively working against the gospel. Much like Peter with Ananias and Sapphira (5:1-11), Paul spoke

---

53 A Jew born outside of Israel would have both a Hebrew (synagogue) name and a Greek or Latin name. Saul/Paul embraced both names and backgrounds, depending on his immediate audience. He did not change his name from Saul to Paul, a common myth.

under the power of the Spirit and blinded Elymas, the sorcerer. This display of power convinced the audience, including the proconsul, leading to their belief in Christ.

As they worked through southern Galatia, many people believed. However, a coalition of legalistic Jews had followed them and "INCITED THE GOD-FEARING WOMEN OF HIGH SOCIAL STANDING AND THE PROMINENT MEN OF THE CITY" to stand against and begin persecuting Paul and Barnabas (vs. 50). So they continued to Iconium.

Chapter fourteen tells the second half of the first tour. Luke noted that "THE SAME THING HAPPENED IN ICONIUM," that is, the legalistic Jews harassed those who did believe Paul and Barnabas' message of the Messiah (vs. 1-7). Again, they performed miracles. This time, though, their lives were threatened (for the first time), and they had to leave quickly.

In Lystra (vs. 8-18) the welcome was not at all what they expected. Rather than rejecting the apostles, after seeing a man healed who had been "LAME FROM BIRTH," the crowd instead began to worship them! Paul and Barnabas would not accept this, of course, but even then "THEY SCARCELY PERSUADED THE CROWDS NOT TO OFFER SACRIFICE TO THEM." In what would become a trend (see 17:13), the troublemaking Jews from previous places – both Antioch and Iconium in this case – had followed them to stir up trouble. Not only were they successful in threatening Paul's life, this time they got the crowd to stone him, presumably to death (vs. 19-20).[54] He remained alive, however, and encouraged the believers before moving on to one more city, Derbe.

This concluded the first missionary tour. From Derbe, Paul and Barnabas circled back to the places they had already been where they "STRENGTHENED THE SOULS OF THE DISCIPLES AND ENCOURAGED THEM TO CONTINUE IN THE

---

54 Some understand this to be the time Paul referred to in 2 Corinthians 12 when he went to heaven. However, Paul said that took place "FOURTEEN YEARS" before he wrote that letter, which would have been approximately seven or eight years before this missionary tour.

FAITH" (vs. 21-28). They also established formal leadership in the individual churches by appointing elders for them. Back in Antioch, they reported the wonderful news of what God had done and spent time recovering and preparing for their next ministry.

Chapter fifteen introduces the first major theological issue the early Church faced. About A.D. 50 (17 years after Acts 2), as the church at Antioch continued to grow with no sign of slowing down, some of the Jewish believers felt it necessary to "correct" an issue about which they had some concern. Specifically, the Gentiles were not being circumcised "ACCORDING TO THE CUSTOM OF MOSES" (vs. 1). In Exodus 12:48, circumcision was required of Gentiles for them to participate in Passover; spiritually, circumcision made them just like a natural-born Jew.

As Gentiles were being saved, many Jewish believers thought that they were essentially joining their Jewish Church, which required becoming a Jew (vs. 1-5).[55] To sort this out, Antioch sent "PAUL AND BARNABAS AND SOME OTHERS" to Jerusalem to meet with "BOTH THE APOSTLES AND THE ELDERS...TO DELIBERATE ABOUT THIS MATTER" (vs. 6).[56] During the discussion, Peter recounted what had happened to Cornelius (vs. 7-11), while Paul and Barnabas shared their ministry among the Gentiles (vs. 12). Finally, James, the brother of Jesus and Chief Elder or Lead Pastor of the Jerusalem Church, stood up and spoke. After reminding the crowd that Gentiles were always part of God's calling, he concluded that "WE SHOULD NOT CAUSE EXTRA DIFFICULTY FOR THOSE AMONG THE GENTILES WHO ARE TURNING TO GOD" (vs. 19). He suggested only that they refrain from a few things that

---

55 This group was probably the source of the Jewish opponents that Paul faced throughout his career, as they followed him around, adding the requirement of circumcision to his message of faith alone.

56 The mention of elders here, distinct from the apostles, shows that the Seven from Acts 6 were not the only ones the apostles had placed into leadership in the Church. It is significant that they appointed "elders" to lead, not additional or new "apostles." Thus, even this early, we see the two-fold distinction of elders and deacons that Paul taught further in 1 Timothy 3:1-13 and mentioned in Philippians 1:1.

were either blatant sin or that could cause Jews to stumble. So the church sent an official letter back to Antioch via Paul's team, encouraging the believers and giving the results of their conference (vs. 22-35).

The chapter concludes with Paul preparing for a second missionary tour (vs. 36-41). Barnabas wanted to include his nephew John Mark again, but Paul was vehemently against him because the young man had quit on the previous tour. Apparently, the culture shock was more than the young missionary could handle. The argument ended with the two apostles splitting ways. Barnabas took John to Cyprus, while Paul invited Silas to join him.

Chapters sixteen through eighteen record Paul's second tour. Paul and Silas visited the churches Paul had established previously (15:41; 16:1-5), especially encouraging the Gentile believers with the good decision from the Jerusalem Council. Along the way, they found young Timothy and invited him to join them as an apprentice. Because of their ministry and his mixed heritage, Paul thought it wise to have Timothy circumcised. This would both bring future benefits and cause future problems.

Although Paul wanted to move north out of southern Galatia "INTO BYTHINIA...THE SPIRIT OF JESUS DID NOT ALLOW THEM TO DO THIS" (vs. 6-10), so they continued west to the Aegean Sea between Asia Minor (modern Turkey) and Greece. It was at this point that Luke joined their team as well. Here Paul saw a vision of a Macedonian man asking him to come help his people, so they took that as God's direction and embarked across the sea. Although Thessalonica was the capital of Macedonia (and probably their primary destination), Philippi was a leading city as well, so they stopped there first. Because there was no synagogue, they knew the Jews would be praying by a river, so they met them there on the Sabbath (vs. 11-15).[57] The first respondent was Lydia, a merchant from Thyatira in Asia Minor, who had

---

57   Ten Jewish men were required in a city before they could build a synagogue, so Philippi must have had only a small Jewish population. In places without a synagogue, the Jews would meet by "living water," wherever they could find flowing water, like a river.

a home in Philippi. She believed and welcome the apostles into her home as their temporary base.

At some point during their ministry, a demon-possessed slave girl began harassing the apostles, so Paul cast out the demon (vs. 16-24). This caused a great problem for her owners, so they brought Paul and Silas to the magistrates to have them arrested for stirring up trouble against Rome. Recognized only as Jews, Paul and Silas were severely beaten and secured in stocks in the maximum-security prison. This did not dampen their spirits, though, and they continued to pray and sing praises to God throughout the night (vs. 25-34). At midnight, God sent a great earthquake that opened all the prison doors and unlocked all the prisoners' bonds. The jailer, thinking he would be executed due to the loss of his prisoners, drew his sword to kill himself. Paul stopped him, and the man listened to Paul preach the gospel. He took Paul and Silas into his home, cared for their wounds, and his family believed in Jesus that night.

The following morning, when the magistrates sent word for Paul and Silas to be released, Paul revealed that they were Roman citizens, who had been arrested, beaten, and imprisoned against their Roman rights (vs. 35-40). Paul never hesitated to use the freedoms his citizenship afforded him, but he did not abuse them either. Not holding this violation against the magistrates, Paul and Silas left Philippi after leaving a word of encouragement with the infant church there.

Chapter seventeen continues the second missionary tour. It seems that Luke and Timothy stayed at Philippi while Paul and Silas traveled the 100 miles (160 km) to Thessalonica (vs. 1-9). Unlike Philippi, Thessalonica was big enough for a synagogue, and Luke noted that the apostles spent three Sabbaths there. Overall, they were probably in Thessalonica for a couple of months, because they also spent time in at least one home teaching the Gentiles as well. There was a great response from the Gentiles and a few of the Jews. This time it was unbelieving Jews who dragged Paul's host, Jason, to the magistrates, charging him with treason against Rome. The magistrates, however, saw that this was a religious argument, not a political one, and let him off with only a fine. In order to not cause more trouble, the fledgling church sent Paul and Silas to Berea, about 50 miles (80 km) away. Timothy may have joined them by this point and stayed to minister on Paul's behalf in Thessalonica.

The Jews in Berea were more attentive than in Thessalonica, so they responded favorably to Paul along with many Gentiles (vs. 10-15). However, the unbelieving Jews from Thessalonica made the trip to harass them in Berea as well, so Paul left for Athens, leaving Silas and Timothy behind to serve the new Macedonian churches.

Although Paul received a hearing from some of the great philosophers and thinkers of the day in Athens (vs. 16-34), the response there was very weak. Paul had capitalized on the void in their religion, proclaiming to know the highest of gods, the creator of all things. It seems they were polite and attentive until he came to the message of Jesus' resurrection. At that point, most just scoffed and stopped listening, though a few believed.

Chapter eighteen concludes the final leg of Paul's second tour. After a disappointing response to the gospel in Athens, Paul moved west to Corinth, where he found a friendship with Aquila and Priscilla, Jews who had just been expelled from Rome (vs. 1-4). Not only did he share the gospel with them and the other Jews in the synagogue, but he was also able to work his trade with them. When Silas and Timothy finally arrived with good news from Macedonia, Paul's mind was set at ease, and he threw himself into the work at Corinth (vs. 5-11). For at least 18 months, Paul preached the gospel with great response from both Jews and Gentiles.

Not everyone received his message well, though (vs. 6, 12-17). Some unbelieving Jews attacked Paul, dragging him to Gallio (around A.D. 52).

As in Thessalonica, Gallio refused to get involved in a religious battle, so they beat one of the believing Jews right in front of him, while he ignored it. Shortly after this, Paul left Corinth (vs. 18-22). On his way back to Antioch and Jerusalem, he stopped in Ephesus, leaving Aquila and Priscilla there with a promise that he would return if God would allow him.

While Paul was back home, Apollos from Alexandria, Egypt, arrived in Ephesus. He was a brilliant orator and theologian, and he knew the facts about Christ but did not yet know of the baptism of the Holy Spirit (vs. 24-28). Aquila and Priscilla took him into their home and taught them what they had learned from Paul. This made him a powerful companion to the ministry, and he moved on to Achaia (Corinth and Athens) to serve the believers there.

Chapters nineteen and twenty tell of Paul's third and last recorded missionary tour. Leaving Antioch, he returned to the churches he had founded, "STRENGTHENING ALL THE DISCIPLES" (18:23), until he found his way back to Ephesus. Apollos had gone to Corinth, and Paul found a small group of Ephesian believers who had heard the gospel but nothing more (vs. 1-7). When Paul laid his hands on them, they received the Holy Spirit, as demonstrated by speaking in tongues and prophecy. This event marks the third and final time speaking in tongues is mentioned in Acts (2:1-4; 10:46).[58] Paul preached in the Ephesian synagogue for three months with a mixed response (vs. 8-10), so for the next two years he used the community lecture hall to preach and teach, a seminary of sorts for "ALL WHO LIVED IN THE PROVINCE OF ASIA."[59]

As a demonstration of the power that the Holy Spirit afforded to Paul,

---

58 Of all the places Paul had yet to travel, this was the last recorded instance in Acts of tongues or prophecy occurring at salvation. This is significant when studying the purpose and extent of these gifts.

59 The province of Asia included most of southern modern Turkey, including all the areas Paul had already preached in southern Galatia and places he had never been like Colossae, Laodicea, and Hierapolis.

Luke recorded that Paul did many healings and exorcisms in Ephesus (vs. 11-20). It was apparently a place full of sorcery and dark magic, and God's power was useful in proving Paul's message to be true. At one point the believers in Ephesus destroyed nearly $3 million worth of spell and enchantment books, as they turned their lives to Jesus.

After those two years, Paul intended to return to Jerusalem, through Macedonia, and then to Rome (vs. 21-41). He sent Timothy and Erastus to prepare the churches in Macedonia for his arrival, while he continued his work in Ephesus. During this time, there was a huge uproar and a riot against Paul, started by businessmen who crafted idols. Their business had suffered because of the number of Ephesians who had believed in Jesus. The mob did not know why they were rioting, but they loudly protested for two hours. Finally, an official got them to quiet down and dismissed the mob, stating that there was a proper way to file a complaint and that the businessmen were free to do so if they wished. It is a wonderful peek back into the ancient world, realizing that it is not much different than today.

Chapter twenty shows Paul finishing his third tour as he made his way from Ephesus back through Macedonia and to Greece, "WHERE HE STAYED FOR THREE MONTHS" (vs. 1-12). During that time, he ministered to the churches, having a companion with him from each of the major churches in the region. Due to a death threat, Paul returned the way he had come. One Sunday he taught in a house until midnight. The story of Eutychus falling asleep in a window and falling to his death is a common children's story. Paul resuscitated the boy, continued to talk with the believers, and left around dawn. It was likely the last time he would see them.

The rest of the chapter is the farewell Paul gave to the elders of the church at Ephesus (vs. 13-38). Needing to travel quickly, he knew that he could not spend time in Ephesus, so he called for them to come to him. When they did, he gave them final instructions on how to continue the ministry there. He was especially insistent that they focus on teaching solid doctrine, knowing that false teachers would certainly arise in that church, even from among their own ranks, if they were not diligent. It was a sad goodbye to a dear friend, not knowing all that awaited Paul in Jerusalem.

Chapter twenty-one finally brings Paul to Jerusalem, after a series of short stops along the way. The "we" throughout the chapter tells us that Luke had joined Paul again in Troas like he did the first time (16:11). In Tyre, the believers repeatedly told Paul to not go to Jerusalem, but he would not stop (vs. 1-9). Again, in Caesarea, the Holy Spirit used a prophet to tell of the danger awaiting Paul in Jerusalem, and those believers begged him to stay as well, but again he refused (vs. 10-14).[60]

Arriving in Jerusalem Paul was greeted warmly by the believers and the church elders (vs. 15-26). Though they celebrated the ministry God had done through him, they warned that his detractors had spread lies about him even throughout Jerusalem. In response, they thought if the Jews could see him participating in a traditional Jewish vow ceremony before God, they would realize the truth that he was not against them. Paul agreed and completed a seven-day vow of purification, which was completed with a sacrifice in the Temple. Near the end of that week, as Paul prayed in the Temple, he was dragged out by an angry mob which assumed he had taken a Gentile into the Temple with him.[61] As they began to beat Paul, he was rescued by some Roman soldiers and carried out of harm's way, but under arrest. When Paul asked to address the crowd, the officer was startled to realize that Paul was not the wanted criminal the centurion thought he was.

---

60 Notice that Paul did not disobey the Holy Spirit here. The Spirit did not tell him to stay away from Jerusalem, only that danger awaited him there. It was the believers who took that as a sign that he should not go.

61 Since it was Trophimus whom they protested as being in the Temple, this indicates that Luke was not prohibited from being there, suggesting that he was probably Jewish.

Chapter twenty-two records Paul's speech to the mob. Essentially, he just told them his story – who he was and where he came from (vs. 1-21). His pedigree was thoroughly Jewish, a student of the famed Gamaliel, and an ardent follower of the Law. He was so zealous that he used to persecute followers of The Way with his own hands. People in Jerusalem could still vouch for him as he spoke. However, he was confronted by Jesus himself and became a believer. He was baptized and became an outspoken witness for Jesus. However, Jesus warned him that the Jews would not accept his message, and he would preach to the Gentiles instead.

This, of course, was the whole issue for the Jews – Paul's proximity to the Gentiles, so they began to riot again (vs. 22-29). Once again, the Roman soldiers rescued him, but this time they intended to determine why he caused such volatility among the crowd since they did not understand the Hebrew language Paul spoke. As they prepared to beat his confession out of him, he nonchalantly asked if they should be doing that to a Roman citizen without a trial; they were not. From this point on they were afraid to do anything with him.

Chapter twenty-three begins a series of imprisonments and defenses that Paul made on his own behalf, which continues through the end of the book. The Roman official needed to know exactly what the Jews had against Paul (22:30), so he brought him before the Sanhedrin in Jerusalem (vs. 1-11). It turned out that Paul, a Pharisee himself, wisely pitted the Pharisees against the Sadducees on the council. Since Sadducees did not believe in a resurrection, Paul stated that the charge against him concerned his message of a future resurrection. Naturally, the Pharisees sided with one of their own on this, which created such an outburst that the soldiers had to rescue him a third time. They kept him in the Roman fortress overnight to protect him. That night Jesus told Paul that he would indeed go to Rome.

As the Romans tried to figure out what to do with Paul, his nephew heard of a conspiracy to kill him (vs. 12-22). Paul had him report this news to the official, who realized this had become a bigger issue than he could handle, so he prepared to transfer Paul back to Caesarea, where he could stand in a Roman trial before Felix, the governor (vs. 23-35). (The exaggeration of the official's personal heroics in his note to Felix is humorous and something we still see in politics and business today.) Felix agreed to hear the case when Paul's accusers arrived.

Chapter twenty-four continues the story in Caesarea. The high priest, with his attorney and some others, finally arrived five days later to present formal charges against Paul (vs. 1-9). They stated that Paul was an international cult leader who attempted to desecrate the Temple. In his defense, Paul presented the facts that he had been in Jerusalem for less than two weeks, and none of the charges against him could be verified (vs. 10-21). He calmly stated the truth of what happened, including his statement before the Sanhedrin that he was on trial "CONCERNING THE RESURRECTION OF THE DEAD." It seems that Felix was familiar with Christian teaching and decided to give Paul some liberty but still wait for the Roman commander to present his case in person. At the end of the chapter, though, Luke noted that Felix just wanted Paul to bribe him for his release, so he talked to Paul frequently (vs. 24-27). This went on for two years until Felix's term expired, and he was replaced by Porcius Festus.

Chapter twenty-five introduces two more officials to whom Paul was able to preach (9:15). After only two weeks in office, Festus agreed to take up Paul's case (vs. 1-12). The Jews in Jerusalem had already tried to get Festus to transfer Paul back to Jerusalem so they could kill him, but he insisted that all their business take place in Caesarea. Once again Paul's accusers could produce no proof of their accusations against him, while Paul simply stated his innocence. When Festus seemed inclined to transfer him back to Jerusalem for another trial, Paul had enough and exercised his right as a Roman citizen to appeal his case to Caesar himself.

Luke's detail of the proceedings is fascinating and reminds us these were real people, not fictional characters of a story. Verses 13-22 record a conversation between Festus and King Agrippa, during which Festus talked about Paul's case and asked Agrippa for advice. Agrippa wanted to hear Paul for himself, and Festus' obliged. Like the commanding officer (23:26-30), Festus exaggerated the reason for this additional hearing with Agrippa. He claimed he needed a second opinion to give cause to send Paul to Caesar, and Agrippa would counsel him on the matter.

Chapter twenty-six gives Paul's fifth recorded verbal defense since he arrived in Jerusalem. Because Agrippa was familiar with Jewish customs and issues, once again Paul began with his background and heritage (vs. 1-23), as he did with the mob in Jerusalem. He recounted the promises that God had made to Israel throughout the centuries, asking if it was impossible to believe that God could raise someone from the dead. He told of his hatred toward the believers until he met Jesus personally, and he recounted his commission to preach the gospel to Jews and Gentiles alike.

Although Festus could not imagine how someone so learned could believe what Paul believed (vs. 24-32), Paul realized that he was making a connection with Agrippa. When he challenged the king to acknowledge the truth of what he had said, Agrippa famously replied, "IN SUCH A SHORT TIME ARE YOU PERSUADING ME TO BECOME A CHRISTIAN?" Paul responded that he did not care if it took a short time or a long time; he wanted everyone who heard him to come to faith in Jesus. As the government officials walked away, conferring with each other, they agreed that Paul was an innocent man. In fact, they would have released him that day had he not insisted on standing before Caesar.

Chapters twenty-seven and twenty-eight tell of Paul's trip to Rome. Under lock and key along with other prisoners, Paul was grateful that Luke and Aristarchus were allowed to travel with him (vs. 1-8). The centurion even permitted him shore leave at various ports to see friends. They changed ships in Lycia and started for Rome, but the weather had started to turn against them.

Luke noted that the port was "NOT SUITABLE TO SPEND THE WINTER IN," so the captain decided to take his chances on the open waters of the Mediterranean, against Paul's warning (vs. 9-20). A "GENTLE SOUTH WIND" convinced the captain that he was right, and they took off. Unfortunately, a hurricane-type storm hit them and drove them toward North Africa, where they were afraid they would be grounded. After three days they had thrown everything overboard and were doing everything they could to keep the ship intact, though no one believed they would survive.

To encourage them, Paul recounted that an angel told him in the night that, although the ship would be lost, all lives would be saved (vs. 21-38). Nearly two weeks later the storm had taken them north to the Adriatic, between Greece and Italy. As they checked the depth, they discovered they were headed rapidly toward land. Some of the sailors tried to escape, but Paul stopped them. Again, Paul encouraged them to eat a little food, because they would survive. Each one ate enough to satisfy himself, and they tossed the rest into the sea. As dawn broke, they attempted to ground the ship onto the shore, but it got stuck on a sandbar and was beaten to pieces while the crew and passengers swam to land.

Chapter twenty-eight concludes Luke's account of Paul's journey to Rome. Because it does not contain the details of what happened after Paul's two-year imprisonment, and because Acts was already part two of Luke's work, some think that he intended to write a third volume, but that is only speculation. There is nothing in Acts or Church history to confirm it as fact.

All the people on board safely reached the shore of an island called Malta (vs. 1-6). The locals saw them come ashore (276 of them, 27:37) and built fires to dry them out and warm them. Famously, a viper bit Paul's arm, but he shook it off into the fire. When he did not drop dead as they expected, they began to believe that Paul was a god rather than a criminal.

Some people use this example in conjunction with Mark 16:18 to prove that Christians can handle poisonous snakes without being hurt. Paul, though, was not "handling" the snake, and God did the miracle so Paul could gain a hearing with the local official. It was not like the self-serving "snake handling" events we see today.

When Paul learned that the official's father was very sick, he prayed over him and laid his hands on him, and the man was healed (vs. 7-10). After this, many others were brought to Paul and were healed as well. Although Luke does not specifically mention it, Paul certainly took the opportunity to preach the gospel while he was there.

They remained on Malta for three months before being picked up by another ship (vs. 11-16). After a few more weeks they made it to Rome. Because of Paul's situation, he was not taken to the prison, but "WAS ALLOWED TO LIVE BY HIMSELF, WITH THE SOLDIER WHO WAS GUARDING HIM." Because he could not make it to the synagogue, Paul asked the Jewish leaders to come to him, and he told them his story in defense of his accusations (vs. 17-22). They were surprised because they had heard nothing about his case, but they were very interested in hearing his message.

On the appointed day, a large group came to hear him teach and discuss the gospel with him, which lasted all day long (vs. 23-28). As was normal, the response among the Jews was mixed. As they left, Paul declared that the Gentiles would certainly accept the gospel, even if the Jews would not.

Luke closed this volume with a note that Paul remained in that situation in Rome for two whole years, teaching everyone who would come to him. The final words in the NET translation state that he taught "WITHOUT

RESTRICTION," an accurate translation of Luke's Greek. Acts ends with Paul preaching the gospel, unhindered and with full Roman protection, from the capital of the known world.

Romans

Practically speaking, the reason that Romans commands the place at the beginning of Paul's letters is not noteworthy. It was not the earliest, but it was the longest of Paul's inspired writings, and a quick look at his letters in any Bible shows they are ordered from longest to shortest, first to churches, then to individuals.

Theologically, however, Romans most certainly deserves the foremost position, as history has repeatedly shown. John Chrysostom famously had the letter read aloud to him once or twice a week in his later years. Martin Luther called it "the chief part of the New Testament and the very purest Gospel."[62] In fact, the Protestant Reformation began precisely because Luther, a Roman Catholic monk, finally read Romans in Greek for the first time and came to faith in Jesus alone for salvation. According to Luther, in Romans he found

> ...most richly the things that a Christian ought to know; namely, what is law, Gospel, sin, punishment, grace, faith, righteousness, Christ, God, good works, love, hope, the cross, and also how we are to conduct ourselves toward everyone, whether righteous or sinner, strong or weak, friend or foe.[63]

---

62 Martin Luther, *Commentary on Romans* (Grand Rapids, MI: Kregel Publications, 1976), xiii.
63 Luther, xxv–xxvi.

More than any other biblical writing, Romans is a theological textbook, addressing every major area of Christian doctrine, as Luther noted. Because the church in Rome had no apostolic founding or teaching (compare 1:9-15 with 15:17-24), Paul thought it necessary to give them the full account of God's work, specifically about salvation. This is especially evident in the keywords *law, sin, faith*, and *righteousness*.[64] Writing with logical precision, Paul carefully laid out the gospel of salvation as the gracious gift of God's very own righteousness (5:17) – who needs it, why we need it, how we obtain it, and what effects should occur in the one who has it. The Christian who does not know Romans well is infinitely poorer than the one who does, both in his theology and his practice.

Paul wrote Romans during his third missionary journey, probably from Corinth. It was on his next trip to Jerusalem that he was arrested, imprisoned in Caesarea, and finally sent to Rome to stand trial before Nero (see Acts 20-28). Within about four years of writing to this church, the apostle was finally able to meet with them and "IMPART . . . SOME SPIRITUAL GIFT TO STRENGTHEN" them (1:11).

Chapter one begins with Paul's traditional greeting with his name (vs. 1), the recipients (vs. 7), and a prayer of thanksgiving (vs. 8). However, it is also very untraditional in that he took five verses to set the tone for the letter, specifically the foundation for his gospel message and his authority as an apostle (vs. 2-6). This, he wrote, was solely through the resurrection of Christ, at which point he was appointed by God to be "THE SON-OF-GOD-IN-POWER," having accomplished everything necessary to fulfill the role God "PROMISED BEFOREHAND THROUGH HIS PROPHETS IN THE HOLY SCRIPTURES."

In verses 8-15, Paul revealed his long-time desire to visit the Roman

---

64 These four words, respectively, are the most-used non-personal nouns in the Greek text of Romans: νόμος (*nomos*, law, 74x), ἁμαρτία (*hamartia*, sin, 48x), πίστις (*pistis*, faith, 39x), and δικαιοσύνη (*dikaiosune*, righteousness, 34x), occurring almost 200 times together.

believers. As the apostle to the Gentiles (Acts 9:15; Galatians 2:9), he desperately wanted to visit them to "IMPART . . . SOME SPIRITUAL GIFT" and to "BE MUTUALLY COMFORTED BY ONE ANOTHER'S FAITH," but he was always stopped (vs. 13; cf. 1 Thessalonians 2:18).

The crux of the chapter, even the book, is established in verses 16-17. Because Paul so badly wanted to "PREACH THE GOSPEL TO" the Romans but was unable to do so, he did the next best thing – wrote this letter about the gospel. No matter where it led him or what he faced because of it, Paul would never be ashamed of this gospel, because it alone "IS GOD'S POWER FOR SALVATION TO EVERYONE WHO BELIEVES." It is this gospel which reveals once and for all "THE RIGHTEOUSNESS OF GOD" that brings true life.

The final section of the first chapter (vs. 18-32) explains the position of the pagan world in relation to God's righteousness, namely, that they "SUPPRESS THE TRUTH BY THEIR UNRIGHTEOUSNESS," thereby bringing "THE WRATH OF GOD...AGAINST ALL [THEIR] UNGODLINESS AND UNRIGHTEOUSNESS." The specific ways a Gentile person, tribe, or nation may suppress God's truth is numerous, but they all follow the same general patterns, often beginning a downward spiral away from him. First, they reject what they know to be true about him – he is eternal and transcendent – by shaping him into the likeness of physical beings, minimizing his full glory. Next, they reject him altogether and begin to worship "THE CREATION RATHER THAN THE CREATOR." Finally, they begin to worship themselves, man becoming god, leaving nothing to the imagination and fulfilling any wicked desire that fills their sinful hearts. As a result, if they do not repent and return to him, there is a point of "no return" at which God will "GIVE THEM OVER TO [THEIR] DISHONORABLE PASSIONS... [AND] TO A DEPRAVED MIND, TO DO WHAT SHOULD NOT BE DONE." At this stage, they become like Israel in the days of the judges where each "GENERATION WOULD ACT MORE WICKEDLY THAN THE PREVIOUS ONE" and "EACH MAN DID WHAT HE CONSIDERED TO BE RIGHT" (Judges 2:19; 21:25). This is the default state of the world without God, not only doing evil "BUT ALSO APPROV[ING] OF THOSE WHO PRACTICE" it.

Chapter two shifts slightly from the blatant paganism of the world to a more sophisticated rejection of God, like in a civilized Gentile society. These citizens would scoff at the notion that they were like "those pagans" Paul described in chapter one. But Paul did not let them off the hook: "YOU ARE WITHOUT EXCUSE, WHOEVER YOU ARE, WHEN YOU JUDGE SOMEONE ELSE." The fact that a person may not engage in the depravity of a pagan nation does not mean he is not equally sinful and separated from God. In fact, the more civilized a person or nation is, the more their "self-goodness" reveals their "CONTEMPT FOR THE WEALTH OF [GOD'S] KINDNESS" that would lead them to repentance and salvation (vs. 1-4). Instead, no matter their background or ethnicity or civilization, their continued rejection of God will only heap additional condemnation on them as well, "FOR THERE IS NO PARTIALITY WITH GOD" (vs. 5-12). The reason is that God gave not only creation as a witness to himself (1:19-20) but the human conscience as well (vs. 13-16). For those not yet given over to their self-destruction, the moral conscience continues to point to an Absolute Morality and the Giver of morals. Thus, the "civilized" nations, so proud of their superiority over the "pagan" nations, also suppress the truth by claiming their morality as their own rather than a gift from God "WRITTEN IN THEIR HEARTS."

Beginning with verse 17, Paul shifted to the final group of people in this world, the Jewish people. If the civilized Gentiles could look down on their pagan brothers, how much more did the Jews look down on all Gentiles "AND BOAST OF [THEIR] RELATIONSHIP TO GOD" (vs. 17-24)? Because they had received their law directly from God, they considered themselves far superior – a guide, a light, a teacher! Yet they, too, violated that law, doing the same things as the Gentiles, proving to be no better and, in fact, dishonoring God even more because of their relationship to him. The people who thought they were the closest to God – even having the physical mark of circumcision to prove it – are just as far away as everyone else (vs. 25-29). It requires an inward change, not an outward change, to actually be in relationship with God.

Thus, in the first two chapters, Paul placed everyone in the human race – Gentile and Jew, civilized and pagan – into the same spiritual sinking ship.

Chapter three begins with a natural question coming from the end of chapter two. If the Jews are just as bad off as the Gentiles, "WHAT ADVANTAGE DOES THE JEW HAVE?" (vs. 1) The answer is, "Many!" although Paul would not mention them all until much later in this letter. At this point, one would suffice to help Paul make his upcoming point – "THE JEWS WERE ENTRUSTED WITH THE ORACLES OF GOD" (vs. 2).

There are some who would like to think that God was present, speaking to all nations throughout the history of the world and that the Scriptures contain only a small sample of the messages just to Israel.[65] However, based on this verse and God's pattern revealed in the Old Testament, it seems that Israel was designed to be God's "showroom" for the world, a place where the nations could come and see the true God on display in the hearts and lives of his people. Except for Jonah's singular trip to Assyria, even the prophets who spoke against foreign nations did so from Israelite soil. Additionally, the Scriptures inspired and preserved by God were written by Jews.[66] There is no excuse for them to not know his will.

This begins a series of piercing, thought-provoking questions that Paul would ask (and often answer) over the next nine chapters, until the end of

---

65 Of course, he was known to some Gentile people (Abraham, Melchizedek, Job, Jethro/Reuel) and spoke to them, but that special revelation diminished quickly after the founding of the Jewish nation.

66 There is some debate over Luke's ethnicity. Colossians 4:11 makes it seem as if the people listed later, including Luke, could not be Jewish, but the grammar does not necessarily demand that interpretation. On the other hand, when Paul was arrested for allegedly entering the Temple with a Gentile, it was "Trophimus the Ephesian" that the Jews arrested him for, even though Luke was with Paul on that trip (see Acts 21:15-30). It seems no one thought it an issue for Luke to enter the Temple. Since the word of God was entrusted to the Jews, it seems that Luke was probably a Grecian Jew, not a Gentile.

chapter eleven. For instance, "IF OUR UNRIGHTEOUSNESS DEMONSTRATES THE RIGHTEOUSNESS OF GOD" is he unjust to punish us (vs. 5-8)? Should we not, instead, do more unrighteousness so that he can be further glorified? The answer, as Paul will carefully unpack, is a resounding "No!"

Because of the Gentile rejection of creation and conscience and the Jewish rejection of those along with God's spoken and written law, Paul concluded that "ALL ARE UNDER SIN" equally (vs. 9-18). He supported this with a series of quotations from various psalms and the prophet Isaiah – the very words the Jews had rejected – culminating in this chilling indictment on unregenerate humanity: "THERE IS NO FEAR OF GOD BEFORE THEIR EYES."

At this point, one would assume all hope is lost. If the Jews cannot obtain God's righteousness and Gentiles are equally bad off, what hope is there (vs. 19-26)? This is the beauty and grace of the gospel: "THE RIGHTEOUS-NESS OF GOD [COMES] THROUGH THE FAITHFULNESS OF JESUS CHRIST FOR ALL WHO BELIEVE." Because all people are equally under sin, God's plan is to declare us righteous "FREELY BY HIS GRACE THROUGH THE REDEMPTION THAT IS IN CHRIST JESUS." Because this is not based on anything we could ever accomplish, God is both "JUST AND THE JUSTIFIER," that is, he maintains his holy justice and righteousness by declaring righteous only those who come to him through Jesus, apart from the works of the law. "WHERE, THEN, IS BOASTING?" There is none because God's righteousness is a gracious gift that cannot be earned, only received through faith, available to everyone who is under sin, Jew and Gentile alike (vs. 27-31).

Chapter four serves two purposes in Paul's explanation of salvation as God's gift of righteousness that comes only through faith. First, by quoting from two passages from the Hebrew Scriptures, he ensured that his Jewish readers could not escape the knowledge that they had this truth in their grasp the whole time. Second, by using two different examples from two different points in Jewish history, he solidified the inevitable conclusion that salvation has always come by grace through faith alone, apart from the law of which they were so proud.

In verses 1-5, Paul invoked the father of the Jewish nation, Abraham, and quoted what seems to have been his favorite go-to verse and example on this topic, Genesis 15:6 (see also Galatians 3:6): "ABRAHAM BELIEVED GOD, AND IT WAS CREDITED TO HIM AS RIGHTEOUSNESS." What more proof is required than that even Abraham's righteous standing with God came through faith alone?

Paul foresaw that some may object because God had not yet given the law. Of course, righteousness could come through faith *before* the law, but what about *after* the law? Paul gladly answered, this time using David as his example, a man who desperately loved God's law, as evidenced in the Psalms (vs. 6-8). However, even David sang of the blessedness of God's forgiveness which comes "APART FROM WORKS." Fine, Paul's readers might continue, but both Abraham and David were at least circumcised, the visible sign of God's covenant law. True, Paul responded, but Abraham's faith came even before his circumcision (vs. 9-12), so circumcision did not provide his righteousness. In short, Abraham had nothing but his faith, and even David celebrated that God's grace came through faith in his day.

Throughout the remainder of the chapter, Paul continued to dismantle various arguments that God's righteousness could be related to law in any way (vs. 13-22). Even the promises that God made to Abraham were given before his circumcision; only his faith was required to activate them. In fact, Paul argued, if righteousness came through obeying God's law, how could anyone ever be sure they were obedient enough? And since everyone is guilty of sin, how much good could make up for our sin? "FOR THIS REASON IT IS BY FAITH SO THAT IT MAY BE BY GRACE WITH THE RESULT THAT THE PROMISE MAY BE CERTAIN" to everyone who believes, both Jews and Gentiles.

Although many will debate what faith is and what exactly a person must believe to be saved and obtain God's gift of righteousness, verse 21 reveals the simple truth: Abraham "WAS FULLY CONVINCED THAT WHAT GOD PROMISED HE WAS ALSO ABLE TO DO." For the past 2,000 years "WHAT GOD PROMISED" is solely based on the death and resurrection of Jesus (vs. 23-25; 1:16).

Chapter five begins the second half of the first major section of Romans. Having shown our need for God's righteousness (chapters 1-3) and that it is accessible only through faith (chapters 3-4), Paul used the next four chapters to explain further what takes place in us once we are saved. The first major change is reconciliation (vs. 1-11). "THEREFORE, SINCE WE HAVE BEEN DECLARED RIGHTEOUS BY FAITH, WE HAVE PEACE WITH GOD THROUGH OUR LORD JESUS CHRIST" (vs. 1). The practical result of this supernatural peace is a newfound joy in God's glory and our sufferings because we see them differently after salvation. Rather than being upset in trouble, we can see the endurance, character, and hope that comes through suffering, because it reveals that "THE LOVE OF GOD HAS BEEN POURED OUT IN OUR HEARTS THROUGH THE HOLY SPIRIT."

This did not used to be the case, because we were enemies against God. However, in an act of supreme grace and love, "CHRIST DIED FOR THE UNGODLY," namely, "WHILE WE WERE STILL SINNERS, CHRIST DIED FOR US." Before Jesus' death and resurrection, full reconciliation with God was not possible; sin could only be covered but never removed (Hebrews 10:11). In Jesus, God gave an initial reconciliation to the entire human race, although it is put into effect fully only for those who believe.

It is impossible to overstate the importance of the second half of this chapter (vs. 12-21) regarding one's entire theological understanding. Here is just a sample of truths readily found in this section.

- Sin and death in this world are the direct result of Adam's sin. Therefore, there was no sin, death, or judgment until after Genesis 3. This affects our understanding of Creation as well.

- Adam's sin was an intentional rebellion against God's command. Paul used four separate words, each revealing a different nuance, to describe how heinous Adam's sin was: *sin, transgression, trespass, disobedience.*

- Every human sinned with Adam. No one can say, "I wouldn't have sinned."

- Jesus' gift of righteousness far exceeds Adam's "gift" of sin and death in every way.

- In the same way that Adam's sin affected the entire race, Jesus' sacrifice also affected the entire race.

- God's grace is greater than any and all sin.

Chapter six portrays the ideal situation for a living Christian. What God's grace and righteousness should accomplish in a believer's life is nothing short of perfection. However, this requires a complete mindset shift in the person himself, namely, that a believer must believe himself to be dead to sin and its power (vs. 1-4). The reality of this change occurs immediately at salvation when a new believer is "BAPTIZED INTO CHRIST JESUS." In 1 Corinthians Paul wrote that the Holy Spirit baptizes or places a person into the Body of Christ (1 Corinthians 12:13). Although water baptism is a symbol of what took place at salvation, it does not cause a real spiritual change in a person. Paul was referring to Spirit baptism in Romans 6 when he wrote that those "BAPTIZED INTO CHRIST JESUS WERE BAPTIZED INTO HIS DEATH." The result of this joining with Christ is that "JUST AS CHRIST WAS RAISED FROM THE DEAD . . . WE TOO MAY LIVE A NEW LIFE." Because of this spiritual reality, our old sinful nature "NO LONGER DOMINATE[S] US." Thus, we should live with this mindset: "DEAD TO SIN BUT ALIVE TO GOD IN CHRIST JESUS" (vs. 5-11). Living this out in practice requires an intentional determination and action: everything we are and have belongs only to Jesus for his exclusive use (vs. 12-14).

The truth that an unbeliever is enslaved to his sin nature is often under-stated (vs. 15-23). The personal, inherent depravity that Paul discussed in the first three chapters does not mean that each person lives as badly or sinfully as he possibly could. Rather, it means that each person is as bad off and separated from God as he possibly could be. The fact that many unbelievers do a lot of wonderful things does not change their spiritual state. They are still, by nature, enslaved to their sin nature, living for themselves and rejecting God and his gift of righteousness. At salvation, God frees a person from the power of the sin nature (but not the sin nature itself) and grants the new believer Jesus' own righteousness. He wants all believers to voluntarily "enslave" themselves to him as their new Master and Lord, but that is often not the case. Many believers continue to live subject to sin and self rather than the Savior, even though they no longer have to live that way. Because of this, although their sins are forgiven, they will never enjoy the fullness of eternal life (knowing God intimately, John 17:3).

Chapters seven and eight demonstrate the wrong and right ways, respectively, of living out in practice what chapter six taught in theory. Continuing his theme from chapter six, Paul used marriage as an illustra-tion of a Jewish believer's tie to the Mosaic Law (vs. 1-6). Just like a marriage bond is broken when one spouse dies, so too when a Jewish person believes and is baptized into Christ and his death, that Jewish believer is no longer bound to the Law. Instead, he "MAY SERVE IN THE NEW LIFE OF THE SPIRIT AND NOT UNDER THE OLD WRITTEN CODE."

The rest of chapter seven is hotly debated as to whether Paul was speaking of himself before his salvation or afterward. Some find it difficult to see a regenerated Paul struggling with sin and the Law, especially given what he had just written in chapter six. However, as a highly respected Pharisee who was zealous for the Law and rising in the ranks more quickly than those around him (see Philippians 3:4-6; Galatians 1:14), even his encounter with

Jesus en route to Damascus would not have caused Paul to drop the "baggage" from being so deeply entrenched in Judaism.

It seems more likely that Paul was reflecting on his early days as a believer, still trying to obey the law under his own willpower (vs. 9). Instead of successful obedience, though, he found himself struggling even harder with sin. He knew that God's law was "HOLY, RIGHTEOUS, AND GOOD," but he could not force himself to obey it because his sin nature rebelled harder when more rules were put into place. So, he found himself doing exactly what he did not want to do, not because he was not trying to obey, but because he was trying too hard. In a sense, obedience had become his god, but willpower has no power to defeat the sin nature. This led to his famous cry, "WRETCHED MAN THAT I AM! WHO WILL RESCUE ME FROM THIS BODY OF DEATH?" (vs. 24)

Chapter eight provides the answer to Paul's internal struggle from chapter seven, the same struggle many believers consistently fight today. Paul learned that the mindset shift required in chapter six is not something he could force himself to do; rather, he needed to submit completely to the Holy Spirit, "THE LIFE-GIVING SPIRIT IN CHRIST JESUS" (vs. 1-11). Rather than insisting that he fulfill the Law himself, Paul realized that Jesus' death made it "SO THAT THE RIGHTEOUS FULFILLMENT OF THE LAW MAY BE FULFILLED IN US." In us, not by us. Submission to sin and the Spirit are mutually exclusive (Galatians 5:17) because sin and the law bring death, but the Spirit brings life.

Because of this truth, our obligation is to live as truly free from sin and alive to the Spirit who is making us alive (vs. 12-13). This is a significant change from the early parts of Romans. In the first seven chapters, the Holy Spirit is mentioned only a few times; in comparison, chapter eight refers to the Spirit nearly twenty times in a dozen verses. Not only does he give us life, but he also assures us that we are God's children (vs. 14-17). He empowers us to understand and endure our present sufferings and anticipate our future redemption (vs. 18-25). He helps us pray in our weakness and struggles and realize that sufferings are necessary to fulfill God's will for us – becoming like Jesus himself (vs. 26-30).

This section closes with a great series of rhetorical questions in which Paul celebrates the dramatic difference between our state in chapter one compared to what God's immense grace and righteousness accomplishes by chapter eight. Consider the benefits for believers:

- No one can stand against us (vs. 31)

- No spiritual blessing is withheld from us (vs. 32; see Ephesians 1:3)

- No one can charge us with any sin (vs. 33)

- No one can condemn us (vs. 34)

- No one and nothing in all creation can separate us from God's love (vs. 35-39)

Chapters nine through eleven form the second of three major sections in Romans. After reading Paul's series of promises at the end of chapter eight, some Jews may have been inclined to doubt the veracity of Paul's claims. "After all," they could say, "God has made many promises to us that he has never fulfilled." Apparently with this in mind, Paul addressed the nation of Israel in God's plan, elaborating on Israel's past, present, and future.

In chapter nine, Paul picked up where he left off in chapter three, elaborating on the advantages that Jews have over Gentiles (3:1). In fact, there are several: "THE ADOPTION AS SONS, THE GLORY, THE COVENANTS, THE GIVING OF THE LAW, THE TEMPLE WORSHIP . . . THE PROMISES . . . THE PATRIARCHS, AND . . . THE CHRIST" (vs. 4-5). For these reasons, the apostle to the Gentiles was so passionate for his kinsmen to come to know the Christ, he went so far as to wish condemnation upon himself if it would guarantee their salvation (vs. 3)!

In response to the inferred question about God's unfulfilled past promises, Paul insisted, "IT IS NOT AS THOUGH THE WORD OF GOD HAD FAILED" (vs. 6-13), as if those promises would never come to pass. On the contrary, Paul said, God did not make his promises to just anyone, but to only certain people – descendants of Abraham through Isaac and Jacob. Additionally, some promises were made only to those who would believe as Abraham did. God's promises, Paul contended, were based on his desire to act, not based on the actions of the Jewish people.

Paul anticipated a second question: "Is THERE INJUSTICE WITH GOD?" (vs. 14-18). If God made promises to only certain people, does that mean that he is not as impartial as he claims? Of course not. A giver can choose the recipients of his gift, and God chose ethnic Israel and believing Israel for different blessings. As a negative example, God chose to reveal his power through Pharaoh, who rejected God and suffered the consequences.

In verses 19-29, Paul anticipated a third question: "If God places people in their current situations, how can he condemn them?" Rather than answering the question, Paul deferred to God's sovereignty in all things. Sovereignty is not about action but authority; sovereignty gives the right to act or not act, independently of anyone or anything else. Because God created people, he has the right to bless some people and not others. Although some scholars want this passage to refer to salvation in general, as if God has chosen to save certain people and not save others, the context is clearly about God choosing the Jews instead of the Gentiles to receive his blessings. However, Paul reminded his readers, Gentiles have always been part of God's plan, as shown in Hosea (2:23 and 1:10). However, according to Isaiah (1:9), only the believing remnant of Israel will be saved, proving again that salvation is through faith, even for the Jews. Paul ended this chapter reaffirming that, in the Church Age, many Gentiles are receiving God's righteousness through faith, even though Israel had failed to receive it through the Law, exactly as Isaiah had prophesied.

Chapter ten continues Paul's teaching on Israel, specifically focused on their present state in the Church Age. Paul's deepest desire and prayer "ON BEHALF OF [HIS] FELLOW ISRAELITES IS FOR THEIR SALVATION" (vs. 1-4). The problem is that they are still seeking to "ESTABLISH THEIR OWN RIGHTEOUSNESS" rather than "THE RIGHTEOUSNESS THAT COMES THROUGH GOD." True righteousness is obtainable only in Christ, because "CHRIST IS THE END OF THE LAW."

The problem with trying to gain righteousness through the law is that no one can live up to it perfectly (vs. 5-8). Instead, Christ has already come down from heaven (without our help) and rose from the dead (again, without our help), so the message of faith is based solely in him.

Verses 9-10 are often used by those who share the gospel and by those who hold to Lordship Salvation, for different reasons. Those sharing the gospel of salvation sometimes say, "You must confess with your mouth and believe in your heart to be saved." This adds the unnecessary requirement of verbal confession for salvation. Lordship Salvation advocates point here and say, "You must acknowledge Jesus as the Lord of your life to be saved." This adds the requirement of full submission, which an unbeliever cannot do.

The correct interpretation is found in the context of the present state of the Jewish people. In verse 13 Paul quoted from Joel 2:32, where "THE NAME OF THE LORD" is God's personal name, Jehovah. In verse 9, a Jew must "CONFESS . . . THAT JESUS IS LORD." In other words, for a Jew to be saved today, he must confess or acknowledge that Jesus is Jehovah, the very thing the Jewish people at large have refused to do for 2,000 years. This is an essential requirement for salvation, something that comes easier for Gentiles than Jews.[67]

Paul concluded this chapter with a series of questions that are often

---

67 This does not always satisfy the question of why Paul specified the "mouth." The answer lies in Hebrew poetry. Notice the AB/BA structure of the passage: "mouth . . . heart . . . heart . . . mouth."
Paul used a standard Hebrew parallel structure to emphasize the completeness of the conversion.
As the book of Hebrews shows and we still see today, confessing a belief with one's mouth means
nothing if the heart does not truly believe it. So, "WITH THE HEART ONE BELIEVES AND THUS HAS
RIGHTEOUSNESS." However, the Jewish people need to confess Jesus as Jehovah, the true gospel,
which no one can know if they do not verbalize it.

used by missionaries because their truth is relevant throughout this age (vs. 13-21). How does a Jew (or anyone) believe if no one will approach him with the truth of the Messiah? A person cannot believe without first hearing the true message of Christ. Of course, Paul admitted, that creation speaks to God's power (Psalm 19:4), but that is not enough. A short series of quotes from Moses and Isaiah shows that Israel has continually rejected the Savior, to their loss and others' gain.

Chapter eleven concludes this middle section of the letter by focusing on Israel's future as a nation. Based on the truths of chapters nine and ten, Paul asked, "GOD HAS NOT REJECTED HIS PEOPLE, HAS HE?" (vs. 1-4) The answer is an emphatic, "No!", and Paul used himself as proof. If God were really through with Israel, how could Paul have come to faith in the Messiah? Instead, there has always been a believing remnant, as in Elijah's day, even though it seems as if no one else believes. So then, even today there is a remnant of Jews who have come to Jesus by grace through faith rather than the law, while the nation at large is prohibited from turning to him quite yet (vs. 5-10).

But Israel's falling away was not "IRREVOCABLE" (vs. 11-16). Even though more Gentiles than Jews are believing, God's purpose is that the Jewish people would become "JEALOUS" that their Messiah is being accepted by Gentiles. And if Gentiles are being saved by the Jewish Messiah through faith, how much more will Jews be saved if they would only respond in faith?

Verses 17-24 contain the famous olive tree analogy, which is often misunderstood and misapplied. A common interpretation is that the olive tree is Israel, so believing Gentiles become part of the "true Israel" or "spiritual Israel." Not only does this contradict many other portions of Scripture, it is indefensible from this passage. Verse 24 shows that the tree in the analogy belongs to Israel; it is "THEIR OWN OLIVE TREE." It is a different matter to say that the tree is "Israel" instead of "Israel's." The olive tree represents something that was given to Israel, which Paul had already enumerated at the beginning of chapter nine – the prophets, covenants, patriarchs, etc. Most importantly, though, the Messiah is Israel's (9:1-5). Salvation is "TO THE JEW FIRST" (1:16) and "SALVATION IS FROM THE JEWS" (John 4:22) because the Savior is a Jew. However, many Jews do not believe, so they have been removed from the tree. Gentiles who believe are "GRAFTED IN," not into Israel to become Jews, but into Christ to participate "IN THE RICHNESS OF THE OLIVE ROOT," which is Christ himself. Thus, there is no Scriptural basis to teach that Gentiles have taken Israel's place as the people of God or that God has transferred his promises from Israel to the Church. Rather, Gentiles who believe get to participate in the blessings of Christ, while the promises made to Israel stand firm (11:1).

The chapter concludes with a final promise that, even though Israel is under a partial hardening by God himself, one day the blinders will be removed and "ALL ISRAEL WILL BE SAVED" (vs. 25-32). In a nod back to the first section (chapters 1-8), as he prepared to move into the final section of the letters (chapters 12-16), Paul responded to those who cannot understand why all people are imputed with Adam's guilt (5:12). It is a gracious act of God who has "CONSIGNED ALL PEOPLE TO DISOBEDIENCE SO THAT HE MAY SHOW MERCY TO THEM ALL." If not everyone were equally guilty, there would have to be many ways and plans of salvation, which could never be considered "impartial." By considering us all the same, each one is equally able to come to Jesus through faith – equally sinful, equally savable. This thought caused Paul to break out in joyful praise to God's transcending "WISDOM AND KNOWLEDGE...UNSEARCHABLE...[AND] FATHOMLESS. ... TO HIM BE GLORY FOREVER!"

Chapter twelve begins the final section of Paul's letter, in which he took the immense doctrine taught in the first eleven chapters and provided several principles and commands that should drive the Christian lifestyle.

The first step of true discipleship after initial saving faith is for a Christian to make the declaration to God that he is "all-in" (vs. 1-2) In chapter six Paul taught that the believer has been freed from the power of sin, so he should live as if this were true. Before getting to the rest of his application, Paul stated how this is done. It is a willful decision to submit one's entire body to God "AS A SACRIFICE" ("PRESENT…YOUR MEMBERS TO GOD AS INSTRUMENTS TO BE USED FOR RIGHTEOUSNESS," 6:13). This will keep us from being shaped by the world system, and instead, we will be able to discern and understand God's good will so that we can live wisely, no matter the situation in which we find ourselves.

As we begin to know and obey God and his Word better, we will begin to think like him, which will result in thinking of ourselves and others properly. This new worldview displays itself in three ways. The first has to do with spiritual giftedness (vs. 3-8). Outside of 1 Corinthians 12, this chapter contains the most compact teaching on the Church as the Body of Christ. Paul emphasized the truth that the members belong to each other and that we are to serve each other in the unique ways God has enabled us. The list of gifts mentioned here focuses primarily on the task or serving gifts (as opposed to the fuller list in 1 Corinthians). The gifts are manifestations of God's grace given to us, and ten years later Peter would write that God considers us managers of that grace (1 Peter 4:10).

Second, we are to focus on the growth of our fellow believers in our general interactions (vs. 9-16). This passage is essentially a series of "proverbs," short principles that stand on their own. They can be memorized as "sound bites" that we can take with us into every situation. Although our English translations do not always reflect it, verses 9-13 comprise one long sentence describing what sincere love ("WITHOUT HYPOCRISY") looks like (see 1 Corinthians 13:4-7). It looks for opportunities to bless others, empathize with them, and "LIVE IN HARMONY" with them.

The third change in our thinking about ourselves and others is displayed in our interaction with unbelievers in the world around us (vs. 16-21). In these final verses, Paul changed his language from "one another" to "anyone" and "all people," not just fellow believers. Whereas Christians are commanded to "LIVE IN HARMONY WITH ONE ANOTHER," Paul understood that was not always possible with unbelievers, so he added the caveat, "IF POSSIBLE, SO FAR AS IT DEPENDS ON YOU, LIVE PEACEABLY WITH ALL PEOPLE." It is impossible to completely "LIVE IN HARMONY" with those who have opposing worldviews (this would be a kind of partnership, 2 Corinthians 6:14-18), but we can strive to live in peace with them, a theme common in the apostles' letters.[68] This kind of peaceful living involves not taking personal vengeance and not allowing the world's evil to overcome us so that we stop living out our new godly nature.

Chapter thirteen continues with our Christian lifestyle in this world, beginning with our interaction with human government (vs. 1-7). The government has always been a favorite "whipping boy" and for a good reason: Corrupt people with power use their power to do corrupt things. Or as Lord Acton famously said, "Power tends to corrupt, and absolute power corrupts absolutely." Since we are all corrupt by nature, as Paul thoroughly taught in the early chapters, only believers can govern out of a godly nature, but even that is not guaranteed. However, human government is not evil; it was established by God to maintain peace and justice among the people. Therefore, we are subject, even to corrupt governments, to obey whatever is within their jurisdiction, including taxes, which Paul had to mention specifically because they have never been desirable in any civilization.[69]

Verse eight has often been used to "prove" that financial debt is a sin in Christianity, but the rest of Scripture does not allow that interpretation. We can certainly find other passages showing the negative side of financial debt

---

68 1 Thessalonians 4:12; Colossians 4:12; Galatians 6:10; Titus 3:1-2; 1 Peter 2:11-12

69 Obviously, God's law still transcends man's law, so when the two conflict, "WE MUST OBEY GOD RATHER THAN PEOPLE" (Acts 5:29).

(Proverbs 6:1-5 and 22:7, for instance), so Paul said that we should not make debt a way of life. However, a renewed mind sees that we can never fully love our fellow Christians, and so that "debt" will always be unpaid, even though we should spend the rest of our lives trying to "pay" it. The reason this is so important is that we cannot know the timing of Jesus' return, and we are to be working faithfully as we anticipate him (vs. 11-14). The closer we get to the end times, the more we are to look and live like Jesus. This includes living "DECENTLY," which Paul clarifies as to "MAKE NO PROVISION FOR THE FLESH TO AROUSE ITS DESIRES" (see 8:5-11; Galatians 5:16-26).

Chapter fourteen deals with another issue in Christianity, namely, the practice of one believer forcing his convictions and preferences on another believer, then condemning him if he does not agree and submit. Paul introduced a new differentiation between believers at this point: strong and weak.[70] Using illustrations such as what we are permitted to eat and which day or days we should set aside as sacred, Paul concluded that the believer who places himself under restrictions that God did not specifically give is "weak," because engaging in such activities would violate his conscience, causing him to sin. A "strong brother," on the other hand, is not burdened by these extra-biblical prohibitions and, thus, can freely participate without sinning, because they are not God's prohibitions at all (vs. 14). Paul did not give an exhaustive list of activities because it can include any restriction that a believer places on himself that God did not command. Not surprisingly, even modern believers still wrestle with the broad categories mentioned like entertainment (TV, movies, music), substances (certain foods, alcohol, some drugs), and special days (when the church gathers, religious celebrations).

However, Paul did not leave the question with just a definition of terms. There are two principles that we are to learn and live considering this truth.

---

70 These are different from his categories in 1 Corinthians 3:1-5. There, "carnal" refers to a believer who is driven by his sin nature, and "spiritual" is a believer driven by the Holy Spirit.

First, "weak" is not God's desired state for a Christian. Because the issue is extra-biblical prohibitions, God wants us to grow from "weak" to "strong" in our faith, so we are not weighed down by them. The second principle is equally important, though. Just because a "strong" brother <u>can</u> participate in these activities, it does not mean that he always <u>should</u>. In fact, Paul commanded "strong" Christians to intentionally withhold from participation if they know that engaging in them could cause a "weak" Christian to fall into sin by participating as well, against their conscience. In this scenario, rather than helping our weaker brothers, the stronger brothers actually become an obstacle to our fellow Christians' growth, potentially destroying God's work in them, the opposite of love. A decade earlier Paul acknowledged that it was "FOR FREEDOM THAT CHRIST HAS SET US FREE." Yet we must "NOT USE [OUR] FREEDOM AS AN OPPORTUNITY TO INDULGE [OUR] FLESH, BUT THROUGH LOVE SERVE ONE ANOTHER" (Galatians 5:1, 13). Continuing his theme from chapter twelve, Paul implored, "SO THEN, LET US PURSUE WHAT MAKES FOR PEACE AND FOR BUILDING UP ONE ANOTHER" (vs. 19).

Chapter fifteen finishes the teaching on strong and weak believers from the previous chapter. Rather than causing weaker Christians to stumble in their faith, stronger Christians "OUGHT TO BEAR WITH THE FAILINGS OF THE WEAK, AND NOT JUST TO PLEASE OURSELVES" (vs. 1-6). This is essentially further teaching on the proper outworking of love from the Christian perspective on ourselves and others that Paul introduced in chapter twelve.

Verses 7-13 help clarify the teaching on strong and weak Christians. While those tensions are certainly true within a group of Gentile believers, they are especially strong between believing Gentiles and Jews. The Acts and Paul's earlier letters show that the early Jewish Christians had a difficult time breaking away from the Mosaic Law, even after their salvation. In fact, an entire doctrinal council was held addressing this issue and, more narrowly, specific requirements within the Law (Acts 15). Not unsurprisingly, many believing Jews still have this difficulty today. In this short paragraph, Paul urged the Jews and Gentiles to love and build up each other, even though they held many differences when it came to which practices were acceptable for Christians. Paul quoted from Psalms, Deuteronomy, and Isaiah to remind the Jews again that believing Gentiles had always been a part of God's plan, and that Gentiles were not "messing things up" by not embracing the Mosaic Law.

The rest of the chapter is much more personal, showing that Paul was drawing to a close. His first comment was to the Jews in his audience (vs. 14-21). Admitting that he was sent to the Gentiles specifically, Paul noted that he wrote a little more boldly to the Jews than he normally would have, because of the great overlap between them in his themes throughout this letter. He mentioned again his desire to finally visit them, but that he ultimately wanted to go all the way to Spain, where he believed the gospel had not yet reached, and he expected that the Roman believers would help him on that journey (vs. 22-24). In the meantime, he was headed back to Jerusalem, carrying the money he had collected for the famished saints there (vs. 25-29). Little did he know that he would certainly find himself in Rome, but as a prisoner rather than a free traveler (Acts 21-28). He did, however, know that trouble was awaiting him in Jerusalem, so he asked that the Romans pray for his safety so that he could come to them (vs. 30-32). As Acts records, God did answer their prayers but not in the way they asked or could have imagined.

Chapter sixteen concludes this letter with Paul's traditional final greetings, yet it is significantly different from his other letters (vs. 1-16). Paul names more people (a total of 26 plus generic "sister, brother, others") than in any of his other letters. This is interesting given the fact that he had never yet been there, yet he refers to many of them as his dear friends. One possible conclusion is that they had served with him (like Prisca and Aquila, vs. 3) at various times outside of Rome. If this were the case, it reminds us that Luke's account in Acts is a broad overview of Paul's ministry with only a few specific incidents and people mentioned.[71] Paul was obviously aware of the various small house groups and their leaders that made up the Roman church, so it is also likely that he had continually inquired about them during his travels, especially since he wanted to minister there. This points to Paul's strategic mind, carefully planning and preparing for his work, even well in advance.

Because of the nature of the essential doctrines in this letter, a final warning was necessary to make sure that the believers understood how to deal with those who would push back and even reject what Paul had taught (vs. 17-20). Contrary to those who insist that Christians are not supposed to judge other people, Paul commanded that we not allow rebels who reject sound doctrine and teach false doctrine to have free reign among our assemblies. Instead, we should avoid them, breaking fellowship until they repent. This will "CRUSH" Satan's foothold within the church and enhance our ministry.

After a final greeting from those with Paul (including Tertius, who actually wrote the letter for him), Paul closed with a benediction praising "THE ONLY WISE GOD" and Jesus for the new revelation of these truths which God had "KEPT SECRET FOR LONG AGES" and had only hinted at "THROUGH THE PROPHETIC SCRIPTURES." It is a fitting conclusion to the greatest book in all the New Testament – the introduction, explanation, and application of God's gift of righteousness to all who believe.

---

71 For instance, we know that Titus was a close companion and minister with Paul (2 Corinthians 2, 7, 8, 12; Galatians 1, 2; 2 Timothy 3; Titus), yet he is never mentioned in Acts.

1 Corinthians

Of all the people to whom Paul ministered in his 30-year service as the apostle to the Gentiles, the church at Corinth is set down as the one that caused him the most personal heartache. Paul founded the Corinthian church during his second missionary tour in the early A.D. 50s (Acts 18:1-17). Luke recorded that Paul had a fruitful ministry there, staying for almost two years.

However, the letters paint a darker picture. Once the church was established and Paul had moved on, it did not flourish quite like others did (Thessalonica, Ephesus, Philippi, etc.). In its early years, Corinth was a corrupted city, full of debauchery. How bad it was during Paul's time is debated, but if the kind of lifestyles these believers had before their salvation is any indication (6:9-11), then the city's pagan history seems to have stayed in force.

Over the course of a couple of years (A.D. 55-56), it seems that several communications traveled back and forth between the apostle and the church, but God preserved only the two we call "1 and 2 Corinthians." In these letters, we discover a congregation with deep factions (ch. 3), worse-than-pagan practices (ch. 5), abuse of the ordinances (ch. 11), and general spiritual apathy.

In fact, Paul was so concerned about their spiritual well-being, he did not send only letters to Corinth but personal representatives as well. Between these two letters, we discover that at least Apollos, Titus, and Timothy all served there at different times at Paul's request.

Because of all this, 1 Corinthians is a treasure for the modern church and is always relevant. In it, Paul not only addressed corrections that he needed to make, but he also answered several questions they must have asked him, providing us with teaching on a wide variety of topics in more detail than any other place in Scripture. These topics include marriage and divorce, spiritual gifts, and the resurrection. This letter is invaluable for sound doctrine and practice.

Chapter one begins with a traditional greeting and prayer of thanksgiving for the believers in Corinth (vs. 1-9). Given the topics that Paul would address in this letter, it is important to remember that he was convinced that most of those in his original audience were genuine believers, even if they were still spiritually immature. No matter their current condition, Paul admitted that they were "SANCTIFIED IN CHRIST JESUS ... CALLED BE SAINTS ... [AND] CALLED INTO FELLOWSHIP WITH HIS SON, JESUS CHRIST OUR LORD." In his greeting, Paul also mentioned Sosthenes, who, according to Acts 18:17, was "THE PRESIDENT OF THE SYNAGOGUE" in Corinth and one of the Jewish converts to Christianity.

Verses 5-7 (along with the lengthy discussion in chapters 12-14) indicates that their use of spiritual gifts, especially prophecy, tongues, and supernatural knowledge, was unusually high compared to other congregations. Unfortunately, these gifts that were meant to build up the church and point to Jesus instead built only pride and were used to create factions around personalities other than Christ (vs. 10-17). Paul, Apollos, and Peter had their devoted followers, while the "super spiritual" claimed their dedication to Christ alone. Verse 17 includes one of Paul's rare mentions of water baptism.[72] It seems that, although he acknowledged the importance of water baptism, it was not something he found necessary to do himself. His primary mission was to preach the gospel of the cross. Others could baptize those who believed his message.

The chapter concludes with a lengthy monologue on the message of the cross and how it is received by unbelievers in this world. Six times in verses 18-31 Paul described the gospel and God's ways as "foolish" or "foolishness." It is foolishness "TO THOSE WHO ARE PERISHING" (vs. 18). The method of preaching was foolish (vs. 21). It was foolishness "TO GENTILES" (vs. 23). (The search for wisdom was a major activity in the cultured Greek world; see Acts 17:16-34.) To the Jews the "CRUCIFIED CHRIST" is not just foolish but a "STUMBLING BLOCK" – the obstacle that (still) keeps them from God. Paul asked his readers to remember when they first believed. It was not because there was something special about them, but because God graciously saved them, exactly the opposite of what Greek wisdom suggested. Before, in their weakness and lowliness, they had nothing to boast about to their countrymen, but now, because of God's grace, they could "BOAST IN THE LORD."

Chapter two continues Paul's exposition on the wisdom of God versus the wisdom of this world. Unlike the philosophers of his day, Paul did not ride into town offering great secrets and eloquent speeches, catering to those who could pay the most money (vs. 1-5). In fact, he did just the opposite. His message was simple and clear: "JESUS CHRIST . . . CRUCIFIED." Rather than great oratory and "PERSUASIVE WORDS OF WISDOM," Paul preached "IN WEAKNESS AND IN FEAR AND WITH MUCH TREMBLING," yet his message was accompanied "WITH A DEMONSTRATION OF THE SPIRIT AND OF POWER," i.e., signs and wonders and miracles (2 Corinthians 12:12). This way when they believed, it would be in Christ, not Paul.

---

72 Most of the time Paul refers to "baptism" in his letters, he meant Spirit baptism at salvation, not water baptism afterward. Proper identification of this difference often clears up a lot of confusion in interpreting his writings.

However, none of this means that Christianity has no wisdom (vs. 6-16). On the contrary, true wisdom and knowledge are not available without the proper fear of God (Proverbs 1:7; 9:10). This wisdom and knowledge is not accessible even to "THE RULERS OF THIS AGE," as revealed in the fact that they murdered God's Son. With the indwelling Spirit of God comes access to the very mind of God, "SO THAT WE MAY KNOW THE THINGS THAT ARE FREELY GIVEN TO US BY GOD," also called "THE DEEP THINGS OF GOD." Making a clear distinction between saved and unsaved people, Paul taught that only true believers can understand spiritual things. Unbelievers can grasp the words, but not the full spiritual meaning.[73] Again, these things "ARE FOOLISHNESS" to the unbeliever, but the believer has the very "MIND OF CHRIST" himself. It is through the full knowledge of Christ that we are given "EVERYTHING NECESSARY FOR LIFE AND GODLINESS" (2 Peter 1:3), the very message Paul needed the Corinthians to hear.

Chapter three provides our first look at the spiritual level of these believers. In chapter one Paul said that they were divided rather than united, but verses 1-4 finally reveal why. For Paul, all people can be classified into three spiritual states. First are the "unregenerate," those who have not believed in Christ for salvation. Their lives are driven by their sinful natures. Second are the "carnal" or "fleshly," those who have believed in Christ for salvation (truly saved) but are still driven by their sinful natures, like the unregenerate. Paul also refers to these as "INFANTS IN CHRIST," because they have no spiritual maturity yet. A bystander may not be able to tell the difference between an unregenerate person and a carnal Christian.[74] Third are the "spiritual," those

---

73 This is why it is important for Christians to not try to change the world on the basis of morals and ethics instead of the gospel. The only biblical command for unbeliever is to believe the gospel. Only believers have the power to live out God's standards in this world.

74 This is one of the most devastating passages for proponents of Lordship Salvation, who teach that a Christian cannot live extended periods of time in sin. Whereas they would question the person's salvation, Paul questioned only their maturity, while still acknowledging they were truly "IN CHRIST." While a Christian *should* not live like this, it is biblically wrong to say that he or she *cannot* live like this.

who have believed in Christ for salvation and are driven by the Holy Spirit. Continuing the infant analogy, Paul said that the Corinthian believers had been saved long enough to be able to handle "SOLID FOOD" (probably "THE DEEP THINGS OF GOD" in 2:10), but instead they were still dependent on "MILK."

These people were so wrapped up in individual accomplishments and recognition that they had turned the church of God into personality cults behind the apostles (vs. 5-9). Could they not see that Paul and Apollos and the others were simply servants carrying out God's work? One of the greatest principles any church leader or member must hold to is that, no matter who "PLANTED" or "WATERED ... GOD CAUSED IT TO GROW." Those who faithfully carry out the planting and watering will receive rewards based on their work, but no one can grow the church of God except God himself.[75] We simply have the privilege of working alongside him.

Quickly changing analogies, Paul shifted from a field to a building (vs. 9-15).[76] Now he was a builder, laying the foundation for the Corinthians upon which they could build their lives and church. Paul reminded them that nothing is worth building if not built on Jesus; he is the only solid foundation (see Psalm 127:1 and Matthew 7:24-27 for similar concepts). However, it is left to each Christian how he or she will build on that foundation. Some will build with high-quality materials ("GOLD, SILVER, PRECIOUS STONES") while others will use low-quality materials ("WOOD, HAY, OR STRAW"). These materials are the works that we accomplish in this life.[77] On "THE DAY" (the Judgment Seat of Christ, 2 Corinthians 5:10) those works will be tested by God's judgment fire.[78] Those buildings that survive the judgment will bring

---

75 Jesus plainly declared, "I WILL BUILD MY CHURCH" (Matthew 16:18).

76 Much has been written about Paul's liberal use of mixed metaphors throughout his writing. Pay attention or risk getting lost as he jumped from one illustration to another with no warning, as shown in verse 9.

77 Paul's word selection in 2 Corinthians 5:10 when referring to the same judgment shows that he meant the *quality* of our works, probably based on our hearts and motives, not just the *quantity*.

78 This reveals that a judgment of fire will not be limited only to unbelievers. Those who read every

reward; those that do not survive will reveal only loss. However, Paul was quick to add that reward was the only loss, never salvation itself.

Because of the coming judgment of our works and lives, Paul closed this chapter with a warning (vs. 16-23). We must be mindful that God's Holy Spirit indwells us, so we should manage our lives well. We must intentionally trade in worldly wisdom, which is not wisdom at all, for godly wisdom which will benefit us eternally. We must give up our silly factions and temporal desires, remembering that we can inherit all things with Christ, if we would remain faithful to him, as he remained faithful to God.

Chapter four is a mixture of harsh correction and urgent pleading for these believers to change their hearts and ways. After mentioning multiple times about the personality factions in this congregation, Paul said that there was nothing they could say to affect him (vs. 1-5). As far as he was concerned he simply needed to remain faithful to Christ, who will be the ultimate judge. He was sure that Jesus had nothing against him at that time, so what the Corinthians thought was "A MINOR MATTER" to him.

Yet what they thought was also a major matter, because it revealed their hearts and immaturity, so he attacked their sinful actions (vs. 6-13). He noted that it was arrogance and condescension at the heart of the matter. Paul insisted that they "LEARN 'NOT TO GO BEYOND WHAT IS WRITTEN,'" something he and Apollos practiced.[79] This obviously refers to the Scriptures available to them, which probably speaks to the special revelation they had received (see 1:5-7). Since everything they had was given to them, why did they think they had reason to boast about anything?

The Corinthians continually flaunted themselves, parading around as if

---

instance of judgment fire as a reference to hell are unable to properly interpret passages like this, John 15, and the warnings in Hebrews. Christians will indeed be judged by God's holy fire at the Judgment Seat of Christ.

79 This should be held as a defining principle for Christians today as well. What the Bible says, it means. What it does not say, we should be very careful in saying or demanding of ourselves and others.

there were something special about them. Paul, on the other hand, remarked that the apostles were noticed only as "A SPECTACLE . . . FOOLS . . . WEAK . . . DISHONORED" by the world's standards. In fact, while the Corinthians enjoyed their wealth and privileges, all the while exhibiting self-righteousness, Paul's team was "HUNGRY AND THIRSTY, POORLY CLOTHED, BRUTALLY TREATED, AND WITHOUT A ROOF OVER [THEIR] HEADS." They worked hard, were verbally abused, persecuted, and lied about. His conclusion: "WE ARE THE WORLD'S SCUM."

Now, that rant was not meant to shame his readers, just point out the nature of things, and to correct their thinking and grow them (vs. 14-21). No matter how many great heroes of the faith they could point to, only one could they call their "FATHER," and he deserved their respect. So that he would not have to come to them himself "WITH A ROD OF DISCIPLINE," Paul sent Timothy ahead to help bring them back to where they were when Paul had left them.

One interesting point Paul made was to remind them that God's work comes with God's power. When he was there, he performed demonstrations of God's power to identify himself as a genuine apostle (2 Corinthians 12:12). He wondered if these so-called leaders in the congregation, who were stirring things up, could do anything more than talk. He doubted it.

Chapter five contains some of the harshest words from Paul in any of his inspired letters. The reason had to do with a situation he found appalling: a Christian man[80] was having an affair with his step-mother (vs. 1-5). Not only was this something that the surrounding pagan culture would apparently not even consider, rather than exercising discipline, the congregation applauded it! Paul was quick with his verdict. If they had not done anything about it by the time he arrived, Paul would excommunicate the man himself.

---

80 Even in this horrific sin, Paul never questioned the man's salvation, only his actions and the congregation's response.

Although the congregation must have thought that they were showing their "tolerance" and "inclusiveness," Paul used an analogy of bread and yeast (vs. 6-8). Like a tiny bit of yeast permeates the entire loaf of bread, so even a little sin can permeate a church – and this was not just a little sin. At the Passover, the Jews eat unleavened bread. Since Jesus was the ultimate Passover sacrifice, how could they tolerate any sin at all in their midst?

In an earlier letter, Paul had told them to not associate with immoral people (vs. 9-13). They took this to mean they should keep away the immoral people outside the church but still love everyone and everything inside the congregation. Paul had to correct their thinking. It is impossible to dissociate with all immoral people because we still must function in this world. Instead, his command concerned those inside the church. Contrary to modern opinion, a congregation *is* to be in the business of "judging" each other, to help keep each other right before God. Blatantly unrepentant people are to be removed from the congregation until they repent (after following Jesus' steps laid out in Matthew 18:15-18).

Chapter six addresses three more issues that are all particularly relevant for the modern church. First, Paul taught how believers are to handle conflict with each other (vs. 1-8). It seems that the Corinthian believers were dragging each other to court to settle their differences. While this seems natural (especially in today's litigious American society), the apostle said that unbelievers had no business arbitrating disputes between believers. According to 2:15, spiritual people should be able to discern all things, so Paul stipulated that the elders of the church (who should be spiritual people) should take care of the disagreements between congregation members. Paul claimed that it is better to lose an argument than for two believers to sue each other in a secular court.[81]

---

81 Part of the difficulty with this today is that there are multiple local churches in a city. Corinth had one church with elders leading and ruling over all the believers there. Even still, disputes between believers in different local churches today could be addressed by the elders of both churches, if those

Second, Paul addressed the issue of sanctification, the maturing process that God intends for all believers to go through (vs. 9-11). Not only can unrighteous people not understand spiritual matters, but they will also have no inheritance in the Messianic Kingdom that is awaiting believers.[82] Every believer should be able to look at his past (or potential) life and say, "God saved me from this." The list of sins given contains only lifestyle sins, i.e., habitual sins that control one's life. Even as depraved as some of these are, they are no match for God's cleansing power in a believer's life. Paul did not allow anyone to say, "That's just the way I am" or "I was born that way."[83]

Third, Paul addressed sexual sin specifically (vs. 12-20). Even though Christians are not under the Mosaic Law, we cannot engage in just anything we want. One of Israel's greatest downfalls was sexual sin. It was pervasive among the pagan cultures and religions, leading to some of Israel's great defeats, and it continues to pervade modern culture, affecting the church in the same way. Paul reminded the Corinthians that, as the Body of Christ, engaging in sexual sin has the same effect as Christ hiring a prostitute. How could we do that? We must remember that we have already been purchased (redeemed) to be used by God, for God, and his own Holy Spirit indwells us to keep us from sin and help us glorify God.

Paul's mention of both "PASSIVE HOMOSEXUAL PARTNERS" and "PRAC-TICING HOMOSEXUALS" is significant (vs. 9). Those who insist on normalizing homosexuality within the Church have attempted to redefine these to mean abusive actions, not relationships between a loving same-sex couple. However, the words Paul used refer to actions, not intention or relationship. The first word is μαλακός (*malakos*), which means "soft" and can refer

---

churches practiced biblical church government and Christian discipline.

82 Believers can lose reward in the Messianic/Millennial Kingdom based on how we live in this life, but unbelievers have no entrance to the Kingdom at all or reward to lose. To view this passage as potential loss of salvation is a misunderstanding of the doctrines of salvation, eternal security, and inheritance or reward.

83 This is highly relevant since Paul specifically mentioned the actions of both active and passive homosexual partners in his list. According to Paul, "gay" is not a state of being but a choice of action.

to anything, including clothing or a cushion. When applied to a person in ancient Greek literature it meant "effeminate," generally, and "men and boys who are sodomized by other males in such a relationship."[84] The second word is ἀρσενοκοίτης (*arsenokoites*, from *arsen*, "male," and *koite*, "bed" and by extension, "intercourse"). It is the standard Greek word for a male homosexual, the "one who assumes the dominant role in same-sex activity."[85] Since this activity was restricted or limited in various regions throughout the Roman Empire, there is no legitimate basis on which to say that Paul was referring to anything but the homosexual act itself. All homosexuality is sin and unrepentant engagement by a Christian will cause him or her to lose reward or inheritance in Messiah's Kingdom.

Chapter seven introduces a new section of this letter in which Paul answered some specific questions from the church – marriage, divorce, and remarriage (ch. 7); Christian freedom (ch. 8-10); spiritual gifts (ch. 12-14); and the resurrection of the dead (ch. 15).

Regarding marriage and sexuality, Paul made four specific clarifications. First, sexual relations are to be maintained as a normal part of a Christian marriage, and this is the limit of sexual activity for a Christian (vs. 1-7). Within marriage, sex is not to be used to manipulate one's spouse, but each spouse is to consider his or her body the possession of the other. If a couple is to go without sex for a long period for any reason, it should be by mutual consent with a plan to resume as soon as possible.[86] He did note that this was a personal concession of his (albeit inspired). It seems he was not married and thought celibacy to be a perfectly good option (and possibly even a spiritual gift).

Second, for Christians who are not married, Paul recommended that

---

84 BDAG, s.v. "μαλακός," 2.

85 BDAG, s.v., "ἀρσενοκοίτης".

86 Paul's mention of prayer seems to indicate that this can be considered a type of fasting. However, medical issues and other reasons may also require periods without sexual activity.

they remain unmarried as he was (vs. 8-9). However, if they simply could not contain their sexual desires, then they should get married, so they would not fall into sexual sin.[87]

Third, for Christians who are married, Paul had nothing more to say than what Jesus had already taught, namely, that they should remain married and not get divorced (vs. 10-11). The occasion of adultery was Jesus' sole exception (Matthew 19:9). If a Christian couple divorces (except for infidelity), they must remain unmarried or be reconciled to each other. Anything else disobeys Jesus and Paul.

Fourth, in the case of a mixed marriage between a believer and an unbeliever, Paul was more lenient in matters of divorce and remarriage (vs. 12-16). His one rule was that the believer should not be the one to file for divorce. However, if the unbeliever files, the believer is to let the unbeliever go, and then the believer is free to remarry.[88] The reason that the believer should not leave is due to the spiritual influence he or she can have with the unbelieving spouse and children (see also 1 Peter 3:1-6).

The problem is that marriage is a lifetime commitment, often entered by those too young and immature. Over time, people think the grass is greener somewhere else, so they look for reasons to escape what they feel is a boring, stagnant relationship. Paul said that should not be. With the few exceptions just mentioned, believers should remain in whatever state they find themselves (vs. 17-24).

Because of the expected persecution he knew would be coming from the Roman Emperor, Paul thought it wise to avoid marriage altogether at that time (vs. 25-40). This is not because he disliked marriage (as he is often accused) but because marriage takes commitment and time, both of which could be used to further the Church if people did not marry. However, for

---

87 This is a fascinating line of reasoning and doctrine that deserves more treatment than it has received.

88 While this sounds as if it should be simple, divorce almost never is. I have written at length about this in my book, *Marriage, Divorce, and Remarriage: Fresh Help and Hope from the Bible* (Xulon Press, 2007).

those who choose to marry, they should do so knowing that must be their top priority. At the end, he also mentioned that widows (and presumably widowers) are free to remarry as well, if they do so "IN THE LORD."

Chapter eight started a new broad topic with several different parts: freedoms available to believers. The Corinthians' first question had to do with meat that had been sacrificed to idols in the pagan temples. However, before answering that, Paul made a quick detour. When seeing a fellow believer do something we think is wrong or questionable, we sometimes say, "They just don't know better." However, Paul wrote that knowledge was not the issue; in fact, knowledge could be misused (vs. 1-3). The issue was not knowledge but brotherly love.

It seems that he had taught them on this subject already, so he knew what they knew (vs. 4-6). They knew that "AN IDOL IN THIS WORLD IS NOTHING," and they knew that "THERE IS NO GOD BUT ONE." Because of this, any food that had been offered to idols (representing various false gods) should mean nothing to these believers in the only true God.

The problem was that not everyone was aware that these idols were nothing (vs. 7-13), including some of their fellow believers who had come out of these pagan religions. They may have even been the ones who asked the question: Is food offered to idols fit for a Christian? For some former pagans, eating this food would defile their conscience, causing them to feel as if they were worshiping those false gods again. They genuinely thought they were sinning against the true God by enjoying food that had been dedicated to a false god. For this reason, Paul encouraged the believers to exercise brotherly love by refraining from eating this type of meal if a fellow believer might cause himself to sin by participating with them.

This is why the issue was really about brotherly love not knowledge of the truth. For Paul, there were many things that he would rather not do – even though they were perfectly fine – if participating in them would cause a fellow Christian to sin against God, even in his conscience.

Chapter nine continues the teaching on Christian freedom from chapter eight, expanding out from the initial question about food dedicated to idols. To expound on that more, Paul demonstrated how he treated others. There should have been no question as to whether Paul was an apostle, which meant he should have full access to the freedoms we have in Christ (vs. 1-3).

When asked about how to live out his freedoms, he pointed to his ministry (vs. 4-12a). As an apostle, he had the right to have a wife and have her travel and minister alongside him. As an apostle, he had the right to be financially supported by the people he had pointed to Christ and the churches he started. The other apostles apparently did that, and he had those rights as well. In fact, it made no sense that his spiritual children should not take care of his financial needs, and he gave a series of illustrations to prove it.

As he showed in chapter eight, however, the question is not one of rights and freedoms but love. The fact that he had those rights did not mean that he could or should force them on others. In fact, in many cases he did not exercise his rights, "SO THAT WE MAY NOT BE A HINDRANCE TO THE GOSPEL OF CHRIST" (vs. 12b-18). Paul chose to forego his rights and freedoms because he had been charged (and may have been accused even in Corinth) of being like the traveling charlatans, snake-oil salesmen, who scammed the public, collected the money, then left town. Because of his itinerant ministry, Paul chose to not take funds from the places he preached, so that when he left town, the new believers would not feel like he had taken advantage of them, thereby hurting the gospel ministry there.

Broadly speaking, then, Paul chose to use his freedoms to make the most of the opportunities for the gospel, adjusting how he limited himself based on the group he was ministering to (vs. 19-23). Rather than flaunting his freedoms, he chose to limit them for the benefit of those around him. This is what he meant when he wrote several years earlier, "FOR YOU WERE

CALLED TO FREEDOM, BROTHERS AND SISTERS; ONLY DO NOT USE FREEDOM AS AN OPPORTUNITY TO INDULGE YOUR FLESH, BUT THROUGH LOVE SERVE ONE ANOTHER" (Galatians 5:13).

Ultimately, he refused to let his personal desires and freedoms control him (vs. 24-27). Doing so could disqualify him from future ministry. Instead, he controlled his desires. Even though it was uncomfortable or restrictive sometimes, it was better that people came to know Jesus than that Paul maintained his rights. A few years later, he wrote to the Philippians, reminding them that even Jesus chose to forego his rights to serve us, an example we are to follow (Philippians 2:1-8).

Chapter ten approaches Paul's discussion of freedoms from a different perspective. In the previous two chapters, it was about not flaunting legitimate freedoms. In this chapter, Paul speaks of wrongly extending freedoms to areas in which we are not legitimately free. Using the Jewish Exodus generation as an example, Paul showed they had experienced all of God's blessings (freedoms), yet they wanted more (vs. 1-6). Paul wrote that we should look to them as examples, considering that the judgments God placed on them were because they went after evil desires, things they were not free to have or do.

Verses 7-10 list four "nots" that Paul commanded the Corinthians: 1) "DO NOT BE IDOLATERS"; 2) "LET US NOT BE IMMORAL"; 3) "LET US NOT PUT CHRIST TO THE TEST"; and 4) "DO NOT COMPLAIN." God judged the Israelites for each of these things, and Christians are not free to engage in them either. In fact, it is when we think, in pride, that we are exercising our freedoms that we are most likely to fall (vs. 12-13). On the other hand, we should not be so fearful about situations that may be tempting, that we do nothing at all. God will help us through any temptation, whether those Paul listed or any others.

It seems that a specific situation the Corinthians faced dealt with attending feasts to pagan gods, more than just purchasing meat in the market (vs. 14-22). The mature believers knew there was nothing wrong with the food, and they did not worship the false gods, so they participated in these feasts and had a good meal. However, the weaker, immature believers considered this to make them "PARTNERS WITH DEMONS."[89] Paul told them all to refrain from such feasts, because it was tantamount to the Israelites testing God in the wilderness, trying to participate with both demons and God, which must not happen. Eating food sacrificed to an idol was one thing; joining in a feast celebrating these demonic gods was not a freedom they could exercise.

He concluded the section with a few final principles about our freedoms (10:23 – 11:1). First, not all freedoms are beneficial to ourselves or others, and the ultimate principle is still love. Second, enjoy everything with a clean conscience, because "THE EARTH AND ITS ABUNDANCE ARE THE LORD'S." Third, enjoy a meal with a clean conscience, unless a weaker believer is present and clearly concerned about it. Fourth, in all things, work to glorify God and not intentionally offend anyone (Jews, Gentiles, or believers). Fifth, imitate Paul and Jesus who both lived for the spiritual benefit of those around them.

Chapter eleven contains two sections which do not necessarily relate to one another but seem to continue either the list of questions that Paul was answering or some issues that needed clarification and instruction. The first section deals with the propriety of women in church gatherings (vs. 2-16), something Paul could "PRAISE" them for. This is a difficult section, which has resulted in a variety of interpretations, but the key is found in verse three, showing that there is a proper order and authority of things. Like the Father is Christ's functional "HEAD" without any thought of superiority, so man is women's "HEAD" without insinuating that women are inferior. However (as he will demonstrate again in chapter 14), Paul expected a certain functional order

---

89 There is an innate sense that pagans realize they are engaging with or worshiping demons, even if they use different words (spirits, jinns, etc.)

in the church gatherings. Specifically, this was displayed by the head coverings the women were to wear. One major difficulty is in determining whether these were cultural issues limited to Corinth or the first century or whether they are timeless principles still applicable today. Another question has to do with the nature of the head covering, whether it required an external covering, like a shawl, or if it could refer simply to her hair. The comment "BECAUSE OF THE ANGELS" in verse 10 has also confounded scholars throughout the centuries, but it may have a connection to Ephesians 2-3, where Paul wrote that the Church is observed by angels to demonstrate God's wisdom.

Although it is impossible to resolve the debate here conclusively, it seems likely that the issue was connected to the abuse of freedoms the Corinthians displayed in the previous chapters, so Paul was correcting the women's loose attitudes of respect to their husbands, particularly in their public worship services. If this were simply a cultural issue, then a modern comparison may be a woman taking her husband's last name rather than keeping her maiden name.[90]

The second section concerns something that Paul could not "PRAISE" them for, namely, their decorum when they attended their love feasts in conjunction with the Lord's Supper celebrations (vs. 17-34). He could not praise them because their factions were on full display during these times, rather than the unity in Christ that should have been obvious. One example was that some did not wait for the whole congregation to be present before they began. They would have eaten their fill before others arrived, leaving them hungry.

Paul used this opportunity to remind them of the sacred importance of the celebration, that he received these instructions directly from Christ, and that it is a proclamation of his death on our behalf. In fact, their abuse of this ordinance had caused some of them to become physically ill and

---

90 I have taught this for several years as a modern application of Paul's general rule of a wife acknowledging her husband's "headship," and Constable seems to consider it one possible application as well.

others even to die. This is one of at least a half-dozen passages teaching that physical death is a potential judgment from God on decidedly unrepentant believers. To not fall under God's judgment, Paul wrote, they (and we) should closely examine themselves before participating in the celebration. He had other things to tell them, as well, that he would hold onto until he arrived.

Chapters twelve through fourteen comprise the longest section in the Bible on spiritual gifts. The Corinthians had no lack of these gifts (1:5-7), yet they apparently misused them because they were "IGNORANT" about them, which Paul intended to correct (vs. 1-3).

In verses 4-11 Paul set out an initial discussion of the gifts in general, resulting in an initial sample list of gifts and several principles. First, the Trinity works together to produce and make these gifts effective. No matter the differences that we see in their outworking, they are designed for unified ministry. Second, Paul called them "MANIFESTATIONS OF THE SPIRIT." Third, each believer receives at least one of these manifestations or gifts. Fourth, they are distributed by the Holy Spirit, as he determines, not all the gifts to the same believer or any individual gift to all believers.

Offering one of his classic analogies, Paul compared the Church to a body (vs. 12-26), demonstrating several similarities. First, just like a physical body, though unified, is made up of many individual parts, so the Church is Christ's Body with many individuals. Second, no part of the Body can lose its membership because each unique role is necessary. Third, no body part has the authority to tell another body part that he is not necessary. Fourth, in a surprising twist, God highly honors the parts that we tend to consider "LESS HONORABLE." Thus, each part is to look out for the others, caring for and honoring each other.

Verse thirteen contains three significant principles. First, it is the Holy Spirit who baptizes (immerses and joins) us into the Body of Christ. This places us "in Christ" (one of Paul's favorite terms). Second, every believer is "BAPTIZED INTO [CHRIST'S] ONE BODY." According to Romans 8:9, "IF ANYONE DOES NOT HAVE THE SPIRIT OF CHRIST, THIS PERSON DOES NOT BELONG TO HIM." Third, salvation and Spirit baptism are not based on a person's past lifestyle. Some of these Corinthian believers were pagans before salvation (6:9-11), but they had all been baptized into Christ.

The final verses provide another sample list, but a more specific one. In this list, Paul used ordinal numbers to present a hierarchical ranking of the gifts – "FIRST . . . SECOND . . . THIRD . . . THEN" (vs. 27-28). He also asked a series of questions, each phrased specifically to assume a negative response. "NOT ALL . . . DO THEY?" No, of course not (vs. 29-30). He closed with an encouragement for the congregation to desire the greater gifts (again, implying that some gifts are greater than others), and he intended to show them which gifts those were.

Chapter thirteen is the famous "love chapter," a section of which is often used in weddings and other celebrations to demonstrate the greatness of selfless love. What is often overlooked is that this is right in the middle of Paul's teaching on spiritual gifts, and love was the comparison Paul used to show which gifts were greater than others.

In verses 1-3, Paul used a series of hyperboles to demonstrate love's greatness compared to even the most extraordinary things. There are some who take Paul's mention of "THE TONGUES OF MEN AND ANGELS" to prove that speaking in tongues means speaking in a heavenly language that is different from human language. However, this is not supported by the text. The metaphor about faith moving mountains is clearly hyperbolic, as was Paul's comment about allowing his body to be burned[91] or giving everything

---

91 The NET translates verse three with "IF I GIVE OVER MY BODY IN ORDER TO BOAST" (also NIV) rather than "TO BE BURNED" (NASB, ESV, KJV) due to a textual variant, which Metzger notes was given a "C" rating by the Editorial Committee of the United Bible Societies' Greek New Testament because of the strong evidence for both readings (Bruce M. Metzger, *A Textual Commentary On The Greek New Testament, Second Edition*, 1994). In other words, it is difficult to determine which was Paul's original thought. Either reading draws the same analogy that, if Paul were to hand over his body, it would not compare with selfless love.

away. There is no justifiable reason to read "TONGUES OF ANGELS" as a specific supernatural language when the others are illustrative.

Verses 4-7 contain a list of fifteen ways that love is the greatest action in which we can engage. It is a wonderful list often cited and should be read at engagement parties and weddings. Speakers at Christian funerals should be able to point to the person in the casket as someone who embodied these principles. Yet, in context, this list also describes how spiritual gifts are to be used within the Church.

Verse eight begins with "LOVE NEVER FAILS," which is often misread as the sixteenth item in the previous list. In reality, it begins the following sentence, showing again that love is greater than the gifts themselves because they will end while love remains. Paul noted that three gifts specifically would end – prophecy, tongues, and knowledge. Verses 8-13 are highly debated in reference to when these gifts will/did end, mainly centered on the meaning of "THE PERFECT" in verse ten.[92] Much has been written on this over the centuries, but there are three primary interpretations.

First, if "the perfect" refers to Jesus, then these gifts will remain until Jesus returns. This interpretation assumes that only Jesus could be called "perfect." Second, if "the perfect" refers to the final maturation of the Church (Ephesians 4:13), then these gifts will remain until the Rapture, when "WE WILL BE LIKE HIM" (1 John 3:2). This interpretation takes "perfect" to mean "mature" considering the immediate analogy of child/adult. Third, if "the perfect" refers to the Scriptures, then these gifts remained only until the completion of the New Testament. This interpretation takes "perfect" to mean "complete" in direct juxtaposition to "PARTIAL" in verses ten and twelve. This last interpretation seems to make the most sense in the immediate context, in the context of the whole New Testament, and in the experience of church history.

---

92 The Greek word τέλειος (*teleios*) can legitimately be translated as *perfect*, *mature*, or *complete*, depending on the context, so none of these interpretations can be dismissed based solely on the translation of this word. The context and analogies must be used to determine Paul's meaning.

Regardless of one's interpretation of the ending of these gifts, the fact is that they would not outlast "FAITH, HOPE, AND LOVE," and that love is "THE GREATEST OF THESE," including the gifts.

Chapter fourteen begins with almost a repeat of 12:31. Paul encouraged the Corinthians to pursue the love he just explained and still be eager for the spiritual gifts, but now he began to emphasize one gift – prophecy – especially over speaking in tongues. Apparently, the Corinthians were elevating tongues above the other gifts, so Paul listed it last in the hierarchical list in 12:28 and minimized it in this chapter, presenting several principles about tongues versus prophecy:[93]

- Tongues were between a believer and God; prophecy was for everyone.

- Tongues built up only the speaker; prophecy built up the whole church.

- Tongues were unproductive for the mind; prophecy used the mind.

- An emphasis on tongues revealed immaturity; an emphasis on prophecy revealed maturity.

- Tongues were a sign for unbelievers (especially Jews); prophecy was not a sign, and it was for believers.

- Tongues were disorganized; prophecy was structured.

Spiritual gifts are designed and intended to strengthen the church (vs. 26), something that tongues could not do without interpretation. Paul's strong encouragement, especially for those who wanted to speak in tongues, was that

---

93 The use of the past tense in this chapter reflects my belief that the biblical gifts of speaking in tongues and prophecy are no longer in effect or normative today. However, even if they were, these rules would still apply, which is not what we see in many or most occurrences. This should give pause to anyone who thinks that what we see today is from the Holy Spirit, because he could not contradict the rules, guidelines, or principles he already gave in the Scriptures.

they should desire something that was truly beneficial to the church rather than just for themselves (vs. 12), because "LOVE IS NOT SELF-SERVING" (13:5).

Paul also gave a few rules for the use of tongues in church gatherings (vs. 26-40):[94]

- No more than two or three could speak in tongues at any gathering.
- They were always to be interpreted, either by the speaker or someone else.
- Those two or three were not to speak at the same time but one after another.
- Tongues were not to be forbidden.

The rules for prophecy were a little different, but anyone could prophesy if he or she received a revelation from God, and every prophecy was to be evaluated to see if it was true. This seems to indicate that tongues were not necessarily considered to be revelatory since no evaluation was required.[95]

The statement that "WOMEN SHOULD BE SILENT IN THE CHURCHES" (vs. 34) has been the subject of a great deal of debate and writing. The natural reading seems to indicate that it applied to the topic at hand, e.g., tongues and prophecy. Some say that it has only to do with the evaluation of prophets, because women were to ask their husbands at home, rather than in the meeting (vs. 35). Still others point to 11:5 that women could pray and prophesy if their heads were covered. If this were only a cultural matter (see notes on chapter 11), then they believe the whole matter should be dropped here as well. Since the context is about orderliness within church gatherings (vs. 33, 40), it is important to consider all possible interpretations in that light.

---

94 Because he spoke specifically about church gatherings, not private homes, some take the mediating position that there are no restrictions on the use of tongues in private (usually private prayer). Whether this is true matters only if tongues are still in effect (see the notes on chapter 13 for a brief explanation of why I believe they are not).

95 The only three occurrences of tongues in Scripture (Acts 2, 10, 19) bear this out as well. In each instance, the message was preached in the common language, while the tongues were spontaneous praises to and about God. In none of those cases was new revelation or a message delivered supernaturally in tongues that needed supernatural interpretation.

Chapter fifteen concludes the teaching portion of Paul's letter. The final topic he needed to address was the resurrection. His opening statement, which he wanted "TO MAKE CLEAR . . . THE GOSPEL," reminds us that some of these believers were still "INFANTS IN CHRIST" (3:1) and that they were still uncertain about some of the basic doctrines of the faith. It was also a good time to remind them of the gospel that they needed to preach in their meetings so that unbelievers could be convicted and believe (14:23-25). The basic message of the gospel is simple: Christ died for our sins and was raised on the third day. Both of these events were prophesied in the Hebrew Scriptures, and they were confirmed by his public burial and post-resurrection eyewitnesses, respectively (vs. 3-11). Not only did he appear to individual apostles and small groups, including Paul himself, but Jesus also appeared to "MORE THAN FIVE HUNDRED OF THE BROTHERS AND SISTERS AT ONE TIME." For anyone who thought that could not possibly be true, Paul challenged them to visit these eyewitnesses, "MOST OF WHOM [WERE] STILL ALIVE" at the time of his writing, twenty years after the fact. Circling back to his theme from chapter one, this is the only message Paul had, and this is what the Corinthians had originally believed.

This simple, verifiable message did not stop people from trying to lead the believers astray, though. Even though Paul said they could talk to eyewitnesses of Jesus' resurrection, those people were almost 1,000 miles (1,600 km) away in Israel, and some of the Corinthians were beginning to believe that the concept of a resurrection was a hoax (vs. 12-19). Paul countered that, if that were true, three other truths would be certain as well. First, no resurrection at all means that Christ was not raised. Second, a dead Christ means that our faith is empty, we are false witnesses, and we are still in our sins. Third, no resurrection means no hope for those who have already died.

Against this false teaching, Paul pointed them back to the Old Testament Scriptures, noting that death has been common since Adam and that their belief in Christ was a belief that he undid what Adam did; thus, a resurrection from the dead is both theologically and logically sound and necessary (vs. 20-28). He also pointed to the prophecies of what Christ is supposed to do: rule in his kingdom until all his enemies are eliminated, including death itself. None of this is possible if Christ is still dead.

Paul's comment about people being "BAPTIZED FOR THE DEAD" (vs. 29-34) has found its way into Mormon theology, where living people can be baptized in the place of their dead relatives to create a retroactive salvation for them. This has caused a great debate in Christianity as well. It is possible that these Corinthians had been including the pagan practice of baptism for the dead because they had begun to disbelieve the basic gospel (which does not include water baptism at all, possibly why Paul distanced himself from it in chapter one) and the truth of the resurrection. This view fits the context of Paul's comments about their human thinking, bad company, and command to stop sinning.[96]

Paul anticipated they might ask a further question wanting more detail about the resurrection: "HOW ARE THE DEAD RAISED? WITH WHAT KIND OF BODY WILL THEY COME?" (vs. 35-49). His response indicates that this was not a line of honest questioning but one of defiance. His answer was simple: the resurrection body will be similar but different than our current bodies. Humans were meant to live in physical bodies, and we will live forever in physical bodies, except that they will be better. Some people believe there is a difference between "flesh and blood" and "flesh and bone," representing our current and future bodies, respectively (vs. 50-58).[97] Regardless of the details, Paul was clear that our resurrected bodies will become imperishable

---

96 Another option is that some people had come to believe because of Christians who had died, and their baptism was due to the others' martyrdom. This is certainly more palatable and has a lot of support from conservative scholars, but it does not seem to be the natural reading.

97 Paul here said that "FLESH AND BLOOD CANNOT INHERIT THE KINGDOM OF GOD." Some compare this to Adam's statement that Eve was from his "flesh and bone," indicating that they did not have blood at that time. Since physical life is connected to blood (Genesis 9:4; Leviticus 17:11, 14), their conclusion is that spiritual life does not need blood. For an explanation of this position, see Henry Morris, "Flesh and Bones", https://www.icr.org/article/5946.

and immortal. This will happen in an instant, at the Rapture, both for dead saints and those still alive. At that time, "DEATH [WILL BE] SWALLOWED UP IN VICTORY." This truth should cause us all to live in victory, "KNOWING THAT [OUR] LABOR IS NOT IN VAIN IN THE LORD."

Chapter sixteen concludes Paul's letter with a reminder, a tentative itinerary, and a final greeting. First, Paul reminded them that he had been collecting funds to take with him to Jerusalem for the impoverished saints there. Second Corinthians will come back to this topic, but for now, Paul simply asked them to set a little bit aside every week so that no special collection would be necessary when he arrived (vs. 1-4). We should note that his comment about "THE FIRST DAY OF THE WEEK" does not necessarily refer to an established Sunday church gathering, because the command is for "EACH OF YOU" to set aside funds personally, not corporately. (Although, it does not contradict a weekly gathering either.) Additionally, this was not a "tithe" for the church but a special gift for the Jewish saints. To use this passage to teach a necessary weekly tithe is not correct.

Second, Paul informed them of his traveling plans (vs. 5-12). Writing from Ephesus, he intended to finish visiting his churches in Macedonia before going to Corinth, where he might have stayed the winter because he did not want to see them only in passing. (These types of statements help us, who are so far removed from the immediate situation, to remember the real humanity of the people involved. Paul did not like to travel in the winter either.) Instead, he might send Timothy or Apollos in the meantime.

Finally, Paul ended with his common greeting of personal names and encouragements, including a note that he signed it with his own hand, a type of authentication in a time when he was being misrepresented.

2 Corinthians

Second Corinthians is arguably the most personal of Paul's nine letters to local churches (not including those to Timothy, Titus, or Philemon). Over thirteen chapters he shared his physical and emotional distress, he encouraged a volatile group of believers as he defended his apostolic authority over them. The first section (chapters 1-5) contains the major key to the letter's theme (1:3-4) and reveals the apostle as weak and sickly, battling heartache and depression. In this letter, Paul truly wrote out of his pain. (See the introduction to 1 Corinthians for more information regarding this church.)

Paul's exact location at the time of this writing is uncertain, but his account of waiting for Titus at Troas then going to Macedonia (2:12-13; 7:5-7) seems to place him in Macedonia (near Philippi, Thessalonica, or Berea) in Acts 20, so he probably wrote this letter around A.D. 55-56. Since he was in Ephesus headed for Macedonia when he wrote 1 Corinthians (16:8), it is probable he was still traveling on that itinerary.

Chapter one breaks slightly from the traditional letter format of ancient times. Following the writer's name and intended recipients, we find Paul's standard blessing of "GRACE AND PEACE" (vs. 2). Often there would be a short prayer of thanksgiving for the readers as well (see Romans 1:8; 1

Corinthians 1:4; *et al.*), but Paul chose to focus his attention immediately upon God, the Great Comforter. Paul was quick to declare a major reason that they were comforted "IN ALL OUR TROUBLES" was "SO THAT WE MAY BE ABLE TO COMFORT THOSE EXPERIENCING ANY TROUBLE" (vs. 4). The cliché, "Blessed to be a blessing," is more appropriately stated, "Comforted to extend comfort." This is not only a major theme of this letter, but it is also a timeless principle that believers would do well to remember and faithfully live out today. Whenever we gain comfort in a time of testing or trial, God wants us to hold onto that so we can share that with others.

The reason for Paul's introductory remarks is obvious very quickly: he and Timothy were sick and discouraged (vs. 8-11). Consider his description of their current state: "AFFLICTION . . . BURDENED EXCESSIVELY, BEYOND OUR STRENGTH . . . DESPAIRED EVEN OF LIVING . . . SENTENCE OF DEATH . . . SO GREAT A RISK OF DEATH." Whatever the situations they faced that combined to bring them to that point, Paul's only hope was that the believers would join with him in prayer and that God would deliver them from death again.

Paul revealed the second purpose of his letter in verses 12-22. He had intended to visit Corinth again, so he could provide them with a spiritual blessing and experience mutual comfort and growth (vs. 15; see Romans 1:11-12). While he was with them, he expected that they would help him get to Macedonia and back to Judea. Although he deliberately chose to not ask for ongoing financial support, Paul knew he had that right and was not hesitant to seek monetary help when he thought it necessary (see 1 Corinthians 9:1-12). However, as he would explain shortly, he had to change those plans. Unfortunately, it appears that someone in the church had used Paul's delay to malign the apostle and make it seem that he was two-faced, promising one thing yet doing something else. Paul questioned his accusers and those who listened to them: "Is this my normal method that you have to come expect? Is this the gospel I preached to you, how I presented Christ? Have my co-workers, Silas or Timothy, ever given you that impression?" His answer was, "Of course not. God speaks only truth, and we glorify him by doing the same." Paul claimed that the truth of his promises (and plans) was based on God's strength, our unity in Christ, and the Spirit's indwelling and sealing (vs. 21-22).

Chapter two best starts with 1:23, where Paul began to explain his reason for not visiting them as he had planned. Due to some issues within the church (especially factions and immorality; see 1 Corinthians 3 and 5), Paul's previous visit had been "PAINFUL" for all of them, and he did not want to do that again (vs. 1-4). Instead, he chose to write this letter to "test the waters" and see if they had responded appropriately to his previous correction. Verses 5-9 reveal that they had obeyed his instructions, disciplining their sinning member (see 1 Corinthians 5:1-5). However, upon his repentance, they had not forgiven him, so Paul urged them to extend grace and forgiveness, so the man would not be "OVERWHELMED BY EXCESSIVE GRIEF TO THE POINT OF DESPAIR" in his spiritual life.

Interestingly, Paul noted that his command to excommunicate the man had been obeyed "BY THE MAJORITY" (vs. 6). This is an early hint that there were still those in the Corinthian church who refused to acknowledge Paul's apostolic authority (see 1 Corinthians 3:1-4). Later parts of this letter confirm that to be true.

Paul had been so desperate to hear from Titus about the situation in Corinth (whether they had obeyed or rejected him) that even preaching the gospel, which was his driving passion (1 Corinthians 9:16-23), could not ease his mind and heart. It seems he cut short his ministry in Troas so that he could find Titus and find out about Corinth (vs. 10-13).

In the final few verses, Paul reminded them again of his love for them and for the gospel, even though he was being charged with greed and preaching only for money (vs. 14-17). This self-defense will continue into chapter three.

Chapter three continues Paul's defense of his apostolic ministry and authority in Corinth. It seems that one of the attacks his accusers used was that he had no credentials. Officially, that was true. However, Paul took the firm stance that, since he was commissioned by Jesus himself (Acts 9:15-16; Galatians 2:6-10), he did not "NEED LETTERS OF RECOMMENDATION" either to or from the churches he started (vs. 1-3). On the contrary, the churches themselves and the stories of life change through Christ were all the credentials he needed to prove the authority and authenticity of his message. What could be better proof than the Corinthians themselves?

"DO YOU NOT KNOW THAT THE UNRIGHTEOUS WILL NOT INHERIT THE KINGDOM OF GOD? DO NOT BE DECEIVED! THE SEXUALLY IMMORAL, IDOLATERS, ADULTERERS, PASSIVE HOMOSEXUAL PARTNERS, PRACTICING HOMOSEXUALS, THIEVES, THE GREEDY, DRUNKARDS, THE VERBALLY ABUSIVE, AND SWINDLERS WILL NOT INHERIT THE KINGDOM OF GOD. SOME OF YOU ONCE LIVED THIS WAY. BUT YOU WERE WASHED, YOU WERE SANCTIFIED, YOU WERE JUSTIFIED IN THE NAME OF THE LORD JESUS CHRIST AND BY THE SPIRIT OF OUR GOD." (1 Corinthians 6:9-11)

Additionally, Paul needed nothing for his own benefit either, because God had both called him to that ministry and made him adequate to accomplish it (vs. 4-6).

For the rest of the chapter, Paul used the example of Moses receiving the stones tablets with the Ten Commandments as an illustration of the difference between the old spiritual life under the Law and the new spiritual life under the Holy Spirit (vs. 7-18). Exodus 34:29-35 records that Moses' face glowed after having seen God, but he wore a veil in the presence of the people when not relaying God's message to them. Paul noted that this veil unintentionally became a barrier between them and God, much like the unbiblical clergy-laity divide in the Church. Rather than seeing it as a visible reminder that they could not approach God's holiness, the people used it to elevate and exalt Moses.

On a spiritual level, the Jewish people still have a veil which they misunderstand, but it is the Law itself, the one that God gave through Moses. Paul was clear in Galatians 3:19-25 that the Law was a temporary guardian over Israel until Jesus came and that it did not have the power to give spiritual life, only point to death. Thus, in a sense, the Law actually kills those who trust in it for salvation (vs. 6), even though the Law itself was holy (Romans 7:7, 12). By clinging to the Law instead of turning to Christ, the Jewish people continue to "veil" their own eyes to the truth of God's plan for them (vs. 15-16). Only the Spirit of God can produce the freedom they are looking for (vs. 17).

Chapter four returns to the theme of Paul's personal struggles in carrying out his ministry, especially toward the Corinthians. Although there was a great deal to discourage them, including satanic opposition, Paul's cure to keep himself from depression was to do the one thing he was called to do: continue preaching the gospel (vs. 1-6). This worked against his discouragement as he was always reminded that "WE DO NOT PREACH OURSELVES, BUT JESUS CHRIST . . . FOR GOD . . . IS THE ONE WHO SHINED IN OUR HEARTS" (vs. 5-6). Paul's proper focus helped him frame his attitude in situations that could throw him off track.

A second key perspective that Paul held was the temporal nature of this world, especially his physical body. A look through Acts and Paul's other letters show that he suffered great physical abuse throughout his ministry, at the hands of both Jews and Gentiles (see 6:4-5; 11:23-27). Too often believers approach this world as if it should be like heaven. Paul knew that his body was fragile, like a "CLAY JAR" (vs. 7). However, he had an "EXTRAORDINARY POWER" from God so that no matter how he was in "TROUBLE . . . PERPLEXED . . . PERSECUTED . . . KNOCKED DOWN," he refused to be "CRUSHED . . . DRIVEN TO DESPAIR . . . ABANDONED . . . DESTROYED" (vs. 8-9). No matter how often he was "HANDED OVER TO DEATH," it was always "FOR JESUS' SAKE" (vs. 11), and he would certainly be resurrected into Jesus' presence one day (vs. 14). "THEREFORE, WE DO NOT DESPAIR," because, no matter what happens to the body, it cannot destroy our spirits, which God continues to renew. Paul's eternal perspective allowed him to press on through temporary pain (vs. 16-18). What a wonderful encouragement this should be to every believer who suffers from terrible life situations or depression!

Chapter five is a kind of "reverse parallel" of chapter four. In the previous chapter, the first section focused on Paul's ministry and the second on his perspective on this life. Chapter five reverses this, with the first section continuing his perspective from chapter four (vs. 1-10) and the second section focusing back on his ministry (vs. 11-21). Some well-known verses are found here and some key truths that make this a favorite chapter of Scripture for many believers.

Verses 1-10 provide us with a great deal of information regarding the afterlife. Paul referred to his temporary physical body as an "EARTHLY HOUSE" and a "TENT," noting that there is a "HEAVENLY DWELLING" awaiting us so that "WE WILL NOT BE FOUND NAKED" (apparently a reference to a bodiless soul). God created us to be both physical and spiritual beings, and Paul said that the afterlife will be no different. Our bodies will be different, but they will still be physical bodies.[98]

A second major truth in this section deals with the believer's state of existence between death and the resurrection. Although some people believe in "soul sleep" (where the soul is unconscious), the apostle knew of only two states: "ALIVE HERE ON EARTH" (or "at home in the body") and "AT HOME WITH THE LORD" (vs. 6-8). He specifically noted that being on earth

---

98   First Corinthians 15 is clear that all believers will receive a glorified body at the Rapture. However, there is a debate over whether there is a temporary body for those who die before then. Some take this passage to indicate that there is a temporary body while others believe Paul was referring to the final resurrected body. This may be one of the things that we cannot be certain about.

means to be "ABSENT FROM THE LORD" (vs. 6). Thus, when a believer dies, he immediately goes into the presence of Jesus in a conscious state of existence, one of many points of lasting encouragement or comfort from this letter.

Following the resurrection "WE MUST ALL APPEAR BEFORE THE JUDG-MENT SEAT OF CHRIST" (vs. 10). Paul had already written about this in 1 Corinthians 3:11-15, explaining the trial of our works by fire. Here he confirmed that it will be not the works themselves that Jesus will judge but the quality of our works. The Greek words translated "GOOD OR EVIL" are quality words (rather than moral words) and should be understood as "beneficial or worthless." Since Paul's ultimate "AMBITION" was "TO PLEASE" Christ because of this judgment (vs. 9), we can interpret this to mean that the motives behind our service for God contribute to their worthiness of reward. Good deeds that come out of a wrong motive are worthless when it comes to rewarding our faithfulness.

The second half of the chapter focuses again on Paul's ministry based on his perspective of pleasing God during this life. "BECAUSE WE KNOW THE FEAR OF THE LORD, WE TRY TO PERSUADE PEOPLE" (vs. 11). Knowing God well results in knowing and living our mission well. In other words, significant ministry is the result of significant maturity. Paul insisted that, regardless of what it might look like to his accusers or the Corinthians themselves, it was the love of Christ that controlled him or compelled him in his work (vs. 14). Knowing what Christ did for us changed the way Paul saw other people, both believers and unbelievers (vs. 16-17).

In the final four verses, Paul used some form of the word "reconcile" four times. This message that he preached was not just "Jesus died for you." Paul knew that one aspect of the good news was a complete change in status from enemies against God to friends with God (Romans 5:6-11). This was part of God's intent in Jesus' death – reconciling all things back to himself (vs. 18-19; Colossians 1:19-23). Paul insisted that even believers must continually "BE RECONCILED TO GOD" (vs. 20) on a practical level, even after salvation.

Jesus became "SIN FOR US," not just so that we could go to heaven but "SO THAT IN HIM WE WOULD BECOME THE RIGHTEOUSNESS OF GOD" (vs. 21). This is the daily aspect of salvation – becoming in practice what God has already declared us to be.

Chapter six contains two primary sections. As Paul wrapped up the self-defense of his authority and ministry that he had spent the past several chapters declaring, he presented the Corinthians with two challenges. First, he challenged them to not turn away from the message he had presented (vs. 1-10). "TO RECEIVE THE GRACE OF GOD IN VAIN" does not have anything to do with losing their salvation. If we were to remove the chapter and verse divisions, Paul had just explained that the purpose of their salvation was "SO THAT IN HIM WE WOULD BECOME THE RIGHTEOUSNESS OF GOD" (5:21). To receive God's grace without growing in righteousness, he explained, would be to receive it "IN VAIN" or "for no purpose." He urged them to reconsider their rejection of his ministry and message because he and his team had "COMMENDED [THEMSELVES] IN EVERY WAY," risking life and limb to make sure the Corinthians had the truth. "Please," he begged, "reciprocate our love for you by turning your affection back toward us again" (vs. 11-13).

Paul's second challenge was toward their thinking and associations (vs. 14-18). For some reason, they had welcomed Paul's accusers and false teachers into their community with open arms (see 11:4). They had no spiritual discernment and apparently were willing to listen to whoever was right in front of them. Rather than simply saying, "Don't associate with them!", Paul challenged their thinking. "CONSIDER THIS: WHAT PARTNERSHIP IS THERE BETWEEN RIGHTEOUSNESS AND LAWLESSNESS . . . CHRIST WITH BELIAL . . . A BELIEVER WITH AN UNBELIEVER . . . THE TEMPLE OF GOD WITH IDOLS?" (vs. 14-16) It seems he thought they could answer that well enough; there is nothing in common at all. Paul would not always be there to tell them which individual to listen to; instead, they needed to be able to identify false doctrine and choose to disassociate from it. Paul reminded them that "WE ARE THE TEMPLE OF THE LIVING GOD," home of the indwelling Holy Spirit (vs. 16-18). Because of this relationship and status with God, they had no business attaching themselves to anything that goes against God, his character, or his truth.

Chapter seven contains one of the most personal parts of this letter. Paul's genuine love and care for his churches were nothing rare; we find it all over his letters. Mentions of his coworkers are also plentiful throughout his writings. What makes this chapter special, though, is that digs to the very heart of his dealings with the Corinthian believers. In the first three verses, he begged yet again that they would embrace him the way he did them. This continued theme hints that it was more than just a few factions; he was afraid they had rejected him altogether, and this chapter finally reveals why.

In his previous letter, Paul had "spanked" them for their sinfulness in several areas (1 Corinthians 3-6), but he had not yet heard back on how well they received it. Titus had gone (either with that letter or later) to evaluate the church and bring news back to Paul. While Titus was gone, Paul was devastated by the thought that he may have been too harsh and possibly crushed them. When Titus finally rejoined Paul in Macedonia (vs. 4-7; 1 Corinthians 16:5-6), he brought great news. The majority (2:6) had accepted Paul's message and repented! This brought such a wave of relief over Paul that he had to write them again, resulting in 2 Corinthians.

Although he was sorry that he had saddened them by his letter, Paul noted that there are two kinds of sadness. The first kind is from God, who often uses sadness in our lives to lead us to repent of sin (vs. 10-12). Repentance is a change of mind, ideally resulting in new actions as well. Their change of actions showed that they truly had a change of heart and mind because of the sorrow they experienced from his letter. This type leaves "NO REGRET" but leads "TO SALVATION" – not just justification from sin, but the full picture of life with God, spiritual growth, and eternal reward. The second type of sadness is "WORLDLY SADNESS" that offers none of that. It leads only to regret, depression, and despair. Judas Iscariot is a sad example of this type of sadness (Matthew 27:3-5).

Paul finished by praising them for their obedience. He had bragged about them to Titus (vs. 13-16) and was glad to hear that he had not lied or exaggerated. This caused Titus to love them even more, which helped him minister to them, which ultimately helped them as well.

Chapters eight and nine contain some of the most well-known passages on giving in the New Testament. When churches hold giving campaigns and pastors preach on tithing, these chapters are likely to come up. "THEY GAVE ACCORDING TO THEIR MEANS AND BEYOND THEIR MEANS" (8:3). "MAKE SURE YOU EXCEL IN THIS ACT OF KINDNESS, TOO" (8:7). "GOD LOVES A CHEERFUL GIVER" (9:7). These and others seem to teach that giving to the church is important, and it is. The problem, however, is that was not Paul's point when he wrote.

In reality, one of Paul's missions, while he preached the gospel and planted churches, was to raise support for other struggling believers, especially those in Jerusalem (1 Corinthians 16:1-3; Romans 15:25-29). Thus, the giving that Paul asked the Corinthians to do was not for their own church; he was encouraging them to give generously for the benefit of others. He noted that the Macedonian churches (Philippi, Thessalonica, Berea) continued to give, even sacrificially, during a difficult period (vs. 1-5). When Titus went to Corinth, Paul instructed him to make sure they did the same (vs. 6-9). It was especially important to Paul that they gave toward this mission because they had already promised that they would and had begun putting money aside for it (vs. 10-11; 1 Corinthians 16:1-3). As he would explain further in chapter nine, Paul was less concerned with the amount they gave as he was that they gave. However, he did want them to consider their better financial situation as an opportunity to serve, since it may not always be that way. One day they might find themselves on the receiving side, subject to someone else's generosity or lack thereof (vs. 12-15).

Titus and another brother were going back to Corinth again, carrying this letter with them and planning to accept the financial gift from the Corinthians (vs. 16-19). Paul noted that, especially with the accusations still swirling about him, he would not accept the gift personally, so as to not add fuel for his accusers (vs. 20-24). As if that were not enough, Paul sent yet another brother with them – for a total of three trustworthy men – to accept the money and return with it, so they could distribute it as necessary. Not only was there great wisdom in having multiple men traveling together for protection, but Paul was also right to "recuse" himself from showing up at Corinth for what could be construed just for money.

Chapter nine continues Paul's discussion on the Corinthians' giving toward his benevolence ministry with some important general principles about giving in the Church Age. We must understand that tithing is strictly an Old Testament teaching and practice. Nowhere is tithing taught or commanded in the New Testament, including in this chapter. Instead, Christians should give generously and graciously for four reasons, one of which is the support of our global Christian family. (The support of local church leaders, local church members, and global missions are the other three.)

Paul was not afraid to be blunt with his churches. He would not let them feign ignorance as if they did not know they should give toward this ministry (vs. 1-4). In fact, he had bragged to the Macedonians about how well the Corinthians were doing with their fund-raising. This is the second time he mentioned about bragging on them (7:14) and the second time he wanted to make sure he was not embarrassed by it. Although some may call this a "guilt trip," it is obvious that, no matter how wrong they could be in some areas, Paul always had great hopes for their growth.

It was important that they did not give just because he told them to do so, though, so he gave three principles of generous giving that are still applicable today (vs. 5-9). First, giving is like sowing. The principle of the harvest reveals that our harvest reflects what we sow, comes later than we sow, and is in proportion to what we sow. Second, giving should be done intentionally and not reluctantly. Third, giving with the right heart ("CHEERFUL") pleases God.

Prosperity Gospel preachers misuse these principles to convince people to give to their ministries, often promising "returns on investment" for every dollar given. Paul did not do that. Giving is a spiritual issue, and God will reward, although not necessarily with more finances in this lifetime. Instead, the harvest may be one "OF RIGHTEOUSNESS," both in the giver and the recipient (vs. 10-15). Ultimately, the reason for our giving should be to glorify God, and it is a privilege to be able to participate in his work in this way. "THANKS BE TO GOD FOR HIS INDESCRIBABLE GIFT!"

Chapter ten begins the final section of the letter and a new defense of Paul's authority over the Corinthian church as God's divinely-appointed apostle, specifically in comparison to the false teachers that had deceived them.

Paul's appeal that they would listen to him was offered in "THE MEEKNESS AND GENTLENESS OF CHRIST" (vs. 1). His comment that he was meek while with them and full of courage only in his letters was a sarcastic retort toward his accusers, who apparently had convinced many of the Corinthians that Paul was a hypocrite. He could talk a big game in his letters, but in person, he carried no power or authority. Paul claimed this was ludicrous (vs. 9-11). The bulk of his argument in this chapter was based on the truth that the most important aspect of this life is a spiritual matter, not a physical one, emphasizing thoughts and not just actions (vs. 3-5). This is why he refused to be held to someone else's human standards (vs. 2); why he seemed harsh when dealing with matters of obedience and disobedience in the church (vs. 6); and why he did not let outward matters distract him from inward realities (vs. 7-8).

In the final verses, Paul denounced his critics for boasting about their accomplishments while minimizing Paul's (vs. 12-18). He pointed out that they simply "COMPARE[D] THEMSELVES WITH THEMSELVES" to brag about how good they were, but he was not about to lower himself to their games. Instead, he would boast only about the work God was doing in and through him and his team, including what God was accomplishing in Corinth. Ultimately, he cared only that people heard the gospel (from him directly or the churches he started) and that they continued to grow in their faith. Nothing else was worth bragging about because that was all God called him to do.

The last verse should be a wonderful encouragement to all who want to be faithful servants: "IT IS NOT THE PERSON WHO COMMENDS HIMSELF WHO IS APPROVED, BUT THE PERSON THE LORD COMMENDS."

Chapter eleven continues Paul's defense of himself to the Corinthian believers. Many of them had been on the verge of rejecting him, but his previous letter brought them back a little. Now he wanted to stop their retreat once-and-for-all. This chapter contains some of the harshest words we have recorded from Paul's hand toward believers or unbelievers (other examples include 1 Corinthians 3:1-3; 5:1-5; 11:17-18; Galatians 3:1-5; 5:12; Philippians 3:2; 1 Timothy 1:20). Reminiscent of a courtroom, at this point in his self-defense he presented four accusations against his prosecutors.

First, he accused the Corinthian believers of embracing anyone and anything except Paul and his message (vs. 1-4), including those who would abuse them (vs. 16-21). Second, he accused them of scorning him because of his gentle demeanor and graciousness (vs. 5-6). Third, he accused both the Corinthians and the false teachers of dismissing his service for Christ, including taking support from other churches instead of Corinth (vs. 7-9) and experiencing great suffering for his ministry (vs. 23-33). Fourth, he accused his critics of being agents of Satan who were working undercover, only pretending to be apostles of Christ (vs. 12-15).

Although this was harsh and even full of sarcasm and contempt for those against him, Paul made sure to show his love and concern for the Corinthians (vs. 1-3, 9-11). This was not as much an attack on them as it was their sinful actions and those who led them astray. However, even at this Paul still had the court's attention, and he was not done yet.

Chapter twelve concludes Paul's self-defense with his final three points. First, in verses 1-10 he recounted an experience that happened "FOURTEEN YEARS AGO." He referred to himself in the third person ("I KNOW A MAN"), because even in his self-defense his purpose was to point the Corinthians back to Jesus rather than to himself (vs. 6). Probably shortly after his escape from Damascus (11:32-33; Acts 9:23-25), God gave him a special revelation through a vision in which he stood in heaven.[99] Because this was so early in his Christian life, even before his ministry began, God gave him an ailment to keep him from becoming arrogant for receiving such a revelation. The exact ailment is unknown (although there is much speculation[100]); Paul simply called it "A THORN IN THE FLESH" and "A MESSENGER [OR "ANGEL"] OF SATAN" (vs. 7). In response to his multiple requests to have it removed, God responded only with his abiding grace (vs. 8-10), something Paul would learn to appreciate and demonstrate throughout the rest of his life. God's grace became the source of his boasting, not Paul's accomplishments.

His second point was toward his accusers again. For the second time, he called them "THOSE 'SUPER-APOSTLES'" (vs. 11; 11:5), a snide comment reflecting how they presented themselves compared to him. However, he

---

99 Interestingly, Paul's response to what he saw and heard (vs. 4) was very different than those today who claim to have gone to heaven and return to write books and appear on television.

100 See the notes on Galatians 4 for support that this may have been related to Paul's eyes.

reminded the Corinthians of something he had that those others did not: "THE SIGNS OF AN APOSTLE" (vs. 12). By this, he referred to the miracles ("SIGNS AND WONDERS AND POWERFUL DEEDS," vs. 12) that the Holy Spirit worked through his true apostles to authenticate that their message was from God. Of course, Satan can do miracles, too, but it seems that Paul thought that the believers in Corinth knew the difference between the miracles he did and anything Satan might do.

Finally, part of his critics' accusation always included Paul's greed for money, so he continued to remind the Corinthians how he never asked for anything from them for himself either of the first two times he was there, and that he would not ask again on the third visit (vs. 13-18). Basically, in these three chapters (ten through twelve), plus his remarks at the beginning of the letter, Paul thoroughly dismantled every accusation against him with a supernatural blend of authority and love, harshness and grace. Verse 19 reveals his attitude throughout this heartfelt letter: "Ultimately, I'm not really defending myself here. To reject me is to reject Christ. I just want to build you up."

Paul noted that he had three fears that would make his third visit to them painful again (vs. 20-21): 1) that they would no longer know each other; 2) that there would be schismatic disunity; and 3) that they would be living in unconfessed, unrepentant sin, causing him humiliation before his accusers and grief before God.

Chapter thirteen concludes this letter with Paul urging the Corinthians to examine themselves before God before Paul arrived so that his fears (12:20-21) would not be realized (vs. 1-3). He warned them that he would not be timid in using his apostolic authority to discipline any of them who rejected his letters and teaching, choosing to continue in their sin. He challenged them to make sure they were truly "IN THE FAITH" (vs. 5), probably a reference both to initial salvation and sanctification and to the orthodox teachings of Christianity since he did not specify just "in Christ." Even believers can "FAIL THE TEST" of obedience (vs. 5) and be disqualified from serving Christ (1 Corinthians 9:23-27), something Paul did not want for them. Even if it seemed that Paul failed, he did not want them to fail (vs. 6-9).

Paul claimed that this letter, no matter how harsh it was from time to time, was actually a demonstration of his great love for them (vs. 10). Solomon wrote that wounds from a friend can be good (Proverbs 27:6), and Paul chose to wound them from a distance so that they could enjoy each other in person.

The concluding verse[101] is an inspired acknowledgment of the Trinity. Under the Holy Spirit's guidance (2 Peter 1:21; 3:15-16), Paul referred to the three members of the Godhead as individual persons who are co-equal with each other. Although the word Trinity never occurs in Scripture, passages like this teach this doctrine clearly.

---

101 English translations have it marked as either verse 13 or 14.

Galatians

G alatians is possibly the earliest letter we have from Paul.[102] Unlike most of his other letters, this was written to "THE CHURCHES OF GALATIA" (1:2) rather than to an individual congregation. Paul visited[103] these churches during his first missionary tour (Acts 13-14), before returning to Antioch and subsequently defending God's work among the Gentiles at the Council of Jerusalem (Acts 15). The purpose of that council was to decide what Gentiles were required to do to fully participate in the Church. Specifically, the debate was over the circumcision of Gentiles. After much debate, the apostles and elders finally determined that only belief was necessary, as with the Jews, yet they encouraged the Gentiles to refrain from a few practices that would unnecessarily offend the Jews among them (Acts 15:19-21).

Paul's letter to the Galatian believers is a treatise on justification by grace through faith alone, second only to Romans in its importance to our understanding of the doctrine of salvation. The entire letter is an explanation and defense of that doctrine because the Galatians were turning away from

---

102 This is certainly debated, but it makes the most sense to me when all the available facts are considered.

103 While it is possible that he founded them during this tour, it is also possible (and more likely) that he founded at least some of them during his tenure in "SYRIA AND CILICIA" (1:21), years before Barnabas called him to Antioch (Acts 11:25-26).

it due to a contingent of Jewish legalists who demanded that they accept circumcision as a part of salvation or spiritual maturity. If this letter were written later in Paul's ministry (as some infer from 4:13[104]), after the Jerusalem Council, it seems he would certainly have referred to that decision to shut down the claims of his detractors. Instead, Paul's entire argument was based on the doctrine of justification which came to him directly from Jesus and the Hebrew Scriptures.

Chapter one does not follow the pattern of Paul's other letters, or those of the day, in that he did not offer a word/prayer of thanksgiving after his greeting. Instead, he jumped immediately into the purpose of his letter – "I AM ASTONISHED THAT YOU ARE SO QUICKLY DESERTING THE ONE WHO CALLED YOU BY THE GRACE OF CHRIST AND ARE FOLLOWING A DIFFERENT GOSPEL" (vs. 6). "So quickly" seems to indicate that it had not been long since they had accepted the gospel that they were turning away from, though the Greek word can also mean "so easily." Paul noted that they had deserted, not just the gospel, but the Savior himself, and began to follow "A DIFFERENT GOSPEL," another message they had been given by those who would "DISTORT THE GOSPEL OF CHRIST" (vs. 7). This brought Paul's fiercest condemnation – eternal hell for those who preach a heretical message of salvation (vs. 8-9). Today, this includes many false gospels in religions like Mormonism, Jehovah's Witness, Roman Catholicism, Eastern Orthodoxy, Islam, and so many others.

It seems that Paul's accusers painted a picture of him as a "hit-and-run" charlatan. As some of his other letters show (especially 2 Corinthians), they claimed that he did not genuinely care about his listeners, changed his message to gain favor with his audience, and was in it primarily for what he could get out of it. It seems they also continued to attack his authority as a

---

104 They see Paul's statement, "I PREACHED THE GOSPEL TO YOU THE FIRST TIME" (NASB), to mean that he had been there at least twice before writing this letter. Even so, he easily could have been there more than once in the fourteen years of ministry (2:1) preceding this letter.

genuine apostle (vs. 1). His response was measured but firm.

First, he stated that one cannot work to please both people and God (vs. 10). Second, he insisted that his message was not fluid. In fact, it did not even come from a fluid source, from whom he could have received the wrong message. Instead, Paul's message came from Jesus himself (vs. 2, 11-12). Third, his own story of dramatic life change proved that he broke close ties with his former colleagues and intentionally stayed away from the apostles in Jerusalem so he would not be swayed by anyone's doctrine except the Savior's (vs. 13-24). When he finally did begin to meet with the other apostles, it was with only a few of them and only for a short time. Fourth, he declared that God had chosen him for this very specific ministry, that his previous life was utterly opposed to that calling, and that it required direct intervention by God to set him on the correct path. Thus, anything his opponents claimed could only make him more, not less, insistent on his message.

Chapter two records yet another visit Paul made to Jerusalem, this time with Barnabas and Titus (vs. 1-5). The fact that Luke never mentioned Titus in Acts makes it difficult to make a certain determination, but the "FOURTEEN YEARS" Paul mentioned makes it possible that this was the famine relief visit in Acts 11:30. This interpretation is preferred because this visit was "ONLY . . . A PRIVATE MEETING WITH THE INFLUENTIAL PEOPLE" rather than all the apostles and elders and congregation at the Jerusalem Council.[105] In this meeting, Paul made sure to emphasize that he preached justification by grace through faith alone and did not insist on circumcision for Gentiles (vs. 6-10). The other apostles agreed with his message and agreed that he and Barnabas "WOULD GO TO THE GENTILES AND THEY TO THE CIRCUMCISED." (This also implies that their Acts 13-14 missionary tour had not taken place yet.)

---

105 Some of this depends on whether "FOURTEEN YEARS" goes back to Paul's salvation, including the "THREE YEARS" of 1:18, or if it follows consecutively after those three years. In the latter case, this visit may be the Jerusalem Council in Acts 15, meaning this letter must have been written later. I prefer the former view.

In a show of "goodwill" for Paul and Barnabas' ministry in Antioch, Peter made a visit there (vs. 11-14). Although he had good relations with them for a while, including eating meals with them, when "CERTAIN PEOPLE CAME FROM JAMES"[106] he began to pull away from the Gentiles. This hypocrisy grew to such a level "THAT EVEN BARNABAS" got caught up in it. Because of the public humiliation these Jews imposed on their Gentile brothers, Paul publicly called them out.

Paul used the recollection of this event to segue into his first major doctrinal statement of the letter's body and introduced his main thesis: "WE KNOW THAT NO ONE IS JUSTIFIED BY THE WORKS OF THE LAW BUT BY THE FAITHFULNESS OF JESUS CHRIST" (vs. 16). To the Jews God gave the covenants, promises, etc. (Romans 9:1-5), and Jesus said that "SALVATION IS FROM THE JEWS" (John 4:22). Paul's emphasis that he was a Jew "BY BIRTH" (literally, "by nature") rather than "by conversion" was to show that he was not justified by any of those. Even a Jew must believe in Jesus, something Paul expands in detail in Romans.

One debated point in this passage and several others in Paul's writings has to do with the phrase "THE FAITHFULNESS OF JESUS." Although this is often considered the best translation of the Greek text, most translations offer "FAITH IN JESUS." This seems to do damage to Paul's meaning, emphasizing our faith rather than his work.[107] Much has been written on this, and it is impossible to work through the whole debate here.

Chapter three begins the second of three sections, this time with a question of accusation against Paul's readers. Based on their movement away from faith toward works, Paul believed that they had been put under a spell

---

106 There are some who believe this means that James instigated this display. While this was possible, there is nothing else in Scripture to corroborate this charge.

107 The Greek text of 2:16 reads in part ἵνα δικαιωθῶμεν ἐκ πίστεως Χριστοῦ καὶ οὐκ ἐξ ἔργων νόμου, *"so that we might be declared righteous by faith/faithfulness of Christ and not by works of law."* To translate the first half "by faith in Christ" loses the effect of the parallel between "faithfulness of Christ" and "works of law."

of sorts. Verses 1-5 are a figurative snapping of Paul's fingers or shaking them awake from a spiritual trance. Had they so quickly (1:6) forgotten that they were saved through faith so that they were now willing to require circumcision for new converts in their churches, from their communities?

Using his favorite example (see also Romans 4), Paul pointed them to Genesis 15:6, where Abraham – the great father of the faith – simply believed, centuries before the Law was given (vs. 6-14). At the same time Paul introduced Abraham's spiritual family, consisting of those, and only those, who simply believe as he did. This family included Gentiles, as God had promised in the Abrahamic Covenant (Genesis 12:3). Paul also pointed out that one cannot obey only parts of the Law to be declared righteous. In fact, when one places himself under any part of the Law, he places himself under the entire Law and is subject to every part of it. Yet even that cannot provide eternal salvation because the Law could never do that. This is why Christ had to die, becoming a curse under the Law so he could free people from the Law and receive the promised Spirit.

In verses 15-22 he used classical Greek logic to unquestionably show the difference between the physical promises (plural) that God made to Abraham and his physical descendants and the spiritual promise (singular) that he made to Abraham and everyone who believes. Because the Law came after God made these promises, it could not invalidate the promises. Instead, God designed the Law to protect the Israelite people from defecting from him so they could one day receive the promised Spirit through faith in Jesus. Under the Law, neither a Gentile, a slave, nor a woman could receive an inheritance. In Christ, however, all people can receive the Spirit through faith, whether Jew or Greek, slave or free, male or female (vs. 28). No believer is left out of this spiritual inheritance because we "ARE ALL SONS OF GOD THROUGH FAITH" (vs. 26).

Sadly, many today who attempt to use this passage to eliminate functional roles in the home or church (female elders, feminist theology, etc.)

completely miss the context of spiritual inheritance and are bringing their false theology to the passage for their own purposes. Others go so far to teach that God has even removed the distinctions between male and female to support their depraved belief that God approves of homosexuality in the Church.

Chapter four continues the second section of the letter and the explanation of the inheritance available to all who believe in Jesus. Verses 1-7 contain the wonderful truth that Jesus was born at just the right time in just the right manner to accomplish everything God wanted to do, namely, to adopt rebel humans back into his spiritual family and make us free. This is important because we are all enslaved in sin by nature (vs. 8-12; Ephesians 2:1-3), but in Christ we are freed from that. Paul wondered, then, why someone would place himself under any kind of restrictions again.

Verses 13-20 break from Paul's explanation of his doctrine to a personal appeal to his original readers. He reminded them of how they had received him. Even though he was violently ill, they were not repulsed by him, but rather received him and his message as if he were Jesus himself. In fact, Paul noted that they would have gouged out their own eyes and given them to him if they were able.[108]

This chapter (and the second section) closes with an allegory (an extended metaphor), in which Paul likened the old covenant to Hagar and Ishmael.[109] While he was a legitimate physical son of Abraham, Ishmael was not the son through whom God's promises would be fulfilled. In the same

---

108 This offhand remark in verse 15 possibly hints to Paul's "THORN IN THE FLESH," a constant reminder of his weakness and immense privilege (2 Corinthians 12:7-10).

109 This is the only place in the New Testament that we find the English word "allegory" or its Greek source, ἀλληγορέω (*allegoreo*). An allegory is an extended metaphor, usually with several pieces connecting the two things being compared. This should not be confused with the allegorical method of interpreting the Bible that requires looking "deeper" than the literal meaning of the text, usually due to perceived errors or problems that the interpreter has with the text. The literal interpretation method allows the use of allegory and metaphor as legitimate uses of the language. The allegorical interpretation ignores the literal meaning of the text or supplements it with additional, "spiritual" meanings.

way, while the Law, symbolized by Mt. Sinai, was legitimately God's way of leading Israel during that time, it was never meant to bring righteousness or salvation. As Hagar and Ishmael were slaves in Abraham's household, those who subject themselves to the Law are slaves to it.

Sarah and Isaac (along with Mt. Zion), on the other hand, represent the only true way of salvation, through Jesus. As they were free persons in Abraham's household, those who come to God through faith in Jesus find freedom from the Law. Why, then, would someone place himself back into slavery when he had been set free?

Chapter five begins the third, and final, section of the letter, in which Paul gave practical application of how we should live out our freedom in Christ. He insisted that it was "FOR FREEDOM [THAT] CHRIST HAS SET US FREE" (vs. 1). He could not emphasize enough how foolish (3:1) they were for placing themselves into slavery by adding circumcision to faith (vs. 1-6). They had become so deluded by the Jewish legalists that they had forgotten that physical circumcision (or lack thereof) had no spiritual value in Christ – "THE ONLY THING THAT MATTERS IS FAITH WORKING THROUGH LOVE." Paul became so agitated at the thought of his friends falling for the legalists' false teaching he opined, "If these legalists like circumcision so much, why don't they just finish the job!" (vs. 12)

The key is to use our freedom in Christ for Christ and his purposes, namely, serving one another like Christ (vs. 13). We do this by lining up behind the Holy Spirit and keeping in step with him (vs. 16-26).[110] Paul thought it important to remind them that every believer has two natures that are mutually opposed to one another, that these are in constant warfare with one another, that we can "feed" only one of them, and that each one bears fruit in keeping with its source. "THE WORKS OF THE FLESH ARE OBVIOUS,"

---

110 The word translated "BEHAVE IN ACCORDANCE" in vs. 25 is a military term referring to how soldiers march in line behind the leader. Paul's point was that, if the Spirit has given us life, we should line up behind him and stay in step with him like a soldier marching in formation.

producing all kinds of sinful behavior. "THE FRUIT OF THE SPIRIT," on the other hand, is less conspicuous but still in line with its source. Notice that this fruit comes from the Spirit, not from ourselves (we cannot manufacture it or force it to grow) and that its purpose is for serving one another.

Chapter six closes this letter with some final instructions and thoughts on living out the fruit of the Spirit. Because believers will still be overtaken in sin, it is important that the congregation restore sinning brothers and sisters back to the faith, in the gentleness of the Spirit, and help them carry their burdens as they grow (vs. 1-2). At the same time, each person is responsible for lining himself up with the Spirit, not thinking he is better than the others, because we are each responsible for ourselves before God (vs. 3-5).

Understanding this balance is important because the way we decide to live (flesh or Spirit) will come to full fruition (vs. 6-8). Like a harvest our actions we will reap *what* we sow, *later* than we sow, and *much more than* we sow, so the apostle encouraged his readers to sow life and godliness through the Spirit. Because living for Christ in this world is a difficult task, he encouraged them to persevere, to not waver, and to do good for someone whenever the opportunity arises (vs. 9-10).[111] His closing thoughts returned to those who were enslaving themselves under the Law by submitting to circumcision (vs. 12-15), and he offered a final plea that they would stop their foolishness. In keeping with the comment about his eyesight in chapter four, Paul noted that he wrote with his "own hand" which required him to use "big letters" so he could see them. That, along with his handwriting, was probably a mark of authentication that the letter was truly from him (Philippians 4:18; 2 Thessalonians 3:17).

Verse 16 is often used to attempt to prove that the Church (or all believers) make up the "true Israel" or "spiritual Israel" because of Paul's phrase

---

111 Paul thought our focus in doing good should prioritize "THOSE WHO BELONG TO THE HOUSEHOLD OF FAITH." Even still, that does not mean to ignore unbelievers. We should help them as well, "WHENEVER WE HAVE AN OPPORTUNITY."

"THE ISRAEL OF GOD." This belief system teaches that God has chosen to replace Israel with the Church or that the Church is the spiritual extension of Israel. No matter the phrasing, they believe that the promises God made to Israel will be fulfilled in the Church, not national Israel.[112] Given the context of the rest of the letter, where Paul made a clear distinction between believing and unbelieving Jews (Israel) and all believers in Christ (Church), the grammar shows that Paul put his blessing on two groups: "ALL WHO WILL BEHAVE IN ACCORDANCE WITH THIS RULE" (believing Gentiles) and "THE ISRAEL OF GOD" (believing Jews). The structure of the sentence does not allow for these to be combined into one group in this verse.[113]

---

112   This is often called "Replacement Theology," and it is found in the broader form of Covenant Theology and in much Reformed (Calvinistic) teaching. Ironically, it is also found in much liberal theology, because the replacement or removal of Israel as God's chosen people is a satanic doctrine that has infiltrated many religions and denominations, encompassing those who are otherwise conservative and liberal alike.

113   Paul used the preposition twice: εἰρήνη ἐπ' αὐτοὺς καὶ ἔλεος καὶ ἐπὶ τὸν Ἰσραὴλ τοῦ θεοῦ, *"peace and mercy upon them and upon the Israel of God."* Grammatically, these must be two distinct groups.

Ephesians

Though it is rare for anyone to debate about the author of Ephesians anymore, who received the letter is a different matter. Most English Bibles read "TO THE SAINTS IN EPHESUS" in 1:1, but some of the earliest Greek manuscripts do not include "IN EPHESUS," naming no one specifically. There are several points of interest surrounding this. First, Paul was a prisoner at the time of writing (3:1; 4:1). This took place after his third missionary tour which consisted of almost three years in Ephesus (Acts 19:1-10). Second, Paul normally included many personal names and greetings in his letters, which makes Ephesians odd, because he did not record a single personal greeting, even though he was there for so long. Third, the content is very similar to Colossians, which refers to a letter coming from Laodicea (Colossians 4:16). Ephesus and Laodicea were the "bookend" cities on a trade route through southern Asia Minor, of which Ephesus was first and Laodicea last (see Revelation 2-3). All these details combined give evidence that this letter was probably intended to be a general letter for all the churches in the region. It likely went to Ephesus first, but Paul did not intend for it to remain there.

The layout of the letter is simple. The first three chapters contain heavily concentrated doctrine regarding salvation and the Church.[114] The last three

---

114 Interestingly, for as similar as Ephesians and Colossians are, one distinction may be in their two per-

chapters present a series of broad applications on how members of the Church are to grow and live. As all of this is general doctrine and application, its usefulness and relevance to the Body of Christ are just as poignant today as it was when Paul wrote around A.D. 61. Except for the description of God's armor in chapter six, there is nothing in this letter that even references cultural issues of Paul's time.[115] Ephesians' status as one of the best-loved books of the New Testament is directly tied to the way that it spans and addresses every culture and every generation of believers.

Chapter one does not just open the letter; it also lays the foundation for the two primary doctrines Paul intended to address: salvation (vs. 3-14) and the Church (vs. 15-23). In the first section, Paul demonstrated that all three members of the Trinity are integrally involved in salvation. First, the Father made the plan (vs. 3-6). He determined that all believers would be "IN CHRIST" and would become "HOLY AND UNBLEMISHED." He predestined all believers to be adopted "AS HIS SONS." He also "FREELY BESTOWED ON US ... HIS GRACE." All this was done "TO THE PRAISE OF THE GLORY OF HIS GRACE."

Second, Jesus provided redemption and forgiveness "THROUGH HIS BLOOD...ACCORDING TO THE RICHES OF HIS GRACE" (vs. 7-12). This was according to the Father's plan "THAT HE SET FORTH IN CHRIST." Believers are not only adopted as God's sons but also "CLAIMED AS GOD'S OWN POSSESSION" since that was part of God's adoption plan. This, too, was "TO THE PRAISE OF HIS GLORY."

Third, the Holy Spirit is given to every believer as "THE SEAL...THE DOWN PAYMENT OF OUR INHERITANCE" (vs. 13-14). We received the Holy Spirit, "WHEN [WE] BELIEVED IN CHRIST," and he remains in us "UNTIL THE

---

spectives of the same doctrine. Whereas Colossians emphasizes Christ as the Head of the Church, Ephesians focuses more on the Church as the Body of Christ.

115 Some may argue that his instructions to slaves and masters were cultural, but slavery was not limited to the first century, and his principles are still relevant today, both for true slaves and for employees.

REDEMPTION OF GOD'S OWN POSSESSION" (which Paul earlier wrote would occur later in the resurrection, Romans 8:17-25). Again, this is done "TO THE PRAISE OF HIS GLORY." Thus, every part of salvation – the planning, the execution, and the finalization – demonstrates the doxological[116] center of all things: to God be the glory.

In verses 15-23 Paul gave his traditional prayer of thanksgiving (which usually came immediately after the greeting), asking that God would enlighten these saints so that they would understand three things: 1) "THE HOPE OF HIS CALLING"; 2) "THE WEALTH OF HIS GLORIOUS INHERITANCE IN THE SAINTS"; and 3) "THE INCOMPARABLE GREATNESS OF HIS POWER TOWARD US WHO BELIEVE." This power, he went on to explain, is the same power that raised Christ from the dead and that will one day subject all things to Christ. Until then, Christ is serving as the head of the church, and "THE CHURCH IS HIS BODY."

Chapter two mirrors chapter one, dividing neatly into two sections. The first addresses salvation (vs. 1-10), while the second adds new revelation about the Church (vs. 11-22). In verses 1-3, Paul set out the natural state of unsaved humanity. Without Christ, we are "DEAD IN OUR TRANSGRESSIONS AND SINS," living "ACCORDING TO THIS WORLD'S PRESENT PATH" which is determined by "THE RULER OF THE KINGDOM OF THE AIR" and character-ized by "THE CRAVINGS OF OUR FLESH." We are also "BY NATURE CHILDREN OF WRATH."

This is a horrible picture of the real state of unsaved humanity, so much so that Paul never actually finished his thought. The first two words of verse four, however, change everything: "BUT GOD." Salvation is available for one reason only: God's character, demonstrated by his rich mercy and great love. Even in our sad state, God accomplished two things: he "MADE US ALIVE"

---

116 *Doxology* is from two Greek words (δόξα, *doxa*, and λόγος, *logos*) and means "to speak glory." To say that the Bible has a *doxological center* means that everything is said and done for God's glory above anything else.

and "SEATED US WITH [CHRIST] IN THE HEAVENLY REALMS." He did this, partially, "TO DEMONSTRATE IN THE COMING AGES THE SURPASSING WEALTH OF HIS GRACE IN KINDNESS." Exactly what that means and how it will happen has yet to be revealed. However, the truth is that this change is available to humanity only "BY GRACE THROUGH FAITH," and this package of salvation is accessible only as a gift from God, not through anything that we can do to earn it.[117] Although it is a gift, salvation is also given for a purpose: that we would accomplish the spiritual works that God has prepared for believers to do. Paul will elaborate on these works in the second half of the letter.

While the first half of the chapter displays the "before and after" picture of an individual believer, the second half displays the before and after of believing Gentiles (vs. 11-22). Before salvation, Gentiles were just as bad off corporately as they were individually: "WITHOUT THE MESSIAH, ALIENATED FROM THE CITIZENSHIP OF ISRAEL AND STRANGERS TO THE COVENANTS OF PROMISES, HAVING NO HOPE AND WITHOUT GOD IN THE WORLD." Because God was working primarily through Israel, Gentiles with no association with Israel also had no association with God. "BUT NOW" (vs. 13) is the corporate parallel to "BUT GOD" (vs. 4). Since Jesus' death and resurrection, Gentiles are no longer in that state. Believing Gentiles "HAVE BEEN BROUGHT NEAR"; they have been reconciled with believing Jews into "ONE BODY TO GOD THROUGH THE CROSS." They now "HAVE ACCESS IN ONE SPIRIT TO THE FATHER," because they are "MEMBERS OF GOD'S HOUSEHOLD." This new entity, the Church, was built on the New Testament apostles and the prophets[118] – both Jewish and Gentile – and is a unique entity during this dispensation[119]

---

117 There is a great debate over whether the "GIFT OF GOD" refers to the grace, the faith, or salvation as a whole. Grammatically and theologically it makes the best sense to see all of salvation as the gift rather than just the individual parts of grace or faith. In fact, trying to limit the gift to either one of those creates major doctrinal issues with other parts of the New Testament, while adding nothing to this passage.

118 Since Paul listed the apostles and prophets, specifically, as foundational to the building of the Church, conservative scholars believe that these offices ceased to exist 1) with the death of the last apostle, when the Church was well-established and 2) with the completion of the New Testament, when God stopped giving new revelation in this dispensation.

119 The dispensation of the Church (sometimes called the dispensation of grace) or the Church Age

which serves as the "DWELLING PLACE OF GOD IN THE SPIRIT." Unlike any other entity or group in any other dispensation, the Holy Spirit permanently indwells believers during this age until we are fully redeemed at the Rapture.

Chapter three closes the major doctrinal section of this letter with three sections. The first section begins with "FOR THIS REASON" (vs. 1), but Paul does not actually get to that reason until verse seven – "I BECAME A SERVANT OF THIS GOSPEL." In verses 2-6, Paul took a side trail to explain why the information he gave concerning the Church at the end of chapter two (that believing Jews and Gentiles are now "FELLOW HEIRS, FELLOW MEMBERS OF THE BODY, AND FELLOW PARTAKERS OF THE PROMISE IN CHRIST JESUS") is not found in previous Scriptures. The reason was that it was new revelation, a "DIVINE SECRET ... MADE KNOWN TO" Paul. It had not been "DISCLOSED TO PEOPLE IN FORMER GENERATIONS." It is for that reason that Paul was a servant of that gospel, and his role was "TO ENLIGHTEN EVERYONE ABOUT GOD'S SECRET PLAN" (or "mystery"[120]) about the Church. Not only is salvation going to show God's grace in the future (2:7-13), but the Church is also going to reveal God's "MULTIFACETED WISDOM ... TO THE RULERS AND THE AUTHORITIES IN THE HEAVENLY REALMS." Therefore, Paul asked that his readers not become discouraged about what he was suffering.

The second section also begins with "FOR THIS REASON" (vs. 14-19). Because of the great truths about the present and future of the Church, the apostle worshiped God and asked for yet another series of blessings upon his readers: 1) that God would "GRANT [THEM] TO BE STRENGTHENED WITH

---

began in Acts 2 on the Day of Pentecost (see the notes there) and will last until Jesus collects the Church in the Rapture. This period is characterized by 1) the gospel of the cross as the sole message to the world and 2) Spirit baptism of believers into the Body of Christ (see the notes at 1 Corinthians 12). Neither of these has or will characterize any other dispensation. For more information on dispensations, contact the author at danielgoepfrich.com.

120   In the Scriptures, the word "mystery" does not mean something that is hidden that we must unravel. Instead, it refers to something that was hidden at one time but has since been revealed. The Church was a "mystery" because it was hidden during the Old Testament times, but God had revealed it to Paul, and he was to share it with the world.

POWER THROUGH THE SPIRIT IN THE INNER PERSON"; 2) "THAT CHRIST MAY DWELL IN [THEIR] HEARTS"; and 3) that they would "BE ABLE TO COMPREHEND ... THE BREADTH AND LENGTH AND HEIGHT AND DEPTH" of Christ's love. The ultimate goal of all of this, though, was that they would "BE FILLED UP TO ALL THE FULLNESS OF GOD."

This thought caused Paul to end the first half of the letter with a short hymn of praise (the third section), exalting God and asking that he would be glorified in the Church forever (vs. 20-21).[121]

Chapter four begins the second half of the letter with a major change in Paul's grammar and intent. Ephesians contains a total of 41 imperative verbs (which is already a high percentage[122]); however, only one of them occurs in the first half ("remember" in 2:11). Thus, of the 197 verbs in chapters 4-6, more than 20% of them are commands from Paul to his readers.

This chapter has four natural divisions as the apostle began to outline the aspects of genuine Christian living. First, he said it was to be characterized by unity (vs. 1-6). Rather than the unity that many Christians attempt to create today through social justice and community outreach, Paul said that true Christian unity is found in the great truths (doctrines) of God and his work in us. The unity that exists within God and our unity with him should drive us to "LIVE WORTHILY OF THE CALLING WITH WHICH [WE] HAVE BEEN CALLED." This should define our attitudes and actions toward one another. Since Paul did not define this "calling" in chapter four, it must be a reference to the outworking of the truths about salvation and the Church Paul had already presented in the first three chapters.

Second, Paul noted that Jesus gave his Church special gifts specifically to help individual believers live out that calling (vs. 7-16). Unlike the spiritual

---

121   Ephesians is a treasure in revealing how Paul prayed for those he loved. Rarely are temporal or physical concerns mentioned; his prayers were almost always centered on God's glory and their growth.

122   Out of 327 verbs in Ephesians, 41 imperatives is 12.5% of all verbs in the letter. This is twice as high as the percentage of imperatives compared to all the verbs in the New Testament (6%).

gifts the Holy Spirit gives to each believer (1 Corinthians 12; Romans 12:1-8; 1 Peter 4:7-11), Jesus gave certain people in certain roles to the Church at large; these are the apostles, prophets, evangelists, and pastors and teachers.[123] The purpose of these people within the Church is "TO EQUIP THE SAINTS FOR THE WORK OF MINISTRY, THAT IS, TO BUILD UP THE BODY OF CHRIST." The reason that the Body must be built up is so believers will grow in maturity, in sound doctrine, and in love.

Third, Paul "INSISTED IN THE LORD" that believers should "NO LONGER LIVE AS THE GENTILES DO," namely, "IN THE FUTILITY OF THEIR THINKING" (vs. 17-24). This last phrase sets up the overarching theme of living out the godly wisdom that permeates the rest of the letter. Paul taught that there was to be a stark difference in the lives of believers and unbelievers that stemmed from the heart. Whereas unbelievers live out of "THE IGNORANCE THAT IS IN THEM DUE TO THE HARDNESS OF THEIR HEARTS," believers are to live out of the way they learned Christ: "TO LAY ASIDE THE OLD MAN ... TO BE RENEWED IN THE SPIRIT OF [THEIR] MIND, AND TO PUT ON THE NEW MAN." All of this is the result of the "RIGHTEOUSNESS AND HOLINESS THAT COMES FROM TRUTH," demonstrating the importance of sound doctrine on daily living.

Finally, Paul gave a list of general examples of what this should look like: replace lying with truth; replace sinful anger with productive, godly anger; replace theft with work and generosity; replace language that tears down with language that builds up; replace bitterness with forgiveness (vs. 25-32).

Chapter five continues Paul's admonition from chapter four. In 4:32 he told us to forgive like God; in 5:1-5 we are told to imitate God in every way,

---

123   Whether pastors and teachers are meant to be two distinct groups or one subset within a larger group is debated and beyond the scope of this summary. Additionally, since the apostles and prophets were foundational roles for the Church (2:20), they are no longer necessary and do not exist in the Church today. The New Apostolic Reformation (NAR) holds that these two roles have returned, and they embrace a revived "Five-fold Ministry." We reject this doctrine along with most of the other defining doctrines of the charismatic NAR.

specifically in our love for one another. Connecting back to 2:1-3 and 4:19-20 (and reminiscent of Galatians 5:16-23), Paul insisted that the believer's life should not be characterized by sinful activities, because "THESE ARE NOT FITTING FOR THE SAINTS," who are to be living "worthily" of our calling (4:1). In fact, our future inheritance in Messiah's kingdom will be determined by our current lives, and sinful lifestyles will cause loss of inheritance in the future.

Since these types of sins continue to bring God's wrath on unbelievers, we should not wonder that there would be punishment for believers as well (vs. 6-14). Because of this, we are to live as those enlightened by the light of the world, "TRYING TO LEARN WHAT IS PLEASING TO THE LORD," which was Paul's ultimate ambition (2 Corinthians 5:9). We are also to expose the darkness within the Body in order to purify it.

This brings us to the climax of the second half of the letter – "THEREFORE BE VERY CAREFUL HOW YOU LIVE – NOT AS UNWISE BUT AS WISE" (vs. 15-21). Rather than trying to create a rule or application for every situation (which, in fact, Paul repeatedly opposed; Romans 14; 1 Corinthians 8-10) or trying to find the exact "will of God" for every situation, Paul taught that the believer's primary decision-making tool was God's own wisdom.[124] In wisdom, we should make the most of the opportunities presented to us, know the will of God as it has been revealed, and continually be submissive to the Holy Spirit. In this way, we will live out the calling of love, building up the body.

In verse 18, Paul compared the filling of the Holy Spirit in a believer to a person who is drunk on alcohol. In the same way that the alcohol lowers inhibitions and leads a person to do or say things they might not normally do or say, when a believer is submissive to the Holy Spirit, the Spirit will lead us to live in ways that we may have thought impossible or impractical, but which are genuinely pleasing to God. What the Holy Spirit will never

---

124   Paul's example in this area should resonate with pastors and teachers. We are not called to apply the Scriptures to everyone in our audiences. Our job is to give the believers sound doctrine and help them learn how to study on their own so they can submit to the Holy Spirit, who can apply the Scriptures in their hearts and minds no matter the situation.

do is lead a person to sin.

The final section of this chapter best extends through from 5:21 to 6:9 and provides a series of six examples of what Christian relationships should look like when lived out in godly wisdom as described in the previous paragraph. Although this section does not include every possible relationship, those listed are the most important and most common relationships we will have: husband to wife, wife to husband, children to parents, fathers to children, slaves to masters, and masters to slaves. These last two have implications that work with employees and employers as well, even though they are not exactly the same.

Chapter six starts a new section with verse ten. As noted in the previous chapter, verses 1-9 continue Paul's list of example relationships that he started in 5:22. Thus, this chapter contains only one final section of application followed by Paul's closing greetings.

Verses 10-20 contain the famous armor of God passage. This is a favorite for people who like to "pray on the armor" as if it were theirs to wear and use as they wish. However, that is like David trying to wear Saul's armor (see 1 Samuel 17:38-39). In order to "STAND AGAINST THE SCHEMES OF THE DEVIL" and fight the spiritual battles "AGAINST THE RULERS, AGAINST THE POWERS, AGAINST THE WORLD RULERS OF THIS DARKNESS, [AND] AGAINST THE SPIRITUAL FORCES OF EVIL," Paul's solution was the same as in 5:18 – submit ourselves to the Holy Spirit and hide in God. Although he obviously had the picture of a Roman soldier in his mind, Paul did not call this the "Christian's armor" but "THE FULL ARMOR OF GOD." God wears his armor, and we can be protected only when we are living in submission to him. Each item of the armor is related back to God – truth, righteousness, faith – but "THE HELMET OF SALVATION" is an allusion to Isaiah 59:17, and "THE SWORD OF THE SPIRIT" is the spoken word of God. So, Paul commanded that we should "PRAY AT ALL TIMES," especially for those who are on the front lines preaching the gospel. This was true for Paul, even though he was "AN AMBAS-SADOR IN CHAINS" at that moment.

As noted in the introduction, the letter concludes with no personal greetings at all, only a note that Paul had sent the letter and personal updates with Tychicus (vs. 21-24). If this was meant to be a circular letter, Tychicus might have carried the personal greetings (possibly under a separate cover) to Ephesus, then sent the generic letter on its way.

The last sentence of the letter is especially interesting. "GRACE BE WITH ALL OF THOSE WHO LOVE OUR LORD JESUS CHRIST WITH AN UNDYING LOVE." On its own, this could simply be a general appeal. However, when compared to Jesus' letter to Ephesus, in which he rebukes them for leaving their "FIRST LOVE" (Revelation 2:4), this final exhortation seems to take on a more urgent plea to not depart from their personal relationship with Jesus.

Philippians

Philippians is one of the four "prison epistles," written when Paul was under house arrest in Rome (Acts 28:30-31). Unlike Ephesians, Colossians, and Philemon, which do not indicate how long he had been there, in Philippians Paul implied that he might be released soon (1:19-26), so he probably wrote this letter around A.D. 61-62. Though it contains Paul's typical mix of doctrine and practice, Philippians is also a personal note to his dear friends. The church at Philippi began with a strange mixture of people: a wealthy business woman, a hardened prison warden, and a formerly demon-possessed young woman (Acts 16). They had supported him financially for quite some time, including sending one of their own members to minister to his needs while imprisoned (Philippians 4). This letter was a missionary's report to let them know how he was doing, thank them for their support, and encourage them in their own spiritual growth.

The theme of Philippians is often thought to be Christian joy, and this is certainly a major part of the letter, but the concept of correct thinking, with a special focus on unity, seems to outweigh joy by a little bit. Both are immensely important to Paul's overall point, though.

Chapter one contains an interesting greeting that is different from all of Paul's other letters. Normally he greeted just the saints in a particular city or region, but to the Philippians, he singled out "THE OVERSEERS AND DEACONS" (vs. 1). It is possible that he referred to them because of the thanks he would give for their financial support, something overseen by the elders and probably distributed by the deacons. It is noteworthy as well that he did not refer to his apostleship in this opening. There is nothing in his letter that required him to assert his authority, so he used only the title "SLAVES OF CHRIST JESUS" for Timothy and himself.

His prayer of thanksgiving includes his most common lines, but it quickly moves into specific reasons he thought of and prayed for them often (vs. 3-11). A look at Acts 16 reveals a strong congregation "FROM THE FIRST DAY" Paul arrived in Philippi. His "IMPRISONMENT" certainly referred to his stay in Rome, but it also reminded them of his short imprisonment in Philippi as well, when the prison warden came to faith and joined their ranks. No matter where he was or what situation in which he found himself, they were always ready to help him as "PARTNERS IN GOD'S GRACE." Because of their obvious growth, he knew that God would certainly finish the spiritual work that he started in them. His prayer was that their love would continue to grow as they gained more insight into God's will and work.

Although they were certainly concerned for Paul's well-being, he had good news to report: he had become well-known among the imperial guard since his only "crime" was preaching Christ (vs. 12-18). Additionally, many other believers had begun to use his imprisonment as an opportunity to preach the gospel. Certainly, some were trying to build a name for themselves, but Paul did not mind, as long as the gospel message was pure. He seemed to think that he would be released soon, although that was not guaranteed (vs. 19-26). He honestly was not sure what to think about that. After nearly 30 years of traveling and ministry in some horrific conditions (see 2 Corinthians 4:7-12; 11:23-27), he was ready to go home to be with his Savior. However, if his work was not yet finished, he was content to stay alive, preach the gospel, and reconnect with his friends.

He urged them, then, that they would "CONDUCT [THEMSELVES] IN A MANNER WORTHY OF THE GOSPEL" – the gospel that he continually put himself in danger to preach and that they funded (vs. 27-30). They could do this by standing strong in the face of growing persecution that he knew was coming their way.

Chapter two contains the clearest teaching anywhere in Scripture on what happened to Jesus at the incarnation. Paul opened the chapter by insisting that the believers work to foster unity amongst themselves (vs. 1-4). This unity is to be based in the truth of what occurs in us at salvation and what the Holy Spirit continues to work in us. It should lead us to "HAVE THE SAME ATTITUDE TOWARD ONE ANOTHER THAT CHRIST JESUS HAD" (vs. 5-11).

What is this attitude or mindset we should have? Specifically, rather than clinging to his rights as eternal Jehovah, Jesus voluntarily set aside the independent use of his divine rights so he could take on a fully human nature and live as a human. In Jesus, the divine and the human fused in a way unlike anyone else.[125] Not only did he humble himself by becoming human on our behalf, but his humility also took him all the way through a crucifixion-type death. Because of this perfect example of humility and obedience, he will one day receive everything that is due him, including true worship from everything in creation.[126] Although we are not divine like Jesus, we, too, can voluntarily lay aside freedoms and rights for the spiritual growth of others (see Romans 14 and 1 Corinthians 8-9).

The command for believers to "CONTINUE WORKING OUT [OUR]

---

125 Theologically, this is called the "hypostatic union." It means that Jesus was fully God and fully man in one being.

126 Although some people interpret this to mean that everyone will eventually be saved, the rest of Scripture is clear that many of those acknowledging and worshiping Jesus will be forced to do so at the Great White Throne judgment (Revelation 20:11-15).

SALVATION" refers to the practical aspects of what the Holy Spirit is growing in us (vs. 12-18). Like Jesus, we should strive to "BE BLAMELESS AND PURE . . . IN A CROOKED AND PERVERSE SOCIETY, IN WHICH [WE] SHINE AS LIGHTS IN THE WORLD." Paul said that by their obedience and humility, they would mutually increase his joy, and him theirs.

Paul concluded this chapter with a note about each of their two mutual friends. He wanted to send Timothy to them soon, to bring back news from them (vs. 19-24). His comments about Timothy reflected the love of a father for his son and the concern of the son for his father's work. Epaphroditus was a Philippian who had come from the church, carrying aid and help for the apostle (vs. 25-30). Unfortunately, he became sick and almost died, meaning that Paul ministered to him more than he to Paul. The apostle looked forward to returning Epaphroditus to Philippi to rejoin his family there.

Chapter three was apparently meant to be the end of the letter, as Paul seemed to begin concluding it in verse one. His command for them to rejoice occurs again. Paul knew he was repeating himself, but he thought it was worth it. He warned them about those who had continually dogged him throughout his ministry (dating back at least 14 years earlier to the writing of Galatians). Specifically, these were legalistic Jews who insisted that Gentiles must be circumcised to be saved or at least added it as a requirement for their spiritual growth (vs. 2-11). It seems they emphasized their degrees and certifications to prove their legitimacy, but Paul would have none of that. It was not just that he had more qualifications than they did (although he did). He concluded that none of those things mattered for spiritual growth. In fact, in his life, he began to see them as liabilities instead of benefits. Because of this, he eliminated anything from his resume that would detract from Christ. His only goal was to know Jesus better and love him more.

Of course, he knew that he still had a long way to go, but he was intent on finishing well (vs. 12-16). Not everyone was willing to push forward to spiritual growth, and Paul rebuked them for it. He said that God himself would handle anyone who disagreed with Paul's insistence that this should be every believer's goal. At the very least, he said, we should "LIVE UP TO THE STANDARD THAT WE HAVE ALREADY ATTAINED," rather than going backward in our growth, which circumcision for these Gentiles would do. We must be careful who we choose to follow and attach ourselves to (vs. 17-21). Many charlatans are out there who claim to be Christ-followers, but whose "END IS DESTRUCTION, THEIR GOD IS THEIR BELLY, THEY EXULT IN THEIR SHAME, AND THEY THINK ABOUT EARTHLY THINGS." There are many well-known preachers today who have fallen into that trap, and we should not follow them. Instead, we must keep our focus on spiritual things, because "OUR CITIZEN-SHIP IS IN HEAVEN," and we should be eagerly anticipating the Savior's return.

Chapter four begins with the final greeting for his friends, but Paul had to make a side note first. It seems that there was a specific example of disunity that was hurting the Philippian church, so Paul called out the two women involved (vs. 2-7). They may have been fear mongers, leading others to worry about something, because Paul told them to not worry but rejoice instead, giving thanks, with the promise that God would guard their hearts and minds with his supernatural peace. Instead of worry and anxiety, there are specific areas believers can focus our minds, and we should "THINK ABOUT THESE THINGS" (vs. 8-9).

Paul closed his letter with a specific word of thanks for the financial support they had sent him (vs. 10-20).[127] Although he had come to learn to fully trust God whether he had much or had nothing, he was always grateful to have funds. Over time, as God placed him in various situations, Paul had learned to be content. In one of the often-misused verses of the New Testament, Paul declared his faith that, regardless of his financial situation

---

127 Although he was under house arrest, Paul was responsible for his own rent and probably his other supplies (Acts 28:30-31), so their financial gifts helped him tremendously.

at any given time, God would strengthen him to get through it.[128] He also noted that God would reward the Philippians because of their continued faithfulness in supporting his ministry, even from the very beginning of the church. He promised that their faithfulness was well-pleasing to God. A final comment, connecting back to his report in 1:13, revealed that even some of Caesar's own household (either family or servants) had also come to faith in Jesus, something the Philippians could rejoice over in Paul's continued work.

---

128 Verse 13 does **not** mean that a Christian can do anything. Rather, a Christian can face any situation when standing in the strength Christ gives.

Colossians

Colossians was one of Paul's "prison epistles," written while he was under house arrest in Rome, at the same time as Ephesians and Philemon. (Philippians is the fourth "prison epistle.") It seems that Tychicus carried this letter and the one to Philemon to Colossae after leaving the other in Ephesus (4:7; Ephesians 6:21). There is a great deal of overlap and repetition between Colossians and Ephesians, leading (along with other things) to the speculation that Ephesians may be the letter Paul referred to as coming "FROM LAODICEA" (just ten miles [16 km] away from Colossae) in Colossians 4:16.[129]

Colossians stands apart from all of Paul's other letters (except Romans) as being written to a local church that Paul did not start. Paul specifically named Epaphras as the one from whom they "LEARNED THE GOSPEL," so it is possible that he studied under Paul while Paul ministered in Ephesus, before going back to start churches in Colossae and possibly Laodicea and Hierapolis.

The primary theme of Colossians is the supremacy of Christ and biblical Christianity over anything else that the Colossians themselves would elevate or that others may have tried to impress on them.

---

129 See the introduction to Ephesians for more detail on this.

Chapter one contains Paul's opening greeting and prayer of thanksgiving. It is interesting that Timothy, rather than Epaphras, is mentioned along with Paul (vs. 1). However, since Timothy ended up as Paul's representative in Ephesus, the major city in that region, his role may have taken him to the other churches in the area as well, including Laodicea and Colossae. It was Epaphras from whom they heard the gospel, and he reported back to Paul how it had taken hold in Colossae and how their love and faith were growing significantly (vs. 3-8). As was common with Paul in his prison epistles, he prayed that the Colossians would grow in the knowledge of God's will, "SO THAT [THEY] MAY LIVE WORTHILY OF THE LORD AND PLEASE HIM IN ALL RESPECTS" (vs. 9-14; see Ephesians 4:1; 5:15-17; Philippians 1:27; 2:12-13). One of the special events that occurs at salvation, not mentioned elsewhere quite this way, is the wonderful truth that God "DELIVERED US FROM THE POWER OF DARKNESS AND TRANSFERRED US TO THE KINGDOM OF THE SON HE LOVES" (vs. 13-14).

Outside of Hebrews 1:1-3, verses 15-20 contain the longest, fiercest passage supporting the deity and supremacy of Christ. He was the creator of all things; he sustains all things; he is the head of the Church; and he was resurrected as the first of those yet to come. In him is the fullness of God's deity, and through his death everything in all creation will be reconciled back to God in some way. Although this does not mean that all creation will be saved, this passage and Romans 5 teach that there is a kind of initial reconciliation that happened at the cross, making creation *savable*, even if not all will be saved (full reconciliation with God).

This chapter reveals one of the biggest errors of Jehovah Witness theology. Comparing the NET Bible to their *New World Translation*, we clearly see their denial of Jesus' deity, believing that God created him first, then Jesus created everything else.

Colossians 1:15-17, NWT1

¹⁵He is the image of the invisible God, the firstborn of all creation;

¹⁶because by means of him all other things were created in the heavens and on the earth, the things visible and the things invisible, whether they are thrones or lordships or governments or authorities. All other things have been created through him and for him.

¹⁷Also, he is before all other things, and by means of him all other things were made to exist.

Colossians 1:15-17 NET

¹⁵He is the image of the invisible God, the firstborn over all creation,

¹⁶for all things in heaven and on earth were created by him– all things, whether visible or invisible, whether thrones or dominions, whether principalities or powers– all things were created through him and for him.

¹⁷He himself is before all things and all things are held together in him.

Even the Colossians were included in Jesus' reconciliation, and they would one day stand before him holy and blameless if they continued strong in the faith (vs. 21-29). Paul claimed to be God's servant on their behalf as well, even though they had never yet met, as he suffered for Christ and the gospel. As in Ephesians, he claimed that the doctrine of the Church was kept hidden by God until he was ready for Paul to make it known. Paul's goal in all his instruction was to "PRESENT EVERY PERSON MATURE IN CHRIST."

Chapter two continues the account of Paul's struggle on behalf of the Colossians and Laodiceans (vs. 1-5). He thought that those who had never met him could not quite appreciate the agony he went through for them. This was especially concerning to him because of the detractors that continually came behind him, slandering him and the gospel to the new converts he left in the churches. He needed them to know how much he truly cared for them, even though they had never had personal contact.

More important to Paul, though, was that they continued to grow and mature spiritually and live out the truths they had been taught (vs. 6-15). No matter what people said about him, Paul wanted to be sure that these believers were not dragged away by any false doctrine which diminished the truth about Christ. Because of who Jesus truly is – "ALL THE FULLNESS OF DEITY . . . IN BODILY FORM"[130] – what he did at the Colossians' salvation was momentous. He changed their hearts, they were buried with him in Spirit baptism, and they were "MADE ALIVE WITH HIM" through the forgiveness of their sins. Everything that stood against them (and us) was destroyed when he was nailed to the cross, including "THE RULERS AND AUTHORITIES" with whom we currently do spiritual battle (Ephesians 6:12) and the Old Testament Mosaic Law ("A CERTIFICATE OF INDEBTEDNESS EXPRESSED IN DECREES OPPOSED TO US").

Because of these great freedoms all believers have through Christ, Paul encouraged them to not get bogged down in the legalistic traps of his opponents (vs. 16-23). Focusing on things like dietary laws, required feast days, and circumcision means nothing compared to knowing and loving Christ and, in fact, undermines him and his work in our lives. Even though human commands seem to be spiritual and wise, they come from "A WISDOM WITH NO TRUE VALUE," resulting in a false humility and spiritual weakness rather than maturity and strength.

Chapter three begins the second half the letter, introducing the practical steps believers can take to make sure we do not get caught up in these other foolish things that take us away from Christ. First, the most important step is to keep our minds focused on Christ himself, rather than on other,

---

130 As in chapter one, the Jehovah Witnesses minimize Jesus' full deity to simple "God-likeness" by translating this verse, "It is in him that **all the fullness of the divine quality** dwells bodily." *New World Translation of the Holy Scriptures* (2013 Revision), https://www.jw.org/en/publications/bible/nwt/books/colossians/2.

temporal things (vs. 1-11). Truly spiritual matters are higher than the earthly matters that Paul's enemies focused on. Since our life is bound up in Christ, our focus should remain solely on him. Second, we can work to "PUT TO DEATH WHATEVER IN [OUR] NATURE BELONGS TO THE EARTH." This includes any "FLESHLY DESIRES WHICH DO BATTLE AGAINST THE SOUL" (1 Peter 2:11). These things bring God's wrath against unbelievers (Ephesians 5:6), so we should not be surprised that he hates them in believers as well. Third, we are to "PUT OFF THE OLD MAN WITH ITS PRACTICES" and replace that sinful nature "WITH THE NEW MAN THAT IS BEING RENEWED IN KNOWLEDGE ACCORDING TO THE IMAGE OF THE ONE WHO CREATED IT" (see Ephesians 4:22-24). Although all humanity was created in God's image, that image was damaged by sin. However, the spiritual growth process slowly restores God's image in us as we become "CONFORMED TO THE IMAGE OF HIS SON" (Romans 8:29). This change is God's intention for every believer, and it is possible no matter one's background, ethnicity, or social status (vs. 11).

Because of our new status in Christ – "ELECT OF GOD, HOLY AND DEARLY LOVED" – we should live out Christ's love for our fellow believers (vs. 12-17; also see Philippians 2:1-11; Ephesians 4:1-3). This includes being quick to forgive, peaceful, and thankful. It includes letting "THE WORD OF CHRIST DWELL" in us, as we obey what we learn in Scripture and it overflows in our interactions with fellow Christians. Above all, it includes living as agents of the Lord Jesus, thanking and glorifying the Father in everything.

As he wrote in Ephesians 5:18-21 about submitting to the Holy Spirit in their personal relationships, Paul encouraged the Colossians to do the same (3:18 – 4:1). Assuming that the Colossians would read the other letter (Ephesians) as well, Paul gave a shortened version of his list of example relationships found in Ephesians 5:22 – 6:9, giving only one line each to wives, husbands, children, and masters. He did write a longer encouragement to slaves, possibly due to the situation of Onesimus returning to Philemon in

Colossae along with his letter at this same time.[131]

Chapter four closes this short letter with a series of final requests and a long list of personal greetings. In verses 2-6, Paul asked that they would continue to pray for his ministry, even while he was "IN CHAINS." He pleaded that they would be careful in their own interactions with unbelievers so that they would not unnecessarily turn people off from the gospel. Apparently, they especially needed this with their words, which he contended should be gracious, designed to build up others. Perhaps they were too aggressive in their approach with the pagans around them because Paul's hope was that they would learn "HOW [THEY] SHOULD ANSWER EVERYONE" properly.

Paul clarified that Tychicus and Onesimus were both his ambassadors on this mission (vs. 7-9). Although he did not start the church in Colossae, it seems he did know many of the people there and sent his personal greetings to once again emphasize the personal nature of his care for them (vs. 10-18). The mention of several people who are not named elsewhere alongside other well-known companions gives us a peek into the size of Paul's "organization" of people that worked with him to lead and care for his ever-growing network of churches.

Because Paul did not mention Luke in the same grouping with Aristarchus, Mark, and Justus (vs. 10-11), who he singled out as being "FROM THE CIRCUMCISION" (NASB), many have concluded that Luke was a Gentile. However, there are at least three reasons to recognize his Jewishness. First, Luke's understanding of minute details regarding the Jewish feasts and traditions is unmistakable throughout his writings (Luke and Acts). A Gentile would be unlikely to fixate on those details. Second, Luke was in Jerusalem when Paul was arrested and charged with taking a Gentile into the Temple. However, it was not Luke who was the supposed problem, but Trophimus (Acts 21:29). Third, Paul wrote that it was the Jews to whom God had

---

131 See the notes on Philemon for more information.

entrusted his Word (Romans 3:2). If Luke were a Gentile, he would have been the only non-Jewish writer of Scripture. It is better to see Paul's greeting from Luke and Demas as from special friends, rather than the intention of pointing out their ethnicity.

1 Thessalonians

Thessalonica (modern: Thessaloniki) was "the largest and most important city in Macedonia and the capital of the province"[132], so, after receiving his vision of the Macedonian man during his second missionary tour, Paul probably intended to go there immediately after arriving in Europe (Acts 16:6-10). Since they landed at Philippi, they decided to minister there for a while (maybe a couple of months) before Paul and Silas were arrested and put into jail. Once released, it seems that they left Luke there to help the infant believers, while the rest of the team kept pressing toward Thessalonica. Over a period of only a couple of months, "SOME OF [THE THESSALONIAN JEWS] WERE PERSUADED AND JOINED PAUL AND SILAS, ALONG WITH A LARGE GROUP OF GOD-FEARING GREEKS AND QUITE A FEW PROMINENT WOMEN" (Acts 17:4). This group became the foundation of the church in Thessalonica.[133]

Paul wrote this first letter from Corinth about A.D. 51 after he had been run out of both Thessalonica and Berea and had tried to minister in Athens (Acts 17). While ministering in Corinth, about 6-8 months after having left Thessalonica, Paul finally heard from Timothy again, whom Paul had sent

132 Leon Morris, *The First and Second Epistles to the Thessalonians* (Grand Rapids, MI: William B. Eerdmans Publishing Company, 1991), 2.

133 Read more about this in the notes for Acts 16-17.

back to Thessalonica to check on the physical and spiritual well-being of the believers there. Timothy brought back a good report, and 1 Thessalonians was Paul's response to the church. It is full of love and encouragement for them, along with some additional teaching and instructions. For being nearly 2,000 years old, this letter contains some incredibly relevant and practical examples of how Christian ministry and fellowship should look even today.

Chapter one contains a brief picture of the power of the gospel at work in a person's life, moving him from initial saving faith to full sanctification (spiritual maturity). In verse three, Paul used the powerful triad of faith, love, and hope as he celebrated the spiritual growth his friends were displaying. It seems that he reversed the last two from the normal pattern, putting "hope" last, because Jesus' return (the Christian's "hope"[134]) would be a major emphasis later in the letter. (He did the same thing in 5:8.) Specifically, Paul was encouraged to hear from Timothy of three things about the Thessalonian believers: their "WORK PRODUCED BY FAITH . . . LABOR PROMPTED BY LOVE . . . ENDURANCE INSPIRED BY HOPE" (NIV).

Upon hearing the gospel message, Paul noted that four changes had taken place in the months since he had seen them. First, they "TURNED TO GOD FROM IDOLS TO SERVE THE LIVING AND TRUE GOD" (vs. 9). Because Jews would never engage in idolatry[135], this likely points to a predominantly Gentile congregation. Second, they began "TO WAIT FOR HIS SON FROM HEAVEN" (vs. 10), something that Paul would elaborate on later. Third, they "BECAME IMITATORS OF [PAUL] AND OF THE LORD . . . DESPITE GREAT AFFLIC-TION" (vs. 6). We should note that this is the normal pattern for new believers; they imitate their disciplers first as they learn to imitate Jesus himself. Finally,

---

134 In Titus 2:13, Paul called Jesus' return in the Rapture "THE BLESSED HOPE" (NASB).

135 According to the Hebrew prophets (especially Isaiah and Jeremiah), idolatry was one of the primary reasons that Israel and Judah were taken into captivity by Assyria and Babylon. They learned their lesson well and, after their return from exile, Israel has never repeated that sin again (at least on a national level).

because of their growing obedience, they "BECAME AN EXAMPLE TO ALL THE BELIEVERS IN MACEDONIA AND IN ACHAIA" (vs. 7), with the result that "THE MESSAGE OF THE LORD HAS ECHOED FORTH NOT JUST IN MACEDONIA AND ACHAIA, BUT IN EVERY PLACE" (vs. 8). It is no wonder that Paul's mind and heart were put at ease when he heard Timothy's report (3:6-8; Acts 18:5).

Chapter two is Paul's summary explanation of what solid practical Christian ministry looks like. He did this by reminding the Thessalonians how he ministered to them, namely by 1) using various forms of the key phrases, "you know" or "you recall" or "you are witnesses" (vs. 1, 2, 5, 9, 10, 11) and 2) repeatedly pointing to well-known examples in his own life and theirs. In this chapter, we find at least three keys for effective Christian ministry.

First, he was not afraid to show his agony or struggle when ministering to people (vs. 1-2). In fact, hiding our doubts and pain can actually hurt the gospel message, because it makes us look better than we really are. People need to know that the gospel is necessary because we are not perfect, not because we have it all together. Second, he approached plain people with the plain truth, rather than relying on flattery (vs. 3-8, 10-12). He also made sure that the truth was evident in his life. Third, he chose not to impose himself on others (vs. 9). In fact, he went out of his way to make sure that he would not be offensive to his listeners, even if the gospel itself offended them. This is a principle he practiced in Corinth as well (1 Corinthians 2:1-5) and was probably a major key to his successful ministry.

He ended the chapter with a strong word of encouragement, noting again how well they were living out their faith, especially considering the serious persecution that they had already undergone (vs. 14-16). He reminded them that those who persecute Christians are actually enemies of the entire world, because they try to stop the gospel message that the world desperately needs to hear. These people are displeasing to God and are placing themselves under his wrath.

Chapter three best begins in 2:17, and is probably the most personal section of the entire letter. This serves as a great reminder that 1 Thessalonians is not just "a book in the Bible" but a personal letter between dear friends. For those of us reading since that time, it also reveals what genuine Christian fellowship looks like. Paul could literally say that his absence from them caused his heart to grow fonder toward them (2:17-20). Verse 18 is a subtle, yet powerful, reminder that Satan's forces are still active, and God has allowed them some latitude to work against his servants in this world, yet Paul was ready to stand before Jesus and beam in pride at his spiritual "children" who had grown so well.

Verses 1-5 reveal Paul's concern when he had not yet heard from Timothy. Even the apostle who later commanded us to not worry (Philippians 4:6) could not help but be concerned for his friends. This was especially true because he knew that believers in this world are destined for opposition and affliction, just like Jesus promised, and that had already begun in Thessalonica (John 15:18-20; cf. 2 Timothy 3:12).

However, verses 6-10 show the complete emotional shift Paul experienced once Timothy had found him and delivered his report, and he was able to throw himself into his work in Corinth (Acts 18:5). Verse six contains the only time in all his letters that Paul used "GOOD NEWS" (εὐαγγελίζω, *euangelizo*) for something other than the gospel.[136] Both their faith and love had remained strong (1:3), and their attitude toward Paul had not been swayed by his accusers like the Galatians' had been and the Corinthians' would be later on. Their faith was their attitude toward God, and love was their attitude toward each other. So even in their affliction, they kept the proper attitude toward God, each other, and Paul.

Paul finished with a short but significant prayer. First, he asked that

---

136 This is one good example of how a common Greek word gained a special "Christian" meaning during the early days of the Church. While we all enjoy receiving "good news," ultimately, what news is better than the gospel?

God would clear the way (remember, Satan was blocking it) so he could get back to Thessalonica. Second, he prayed that their love would "INCREASE AND ABOUND," both within their church and in their community. Third, he prayed that they would grow in holiness so they would be ready for Jesus' return.

Chapters four and five each divide into two sections. As Paul began to wrap up his letter, he shifted from reminiscing and loving to giving instructions and commands. He addressed four areas in these final two chapters: practical Christian living, the Rapture of the Church, the Day of the Lord, and congregational living.

In verses 1-12, Paul focused on some very practical, "in-your-face" teaching about how to live a Christian life in this world. He said he had previously told them that certain things were necessary to live in a way pleasing to God and urged them to follow through with what he had taught them even more than they were already doing. The first area was their sanctification[137], especially concerning sexual immorality (vs. 3-8). He gave them both a negative and positive command to help them live properly: stay away from it and get control of their bodies. The second area was their brotherly love (vs. 9-10). He had already praised them for how well they were doing it, so he simply praised them again followed by an encouragement to keep it up and do even more.

The third area had to do with their relationship to the unbelieving world around them, and it had three parts to it (vs. 11-12). First, they were "TO ASPIRE TO LEAD A QUIET LIFE." Christians should not be the ones causing trouble, starting arguments, or making a public spectacle (Romans 12:18). Second, Paul told them to "ATTEND TO YOUR OWN BUSINESS." The opposite of this would be a busybody. While leading a quiet life, we are to keep busy in Christian service. Third, Paul commanded them to "WORK WITH YOUR

---

137   The key word of verses 3-8 is "holy." It appears in some form four times in these six verses. In Paul's letters, "sanctification" means "to set apart as holy."

HANDS." Second Thessalonians 3:10-12 explains this further. Apparently, some had quit their jobs and were relying on personal charity and the congregation to support them, as they waited for Jesus' soon return. Paul said, "Get a job and stop mooching!" Paul's reason for these specific commands was that unbelievers are watching. Immoral people, busybodies, moochers, and troublemakers hurt the Christian name. Unbelievers do not like them any more than other Christians do, and they especially do not like it when Christians are doing these things while talking about Jesus.

In verses 13-18, Paul addressed a serious concern from his friends. He had apparently taught them that Jesus would return before the day of the Lord (see 5:1-2). However, some members of the congregation had died in the intervening months, and the survivors were genuinely concerned their loved ones would miss Jesus' coming. Since the details about the Rapture were new to them, it is conceivable that they were the first ones to ever hear this revelation (vs. 15).[138]

Paul told them that they had no reason to grieve as if there were no hope because Jesus' return is the substance of our confident hope (1:3; cf. Titus 2:13). In fact, rather than missing out on the event, Paul insisted that "those who are asleep through Jesus" (literally) will come back with him. Because of Jesus' death and resurrection, even death itself has changed (1 Corinthians 15:54-55).

The Rapture event includes five parts, only one of which is the actual "rapture."[139] Verses 15-17 reveal that there will be an announcement, Jesus' arrival into the clouds, the resurrection of dead saints, the rapture of living saints, and the eternal presence of the Savior. The last part was Paul's emphasis.

---

138 Paul continued to receive new revelation from God throughout the course of his ministry. Some of this was probably for specific ministry but much of it was recorded in the Scriptures for our instruction and benefit as well as the original readers'. Since 1 and 2 Thessalonians were some of Paul's earliest letters, it is exciting to think that this may have been one of the first times that Paul had shared this information.

139 The word "rapture" means "to catch or seize" and comes from the Latin word behind "will be caught up" in verse 17. (The Greek word that Paul used, ἁρπάζω, *harpazo*, means the same as the Latin word.)

Rather than just "going to heaven," whenever he thought of eternity, Paul could think of only one thing: being with Jesus (2 Corinthians 5:6-8; Philippians 1:21-23). This is why he commanded his readers to "ENCOURAGE ONE ANOTHER WITH THESE WORDS" (vs. 18).[140] Although the doctrine of the Rapture of the Church is often scoffed at by Christians and non-Christians alike, it was one of the earliest doctrines Paul taught about the Church and was a special encouragement to him and those around him.

Chapter five concludes with two final teachings. Regarding the Day of the Lord, Paul noted that the Thessalonians did not need any more teaching (vs. 1-2) because it is a frequent topic in the Hebrew Scriptures, which they studied in the synagogue (both the Jews and the God-fearing Gentiles). The Day of the Lord will consist of the Tribulation wrath and judgments (seven years) followed by the Messianic Kingdom (1,000 years). Because of the truth of these future events, Paul instructed the believers to live properly now, so that they would not become spiritually lethargic[141] and be caught off guard by the Rapture, which will occur before the Day of the Lord (vs. 3-8). It is important to note the distinct shift in emphasis between "we/us" in 4:13-18 to "they" in this section. If "we" are living according to the apostle's instructions in chapter four, we will not be caught off guard like "they" will in chapter five. "They" refers to those unbelievers who will be left behind to face God's wrath in the Tribulation.

Verses 9-10 provide the explanation that pulls this section together. Why can we stand in faith, act in love, and expectantly look forward to our future? Because believers are not destined for the coming wrath. We are destined for opposition in this world (3:4), but we will not go through the

---

140 The Rapture of the Church, our "blessed hope" (Titus 2:13), is such an important truth that some believe it should form the foundation for all Christian counseling because it emphasizes Jesus' care for his Bride, the Church.

141 "Sleep" in verse 7 is not the same Greek word as in 4:13-18. Here it means "lethargic apathy"; in 4:13-18 it referred to the physical death of believers.

wrath of the Day of the Lord because Jesus is "OUR DELIVERER FROM THE COMING WRATH" (1:10). This whole letter is an obstacle for those who believe that the Church will go through even part of the Tribulation period. Verse 11 ends this section like 4:18 did the last one. The Rapture is a wonderful truth that we should use to encourage one another. The teaching about the Day of the Lord should also encourage us because we will not go through it, but it should also cause us to "sober up" about what is important in this life and drive us to grow in our spiritual lives, even pushing one another, so we don't become lethargic.

In the final section of his letter (vs. 12-22) Paul focused on the congregational life of the church, and he gave four sets of commands. First, they were to highly respect the elders of the church (vs. 12-13). Some writers see the lack of specificity in the phrase "THOSE WHO LABOR AMONG YOU AND PRESIDE OVER YOU" to mean that there was no formal structure to the congregations yet. However, Paul had already begun appointing local church elders during his first missionary tour (Acts 14:23), so the structure was established. It is more likely that he did not know who the elders were in Thessalonica because he had left so quickly. Silas and Timothy probably appointed them in his absence. Additionally, the concept of "presiding over" and "admonishing" clearly indicates a leadership structure within the congregation. Second, they were to maintain a balance of unity, discipline, and mutual care for one another within the congregation (vs. 14-15). Third, they were to intentionally hold attitudes of joy and gratefulness, which was important because of their ongoing afflictions (vs. 16-18). Finally, they were to keep themselves open to prophecy from the Holy Spirit, not extinguish his work in their meetings, yet practice discernment in what they accepted as truth (vs. 19-22).

Paul concluded his letter with a benediction, praying that they would be ready for Jesus' return (vs. 23-24), his constant focus.

2 Thessalonians

It seems that Paul wrote his second letter to the Thessalonian church shortly after 1 Thessalonians, in response to some follow-up questions they had for him based on the first letter. Given the travel time between Thessalonica and Corinth, where Paul wrote these letters (compare Acts 17:15; 18:5 with 1 Thessalonians 3:1-6), it is likely that Timothy could have delivered 1 Thessalonians and returned to Paul with their questions in just a couple of months, so A.D 51 or 52 is the probable timeframe.

As with the first letter, Paul included Silvanus and Timothy in his greeting, since they were instrumental in getting the Macedonian churches started (Thessalonica, Berea, and others). It seems the specific reason for their letter was that the Thessalonians had received information that pretended to come from Paul, contradicting what he had previously taught them about the end times, specifically the coming Great Tribulation and satanic world ruler. Paul wrote 2 Thessalonians to remind them of his former teachings and to clarify a few other matters.

Chapter one begins with a similar theme as in 1 Thessalonians – Paul's prayer of thanksgiving for the believers' continued growth and public faith (vs. 3-4). In 1 Thessalonians Paul said he did not find it necessary to tell others about the Thessalonian believers because their reputation preceded him wherever he went (1 Thessalonians 1:7-10). In this letter, he said that he was able to "BOAST" about them "IN THE CHURCHES OF GOD" because of how they were persevering "IN ALL THE PERSECUTIONS AND AFFLICTIONS" that they had to endure. Similar to other passages in his later writings, Paul noted that present suffering prepares believers for the coming kingdom, where someday we will find our "REST" (vs. 5-7).[142] He also reminded them that God will "REPAY WITH AFFLICTION THOSE WHO AFFLICT" them. One wonders if Paul often thought of the many psalms in which David called to the Lord to deliver him from his enemies and encouraged his readers: "DO NOT FRET WHEN WICKED MEN SEEM TO SUCCEED!" (Psalm 37:1)

Paul greatly looked forward to the day when Jesus would finally return as the Righteous Judge. He had already noted that those who afflict Christians "ARE DISPLEASING TO GOD AND ARE OPPOSED TO ALL PEOPLE . . . [AND] CONSTANTLY FILL UP THEIR MEASURE OF SINS" (1 Thessalonians 2:15-16). These, he wrote again, "WILL UNDERGO ETERNAL DESTRUCTION" (vs. 9). Specifically, and most importantly to Paul, they would forever be "AWAY FROM THE PRESENCE OF THE LORD," the presence he so greatly anticipated (1 Thessalonians 1:10; 2:19; 3:13; 4:17; 5:23). Paul's greatest prayer for his Thessalonian friends was that they would be worthy of the Savior at his coming, something Paul was convinced God himself would make sure of (vs. 11-12; 1 Thessalonians 5:23-24).

Chapter two contains the largest section of new teaching in this short letter and has generated a great deal of debate in several areas. It seems possible that someone had sent a letter in Paul's name to Thessalonica, stating that they had missed "THE ARRIVAL OF OUR LORD JESUS CHRIST AND OUR

---

142 The Millennial / Messianic Kingdom described in terms of rest is a major aspect of the book of Hebrews.

BEING GATHERED TO BE WITH HIM," otherwise known as the Rapture of the Church (vs. 1-2). One of their fears that prompted the first letter was that the believers who had died would miss the Rapture (1 Thessalonians 4:13), which Paul addressed. However, it seems a "LETTER ALLEGEDLY FROM" Paul and possibly even a demonic prophetic "SPIRIT OR MESSAGE" claimed that, in fact, they all had missed it and were now living in "THE DAY OF THE LORD" (vs. 2).[143] Since Paul had obviously taught them about the terrors of the great Tribulation, they were scared to be in it and wondered how they could have missed the Rapture.

In this chapter, Paul revealed three events that must happen first, before the day of the Lord could commence. The first is called, variously, "the rebellion" (NET, NLT, NIV, ESV); "the apostasy" (NASB, HCSB); and "a falling away" (KJV). There are three views of what this could be. One common view is that, toward the end of the Church Age before the Rapture, there will be an apostasy or falling away within the Church itself. This is prophesied in 2 Timothy 3:1-5, among other places. There will be people within the Church who are either not believers at all or weak, immature Christians who will fall away from the faith. This is the view promoted in Walvoord and Zuck's *Bible Knowledge Commentary*. The translation "rebellion" presupposes this view. A second view is that this will be a departure from the true faith, <u>after</u> the Rapture, by those who had only professed belief but were not true Christians. Constable promotes this view in his *Notes on 2 Thessalonians*. This view is problematic because Paul thought his readers would see the apostasy, which would be impossible if the apostasy occurs after the Rapture. The third view is that this refers to the Rapture itself. Because the Greek word ἀποστασία (*apostasia*) simply means "departure," and since Paul prefixed it with the definite article ("<u>the</u> departure"), some hold that there is only one specific departure Paul had already taught in Thessalonica – the departure of the

---

143 The "day of the Lord" refers to the seven-year Tribulation and the Millennial/Messianic Kingdom, when Jesus will reign on Earth in Jerusalem for 1,000 years.

Church from this world, the Rapture. This view is held by several conservative scholars and has much to support it.[144]

The second event that must occur before the day of the Lord is that "THE MAN OF LAWLESSNESS" must be revealed. Interestingly, although it is commonly used in Christian churches and theology books, the term "Antichrist" is never applied by the biblical writers specifically to the coming world ruler. In fact, John referred to anyone who denied the Word made flesh as an antichrist (1 John 2:18, 22; 4:1-3; 2 John 7). However, Paul used a series of phrases to describe how evil this man will be: "THE MAN OF LAWLESSNESS ... THE SON OF DESTRUCTION ... THE LAWLESS ONE" (vs. 3-10). He will publicly and unashamedly oppose and place himself above all gods, to the point that he will set himself up to be worshiped in God's Temple in Jerusalem (a fulfillment of Daniel 9:27 and Matthew 24:15). Since his arrival will come "WITH ALL KINDS OF MIRACLES AND SIGNS AND FALSE WONDERS AND WITH EVERY KIND OF EVIL DECEPTION" and since his revealing must take place before the Day of the Lord and since that had not (and still has not) yet happened, Paul assured and comforted his readers (and us!) that they had not entered the Day of the Lord.

The third event that will precede the Day of the Lord is that "THE ONE WHO HOLDS HIM BACK WILL [BE] ... TAKEN OUT OF THE WAY" before he is revealed (vs. 7). Again, there has been great debate over who or what restrains the lawless one. The two most common views are that the Church or the Holy Spirit is restraining him. Those who believe the Church to be the restrainer say that the Rapture will release Antichrist to begin his evil campaign since there will be no godly influence in his way. However, the Church is not more powerful than Satan, except through the power of God, so even that view unintentionally bows to the second. Only the Holy Spirit is

---

144   David Olander, *The Greatness of the Rapture* (Tyndale Seminary Press, 2009); Paul Lee Tan, *The Interpretation of Prophecy* (Bible Communications, Inc., 1982); Andy Woods, "2 Thessalonians 2:3a – Apostasy or Rapture" (http://www.spiritandtruth.org/teaching/topics_by_andy_woods/75_Apostasy_or_Rapture/20150412_apostasy_or_rapture_slides.pdf). Additionally, Pentecost listed it as a possibility in his classic, *Things to Come* (1958).

powerful enough to stay Satan's work in this world. After the Rapture, when the Church has been removed from Satan's attacks and God's coming wrath, the Holy Spirit will release his hold on "THE HIDDEN POWER OF LAWLESS-NESS [WHICH] IS ALREADY AT WORK" (vs. 7).

The chapter ends with Paul's word of thanks, again, that his readers would not have to go through that time and an encouragement to hold fast to what he had already taught them on this subject, rather than being tossed around by false teachings (vs. 13-17).

Chapter three also picks up and expands on a theme from 1 Thessalonians, namely, the Christian's work ethic during the current age. Paul prefaced this topic with his request that the gospel would continue to "SPREAD QUICKLY AND BE HONORED AS IN FACT IT WAS AMONG" the Thessalonians (vs. 1-5). He also prayed that God would protect them from those who would do them harm in this world.

Paul believed their work ethic was an important part of the gospel's effectiveness (vs. 6-15). It seems that some of the believers had quit their jobs and were living off of the generosity of the church community. In 1 Thessalonians 4:11-12 Paul had already gently called them out for this, but they needed something stronger. Here Paul reminded them of his own example among them, how he worked for his own food rather than relying on support from the church.[145] He also insisted that their lazy lifestyle was disparaging to the gospel and that someone who continued to live like that was to be shunned by the Christian community. This was such a big deal that even before Paul had to leave town, he commanded them, "IF ANYONE IS NOT WILLING TO WORK, NEITHER SHOULD HE EAT."[146] This principle is still applicable today.

---

145 In 1 Corinthians 9, Paul argued that he had every right to be supported by the churches he started. However, he thought that some would use that to prove that he was just out for their money, so he chose to support himself instead. If this were true for him, a traveling preacher, it was much truer for those who lived in the cities where he ministered.

146 Since this is not found in either of the Thessalonian letters, the fact that he had told them this previously means that it was one of his personal teachings while still there, or he had sent it back verbally

Paul closed his letter with a personal signature to authenticate it, another hint that there was another letter going around with his forged name on it (vs. 16-18).

---

with Timothy. In either case, this was a challenge for them early in their Christian lives, and he had to address it on at least three occasions (verbally and in both letters).

1 Timothy

In Lystra, while on his second missionary tour, Paul found Timothy, who was already a well-known disciple in the area (Acts 16:1-2). He quickly became one of Paul's closest friends and trusted companions. Timothy appears in Paul's letters more than twice the number of times of anyone else, and his name is mentioned in all of Paul's letters except four, plus once in Hebrews and six times in Acts.

We know only a few things about Timothy's personal life. He was born to a Greek father and Jewish mother (Acts 16:1). He was young, but how young is unknown (1 Timothy 4:12). He seemed to have been sick frequently (1 Timothy 5:23). He suffered a major period of spiritual depression at one point that left him nearly ready to quit the ministry (2 Timothy 1:6-8).

Contrary to popular opinion (too often reinforced in sermons), Timothy was not a pastor or elder of a local church; rather, he was Paul's personal representative and an apostle.[147] Paul had left Timothy in Ephesus when he went on to Macedonia to continue the work there (1 Timothy 1:3),

---

147 There were two types of apostles in the early Church. The Twelve were those who ministered alongside Jesus and saw his death and resurrection (Acts 1:21-22). Other apostles besides the Twelve included James (Jesus' half-brother and Lead Pastor in Jerusalem; Galatians 1:19), Paul (Acts 9:15; Galatians 2:8), Barnabas (Acts 14:14), Silas and Timothy (1 Thessalonians 1:1; 2:7), among others.

yet planned to rejoin Timothy back in Ephesus (3:14; 4:13). Since this event does not line up with Luke's timeline in Acts, it is probable that this took place after Paul's imprisonment in Rome (Acts 28:30-31). This means that both of his letters to Timothy were written after the book of Acts, probably in A.D. 64-66, before Paul's final imprisonment and death in Rome. The purpose of this letter was to clarify the instructions and task that he had left for Timothy to accomplish in his absence. It seems as if Timothy may have written Paul with some questions that Paul needed to answer as well.

Chapter one begins with a slight modification of Paul's traditional greeting. With only the two letters to Timothy as the exception, Paul always offered "grace and peace" to his readers, combining the normal Greek and Hebrew salutations, respectively. To Timothy, though, he offered "GRACE, MERCY, AND PEACE" (vs. 2). It is possible that he included "mercy" because of the difficulty of the work in Ephesus and Timothy's weaker tendencies. In fact, Timothy faced a situation that would become confrontational, as he had to stop false teachers in the church, about whom Paul warned the Ephesian elders a few years earlier (vs. 3-7; Acts 20:28-30). Apparently, they wanted to place the Gentile church under the Mosaic Law, something Paul had fought from the beginning of his ministry (vs. 8-11).[148]

Paul connected to the theme of mercy by reminding Timothy of Paul's own past (vs. 12-17). Even though he "WAS FORMERLY A BLASPHEMER AND A PERSECUTOR, AND AN ARROGANT MAN," God treated him with mercy for one primary reason: so that he could be an example demonstrating "FOR THOSE WHO ARE GOING TO BELIEVE IN HIM FOR ETERNAL LIFE" that God can save anyone.

Paul concluded this opening chapter by charging Timothy with his task: "FIGHT THE GOOD FIGHT," a military theme that permeates both letters

---

148 The entire letter of Galatians was written to combat this false teaching, and Paul had to fight it everywhere he went, as shown in several of his other letters as well.

(vs. 18-20). This would require him to "HOLD FIRMLY TO FAITH AND A GOOD CONSCIENCE." There were those in the Ephesian church who had already shipwrecked their faith, and Paul did not want Timothy to suffer the same fate.

Chapter two begins the actual instructions or clarifications that Timothy needed to finish his task. "FIRST OF ALL," he needed to make sure that the local assemblies prayed for "ALL PEOPLE, EVEN FOR KINGS AND ALL WHO ARE IN AUTHORITY" (vs. 1-8). These prayers had two goals. First, praying for the authorities would affect how the believers lived, leading to a more "PEACEFUL AND QUIET LIFE." Second, praying for all people would result in people coming to believe in Jesus and "A KNOWLEDGE OF THE TRUTH," namely, that Jesus is the only mediator between God and man. Because of this, Paul wanted the men of the various assemblies to pray for their nation and their community regularly.

It is important to note at this point that Paul spent much of this letter giving instructions to various distinct groups of people within the local churches, starting with the "MEN." The fact that he specified that men were to pray did not mean that women were not allowed to, as 1 Corinthians 11:5 shows (written about a decade earlier). However, it is a duty of men, in their God-given roles as leaders in their families, congregations, communities, and even politics, that they should intentionally pray for these areas when they are gathered together. The comment that this should be done "WITHOUT ANGER OR DISPUTE" could show that Paul was addressing a specific issue with a timeless principle. Since it was the men who usually filled government and other public roles, Paul thought that praying together as believers would certainly help influence their communities for Christ.

The second group that Paul addressed was the "WOMEN" (vs. 9-15). This paragraph is often maligned by those who mistakenly think that Paul was misogynistic and chauvinistic. In reality, he offered great latitude toward believing women and had several of them serve alongside him in his ministry.

Even so, he strongly believed in the God-designed order for men and women, and his Holy Spirit-inspired letters kept that balance.

Godly women, he wrote, should "DRESS . . . WITH MODESTY AND SELF-CONTROL." The mention of "self-control" may indicate that some of the women in Ephesus were disrupting the meetings, possibly similar to Paul's warning about the men's anger. In response, Paul gave principles for all believing women. They are to be identified and defined by their good deeds rather than outward adornment. Paul's command that he did "NOT ALLOW A WOMAN TO TEACH OR EXERCISE AUTHORITY OVER A MAN" has been widely debated and often dismissed. While some see this to be a cultural issue in Ephesus that has no bearing on our modern culture, this does not fit the entire context, since he referred to creation for his support.[149] Women are not to take teaching or leadership positions over men in the congregation. Constable notes, "The verbs 'teach' and 'exercise authority' are in the present tense in the Greek text, which implies a continuing ministry rather than a single instance of ministry."[150] Because of the inherent roles in creation and because of Eve's being deceived, Paul supernaturally concluded that this was the natural order in the Christian assembly.

Verse 15 is also often misunderstood, as many believe it limits women to be nothing more than "baby-making machines." This is considered a difficult verse, unfortunately, because of our English translations. The key is found in the two verbs, "be delivered" and "continue." Some translations make them both singular – "SHE WILL BE DELIVERED . . . IF SHE CONTINUES" (NET, HCSB) – while others make both verbs plural – "THEY WILL BE DELIVERED . . . IF THEY CONTINUE" (NASB, NLT, NIV). Of the major translations, only the KJV and ESV most accurately reflect the Greek text – "SHE WILL BE

---

149 This is a great example of the apostle showing that he understood the first chapters of Genesis to be literal and historical events. To build such a controversial topic on a myth or legend (as many read Genesis 1-11 today) would undermine everything that Paul taught.

150 Thomas Constable, *Notes on 1 Timothy, 2016 edition*, 33. Constable's notes on the whole Bible are available for free at www.soniclight.com/constable/notes.htm.

DELIVERED [SINGULAR] . . . IF THEY CONTINUE [PLURAL]."

In the context, "she" goes back to Eve from verse 14, while "they" refers to the Christian women Paul was writing to in verse 9. Even though Eve was deceived, bringing God's curse of a natural struggle against male leadership upon her and all women, she (and her gender) can be delivered from this curse. Rather than spending her life being deceived, like Eve, and usurping roles that she was never designed to fulfill, Eve (representing all women) "WILL BE DELIVERED" from this spiritual struggle by focusing on how God did design her – a nurturer and giver of life. Even for those women who cannot bear children or are past the age of childbearing, the nurture and life they give to others around them – whether men, women, or children – can be done out of "FAITH AND LOVE AND HOLINESS WITH SELF-CONTROL." This is far from saying that women have no role in the church. On the contrary, this gives them great responsibility and freedom to serve within their God-given design and help deliver one another from the consequences of Eve's sin, as they learn to walk in step with the Holy Spirit.

Chapter three continues Paul's instructions for specific groups in the local church, continuing with the elders (vs. 1-7). In the New Testament, the terms "overseer" and "shepherd" describe the main functions of the elders, i.e., they rule over the congregation and protect it (like fathers of a family, vs. 5). Contrary to what many Bible colleges and seminaries may teach, the eldership is not something that a man should wait to see if he is called to. The apostle said that eldership is something worth desiring. It is acceptable for a man to "ASPIRE TO THE OFFICE OF OVERSEER."

The verses describing a local church elder can be taken too strongly or too lightly. On the one hand, these are often called "requirements" or "qualifications" to be an elder. If this were the case, then no one would be qualified, because no one meets these perfectly. On the other hand, if we consider these only "ideals" but nothing more, then they might as well have never been written, because, again, there is no ideal elder. Rather, it is best to see these as "character traits" that the elders live out as an example to the congregation.[151] Understanding that elders are not perfect, yet expecting them to be spiritually mature leaders, finds that balance. As such, this list could be read as "characterized by being ABOVE REPROACH...characterized by being NOT CONTENTIOUS," etc. This also helps gain the proper interpretation of the often-misunderstood "HUSBAND OF ONE WIFE" item. When the Greek phrase is read literally and understood as a character quality, we discover that an elder should be "characterized by being a one-woman type of man," whether he is married or not.[152]

"DEACONS" are the second group of church leaders Paul mentioned and the only other official role given in Scripture for local congregations (vs. 8-13). In a list similar to the elders, Paul gave character traits for these godly servants. The specific mention of "NOT TWO-FACED ... HOLDING TO THE MYSTERY OF THE FAITH" seems to indicate some kind of teaching or counseling ministry with people in the congregation. Deacons are also supposed to "BE TESTED FIRST" before being appointed to this role. Like elders, they should have godly marriages and families (if they are married and have children).[153]

The mention of "women" or "wives" in verse 11 is also widely debated. The two obvious interpretations are either female deacons or the wives of deacons. We do not deny that the Church has historically had women serving alongside deacons, but what their exact role was has not always been clear. Some see Paul's reference to Phoebe in Romans 16:1 to mean that she was a deaconess in Cenchrea, but this is a stretch, grammatically. Additionally,

---

151 It has been noted by several writers that, with the exception of "ABLE TO TEACH," each of these character traits is found elsewhere in the New Testament for all believers. They are not exclusive to elders, but elders should lead the way as examples of what godliness looks like.

152 There are some scholars who believe that an elder is required to married and have children so he can fulfill these "requirements." Another common misinterpretation is that he must never have been divorced (either before or after salvation). Some go so far as to say that he may not have been remarried for any reason, even if his first wife had died. None of these meet the interpretation given above.

153 The best writings I have seen on this topic are Alexander Strauch's books, *Biblical Eldership* and *The New Testament Deacon*. We use these in our church and highly recommend them.

Constable observes that it would be odd for Paul to qualify deacons' wives but not elders' wives. (To say that he meant this to apply to wives of both elders and deacons does not explain why they are mentioned in the middle of his instructions about deacons.) Given Paul's instructions to them, it is sufficient to say that these women did exert some influence in the congregation, so they were to do so faithfully and with dignity, keeping their tongues in check.

In the final three verses closing the first half of the letter, Paul made clear the confession to which Timothy and the believers should hold fast (1:18) and should drive the ministry in Ephesus (vs. 14-16). First, the church is "THE HOUSEHOLD OF GOD"; thus, believers are called to live to a higher standard. Second, the church is "THE SUPPORT AND BULWARK OF THE TRUTH"; thus, our teaching and doctrine must be pure. Third, our message to the world centers on the Eternal Son who became flesh and who will ultimately finish his work after the Church has completed ours.

Chapter four is different from the other chapters around it because Paul broke from his instructions to groups so he could focus on Timothy again. In this chapter, he gave Timothy three sets of warnings or encouragements. First, Timothy was to watch out for false teaching that would arise within the congregation (vs. 1-5).[154] Even though elders and deacons should have godly character traits, Paul had already warned the original Ephesian elders that "wolves" would enter the congregation from within their own body (Acts 20:28-30), and as Paul's representative there, it was Timothy's job to help purge these false teachers from the congregation. The description Paul gave Timothy reveals men who had forsaken the truth of Scripture for sensational teachings that, ultimately, come from demons. As innocuous as they sound, they include teachings even about marriage and food, often focusing on what is forbidden in an ascetic way. In Colossians 2:16-23 Paul

---

154 This is another clue that Timothy was not one of the elders of the Ephesian church. Paul tasked him, not only with selecting and training the elders, but also with keeping their doctrine in check. It seems that he was not the primary teacher in the church, even though he did teach.

wrote that we are not obligated to such unscriptural restrictions.

Second, Timothy was to guard himself and his teaching carefully, so that he did not get caught up in such heresies, even unintentionally (vs. 6-10). Paul noted that even in the first century there were those who focused on their physical health to the neglect of their spiritual health. While physical health does some good in this life, spiritual health is eternal and must be our priority. Paul's comment that God "IS THE SAVIOR OF ALL PEOPLE, ESPECIALLY OF BELIEVERS," points to the fact that no one is outside of God's ability to save. The concept that only a special, elect group can or will be saved is contrary to Paul's teaching.

Third, Timothy was to both "COMMAND AND TEACH THESE THINGS" (vs. 11-16). Apparently, there were some in the church who had dismissed him as their local apostle because of his youth. Paul told him not to let that stop his work there. Instead, he was to be an example of all these things already mentioned, even to the elders of the local congregations. He was to make this his life's focus, and it would be beneficial not only for him but everyone in his care.

Chapter five returns to instructions about certain groups in the church, specifically widows and elders. The church is to be a family of families, meaning that we should relate to each other as fathers, mothers, brothers, and sisters (vs. 1-16). Like one would take care of an aging grandparent, Paul said that the congregation is responsible for widows in their church family, but only under certain conditions. First, if the widow has family still living, they are responsible for her, not the church. Second, only older widows are to be included in this care program. Paul specified "SIXTY YEARS OLD" (vs. 9), but this could be considered descriptive rather than prescriptive, due to cultural life expectancies.[155] Third, she was to be "THE WIFE OF ONE HUSBAND" (vs. 9).

---

155 For instance, if a culture had a life expectancy rate for women of 55 years old, waiting to help widows until they turned 60 would drastically cut down on a church's benevolence expenses, but it would probably violate the spirit of what Paul taught here.

This phrase is the exact opposite of an elder's "HUSBAND OF ONE WIFE" character trait (see chapter three), meaning that she was "characterized by being a one-man type of woman." Fourth, she was to be an example of godliness.

Paul specifically commanded that younger widows were not to be accepted "ON THE LIST" (vs. 11-15). Rather, he said they should remarry and fulfill their roles as described in 2:9-15. In a statement that could have been written today, Paul noted that younger women with no responsibilities and full financial provision "LEARN TO BE LAZY, AND . . . ALSO GOSSIPS AND BUSYBODIES." Although this may seem harsh or unfair, every civilization can verify its accuracy.

Another reason Paul wanted younger widows to remarry had to do with a "FORMER PLEDGE." It seems that the church's provision for older widows was a kind of remuneration for devoted service to the congregation. Because these women had no families and were characteristically godly servants, it is possible that they pledged themselves to their congregation. Early church history shows that this is where the Catholic practice of nuns derived. However, it also may refer to the "women" in 3:11. If so, this group of widows probably served alongside the elders and deacons, probably in ministry toward women.[156]

In verses 17-25 Paul gave additional instruction about the elders, this time concerning the congregation's financial support for them. Many people believe that elders should not be paid by the church, but this passage clearly disputes that notion. First, Paul quoted from both Deuteronomy 25:4 (Moses) and Luke 10:7 (Jesus) to prove that the one who works should receive payment for his work. Even animals get that much. Second, Paul used the same Greek word (τιμή, *timē*) to describe how the congregation treated both widows (vs. 3) and elders (vs. 17). Because this word means both "honor" (non-financial) and "compensation" (financial), some argue that elders should

---

156 In the churches that had a role of deaconess, some of their tasks were to help prepare women for baptism, childbirth, etc.

only be honored but not paid. However, since the word obviously means compensation for widows, and the immediate context is payment for work done, it must mean compensation for elders as well. Elders should be taken care of by those they serve, especially those "WHO WORK HARD IN SPEAKING AND TEACHING," because it does not allow as much time for another form of work to provide for his family.[157]

However, lest anyone think that this elevates elders to a level of "untouchable" clergy, Paul told Timothy that elders were still subject to discipline for sin, just like any other congregation member, and that their discipline should be public within the congregation, "AS A WARNING TO THE REST" of the seriousness of sin. Thus, elders will be examples, either for good or bad. For this reason, elders should be appointed carefully and slowly. Paul's mention of Timothy's stomach ailments at this point (with no other medical context) may indicate that Timothy's role in choosing and appointing elders was a stressful and difficult process for him.

Chapter six addresses three more specific groups within the church and Timothy himself again. First, Paul gave instructions for slaves (vs. 1-2). Similar to the instructions in Ephesians 6:5-7 (written just a couple of years earlier), Paul told Timothy that Christian slaves should respect their masters and work well for them because this glorifies God and keeps a good reputation in the community. For those who have "BELIEVING MASTERS," this is true "ALL THE MORE." Sadly, it appears that it was common then as it is now for Christians to treat unbelievers better than their fellow believers in the business world.

Second, Paul addressed those who would spread "FALSE TEACHINGS AND ... NOT AGREE WITH SOUND WORDS ... AND WITH THE TEACHING THAT

---

157 This distinction that some elders will "WORK HARD IN SPEAKING AND TEACHING" reveals that within a team of elders in a local church, different men will have different responsibilities. Some will teach more than others, and they should receive a higher wage than the others. This also implies that all elders should receive at least some compensation for their ministry.

ACCORDS WITH GODLINESS" (vs. 3-10). It seems that then, like now, "health and wealth" theology (the "Prosperity Gospel") was prevalent. Paul warned Timothy not to get involved with it and to warn the believers to stay away from it as well. It is nothing more than idolatry, loving money more than God, and it always destroys one's faith.

Third, Paul returned to his original encouragement to Timothy, that he should not give up (vs. 11-16). It would be a struggle, one that Paul was familiar with, but Timothy – and we – could do it when we place our full trust in Christ and rest in him.

Finally, Paul closed with a few words to those "WHO ARE RICH IN THIS WORLD'S GOODS" (vs. 17-19). His comments about the "Prosperity Gospel" were not intended to be a condemnation on wealth itself or those who have it. Money is a tool, and Paul made sure to tell wealthy believers to use it to help build God's Church and enjoy what God has allowed them to have. What we do in this life is the foundation for our relationship with God and reward in the next.

2 Timothy

Probably within about two years after writing 1 Timothy, Paul was once again arrested and taken to Rome. This would be his final journey because he was beheaded there under Nero's growing persecution of Christians and Christianity. Paul wrote 2 Timothy from a Roman prison around A.D. 66, the last preserved writing we have from his hand and possibly the last letter he ever wrote.

Second Timothy is a personal farewell note from an old mentor to his young friend and colleague, his son in the Christian faith, a man who was ready to throw in the towel himself as he watched everything they had worked for seemingly going up in smoke. Paul's final few words (only 644 in the Greek text) were full of encouragement and anticipation, not regret or remorse, as he said goodbye until they would meet again in Heaven.

Chapter one opens with Paul's modified greeting for Timothy – "GRACE, MERCY, AND PEACE" – to the man who needed to remember all three of them (vs. 1-2).[158] For the last time, Paul identified himself as "AN APOSTLE OF CHRIST JESUS BY THE WILL OF GOD," faithfully obeying his

---

158 See the notes on 1 Timothy 1 for further explanation about this greeting.

commission even to death.

Knowing the turmoil in Timothy's heart, the "TEARS" that he must have shed knowing that he may never see Paul again, the old apostle reminded him of the work that they were doing and the promises of God (vs. 3-14). He reminded Timothy that "GOD DID NOT GIVE US A SPIRIT OF FEAR," so he was not to be afraid of what was about to happen and "NOT BE ASHAMED OF" God's word or God's man, Paul. He reminded Timothy that God was "THE ONE WHO SAVED US AND CALLED US WITH A HOLY CALLING" into ministry because of his grace and for his own glory, so he wanted Timothy to "HOLD TO THE STANDARD OF SOUND WORDS" and "PROTECT THAT GOOD THING ENTRUSTED TO" Timothy.

Paul also gave him some good news, showing that not all was lost (vs. 15-18). One of their dear friends, Onesiphorus, tracked down Paul when he arrived in Rome so he could minister to Paul in his final days. Unfortunately, others did not, namely, Phygelus and Hermogenes from "THE PROVINCE OF ASIA" (modern Turkey), where Timothy was located at Ephesus.

Chapter two continues with a few analogies, a few commands, and a few reminders. First, Paul used the analogies of a soldier and a farmer to illustrate the focus required to serve God well (vs. 1-7). Just like a soldier cannot be concerned with things around him when he is in training or battle, so Timothy must not let his circumstances take him off mission. Just like a farmer receives the first benefit of his labor in the fields, so Timothy would receive great reward for his ministry if he remained faithful and did not quit. Knowing that all of us have only temporary commissions, Paul encouraged Timothy to faithfully pass on the truth to a new generation – as Paul did to Timothy – who could continue to pass it along faithfully to others.

Second, lest Timothy think (like the readers of Hebrews) that quitting now would not affect his spiritual life and reward, Paul reminded him that there is more at stake than our current comfort – the others who still "MAY

OBTAIN SALVATION IN CHRIST JESUS AND ITS ETERNAL GLORY" (vs. 8-13). The promise is true that those who remain faithful will finally be rewarded for their faithfulness. However, "SINCE HE CANNOT DENY HIMSELF," Jesus will have to punish those who do not remain faithful, and they will lose their reward because he is always faithful.

Third, Paul told Timothy to remind those in his charge to stay true to the Scriptures (vs. 14-19). The false teachers Paul addressed in 1 Timothy were apparently still at work, arguing with "PROFANE CHATTER" that was useless to everyone. He wanted Timothy to keep from getting drawn into it, "BECAUSE THOSE OCCUPIED WITH IT WILL STRAY FURTHER AND FURTHER INTO UNGODLINESS." Paul accused two men by name, calling them out for "UNDERMINING SOME PEOPLE'S FAITH." Only by being diligent to handle the Scriptures carefully can one guarantee his ministry will be approved by God.

Finally, Paul charged Timothy to keep himself pure, which will help him keep his doctrine pure (vs. 20-26). His job was to teach the truth and correct opponents to the truth, with gentleness, not getting dragged into useless arguments that would help no one. This, Paul thought, was the method God may use to bring them "TO THEIR SENSES AND ESCAPE THE DEVIL'S TRAP" of questioning, replacing, and finally denying God's expressed word.

Chapter three begins with a sad look at the state of the Church which is falling further and further from Christ (vs. 1-9). This passage is often used to describe the modern world in which we live, and there are certain similarities. However, it is more accurately a description of the Church that is influenced by the world. Most people of the world have no interest in maintaining even "THE OUTWARD APPEARANCE OF RELIGION," although some certainly do. This is true of many believers, though. Verses 6-9 seem to refer to false teachers who prey on weak and young believers, especially young women who are easily deceived (see 1 Timothy 2:9-15; 5:11-14). Where this falling away will end is unclear, but some believe that the true Church will almost be gone by the Rapture.[159]

In the face of such blatant heresy, Paul commanded Timothy to "CONTINUE IN THE THINGS [HE HAD] LEARNED AND [HAD BECOME] CONFIDENT ABOUT" (vs. 10-17). As he regularly did, Paul pointed to himself as an example whom Timothy had observed and followed. Just like Jesus had told the Eleven that the world would hate them as his followers (John 15:18-21), Paul told Timothy that following Jesus in this world means persecution in this world. None of that, though, is stronger than the inspired Word of God, which is designed and fully capable of equipping God's people for God's work.

Chapter four is a template for leaving this life well. First, Paul charged Timothy with his critical work – "PREACH THE MESSAGE ... WHETHER IT IS CONVENIENT OR NOT, REPROVE, REBUKE, EXHORT ... BE SELF-CONTROLLED ... ENDURE HARDSHIP, DO AN EVANGELIST'S WORK, FULFILL YOUR MINISTRY" (vs. 1-8).[160] Paul knew that Timothy's struggle would seem impossible, because many are not interested in hearing the truth, only myths and things that satisfy their own curiosity but do not lead to spiritual growth and maturity. Paul could do no more. Challenging Timothy to continue to "FIGHT THE GOOD FIGHT" (1 Timothy 1:18), Paul believed that he had, and his most cherished thought was his soon meeting with the Savior.

Paul's final wish on this Earth was to see his friend once more before he died (vs. 9-22). Whether or not Timothy ever made it to Rome, we do not know. Paul asked for his cloak, as it was approaching winter, and his dungeon likely had no heat. He also asked for his "SCROLLS, ESPECIALLY THE PARCHMENTS." Although we cannot be sure, it seems possible that these may have

---

159 See the notes on 2 Thessalonians 2 for more detail about the "falling away" that Paul prophesied there.

160 As a silly comparison, this section always reminds me of "The Empire Strikes Back," when Yoda and Obi-Wan Kenobi were talking to the young Luke Skywalker, who was rushing into an impossible situation. "Be careful...don't let the Dark Side take you...stay strong in the Force."

been some of his personal copies of the Scriptures. Paul must have felt lonely, as so many others were busy in ministry or doing other things. Some had even simply deserted him. He sent his warmest greetings to a few friends that Timothy would see on his way to Paul. He also asked that Timothy would bring Mark with him, another wonderful friend that time and maturity, in both men, had developed. Above all, the old apostle was still "CONFIDENT OF THIS VERY THING" (Philippians 1:6, NASB):

> "THE LORD WILL DELIVER ME FROM EVERY EVIL DEED
> AND WILL BRING ME SAFELY INTO HIS HEAVENLY KINGDOM.
> TO HIM BE GLORY FOR EVER AND EVER! AMEN."

Titus

Titus is one of three letters Paul wrote specifically to individual co-workers in his ministry. (The others were both to Timothy. Philemon was not a co-worker.) Although he is never mentioned in the book of Acts, we can piece together some information about Titus from 2 Corinthians, Galatians, and 2 Timothy. Before Paul left him on the island of Crete, Titus served as an itinerant apostle under the authority of Paul in Corinth and Dalmatia (northeast of Macedonia, in modern Croatia).

Luke does not tell anything of Paul's ministry in Crete in the book of Acts, so it is best to assume that this took place after Paul's release from Rome around A.D. 62. He had about two years to do more travel and ministry before his final arrest and death. It was during this time that he began the churches in Crete and wrote his letters to Timothy and Titus. It seems that Paul's ministry in Crete was either cut short by an outside force or he intentionally left so he could move on to other things. In either case, he left Titus there to continue the ministry, building on the foundation they had started.

The theme of Titus has to do with Christian ministry, namely the good works we are to do in light of Christian faith and doctrine.

Chapter one introduces Titus' mission and the purpose of the letter. Paul began with an introduction that does not match any of his other letters (vs. 1-4). Rather than focusing on his role as an apostle of the gospel, Paul emphasized his work in furthering believers' faith and gave a unique description of his message. Probably knowing his time was short, Paul focused on the eternal faithfulness of God, "WHO DOES NOT LIE," and the truth that he made "EVIDENT" through the message Paul preached. This may indicate that Paul spent much of his last few years building on his previous work, strengthening the saints, rather than starting churches in new areas. Even his work in Ephesus (Acts 18-19) was primarily toward teaching the believers who could then start and grow churches without him.

Titus' mission on Crete was to finish establishing the local churches, presumably that he and Paul started. The most pressing task was to appoint the elders to lead each church (vs. 5).[161] Paul gave Titus a specific set of qualifications for these elders (vs. 6-9). Some are similar to the list in 1 Timothy 3, focusing on the personal character traits of the men, but the emphasis in Titus is more on the men's doctrinal integrity and teaching capability. The reason for this emphasis was two-fold. First, there seems to have been widespread false doctrine being taught on Crete, and the local elders needed to be able to refute it and teach sound doctrine (vs. 10-14). Second, for Paul, false doctrine was directly related to lack of good works (vs. 15-16). This was evident in the lives of the false teachers and the lives of those following their false doctrine.

Chapter two picks up the theme of good works from chapter one. Rather than false doctrine, Titus was to "COMMUNICATE THE BEHAVIOR THAT GOES WITH SOUND TEACHING" (vs. 1). The word translated "sound" means "healthy." Paul used it eight times, all in 1 and 2 Timothy and Titus and all

---

161 Notice that even in Paul's absence, the congregations did not choose their own elders. The initial elders were always appointed by the apostles and were always a plurality in each congregation. After the initial appointment, the elders were to train new elders to replace themselves (like the apostles trained elders to replace themselves, 2 Timothy 2:2). The Scripture never shows a congregational vote to determine the leadership of any local church.

related to correct doctrine, except Titus 1:13 and 2:2, where it refers to a healthy Christian faith.[162] However, even those are in the context of sound doctrine and reliant on it.

Paul elaborated on what the results of healthy doctrine should look like by giving specific behavioral instructions to various groups within the local churches. He commanded that "OLDER MEN" and "OLDER WOMEN" (probably both physically and spiritually) were to have godly lives worth imitating and be integrally involved in the training of those younger men and women, respectively, who are coming behind them (vs. 2-5). Notice that the characteristics Paul laid on these older saints are similar to those for elders, even for those who may never be elders.

Modern believers and unbelievers alike often take issue with Paul's instructions for the older women (vs. 4-5). The notion that "YOUNGER WOMEN" are responsible to "[FULFILL] THEIR DUTIES AT HOME" and be "SUBJECT TO THEIR OWN HUSBANDS" seems out-dated and even oppressive. They argue that women today are more empowered and have responsibilities outside the home. Husbands are to share equally in the household responsibilities instead of leaving them for the woman. Unfortunately, this is based on a twisted and unbiblical view of equality and has led to the weakening of the household structure, even in Christian families, which has, in turn, affected the Church at large. Paul said that when our homes are not working properly, "THE MESSAGE OF GOD MAY...BE DISCREDITED."

As Paul's apostolic representative to Crete, it was Titus' responsibility both to model and teach these behaviors to the believers (vs. 6-8). Additionally, Christian slaves were to act faithfully in full subjection to their masters (vs. 9-10).[163] When the church members lived out these commands, antagonists to true Christian doctrine and the Christian faith would not have any ammunition to discredit Christianity.

---

162 1 Timothy 1:10; 6:3; 2 Timothy 1:13; 4:3; Titus 1:9, 13; 2:1, 2. The only other New Testament uses of the word are Luke 5:31; 7:10; 15:27 and 3 John 2 (all referring to physical health).

163 See the notes on Philemon for information about slavery in Paul's letters.

The last few verses of chapter two again emphasize the importance of godly living, this time in the context of Jesus' return to rapture his Church (vs. 11-14). The story of God's grace is more than just salvation from the eternal penalty of sin. It also serves to instruct us in the way of living properly during this life. Most of what Christians call "struggles" are simply "GODLESS WAYS AND WORLDLY DESIRES" (vs. 12) that the Christian has refused "TO REJECT."[164] The outworking of God's grace and the anticipation of Jesus' imminent return should not only be sufficient for God's people to live God's way (2 Corinthians 12:9), it should drive us in that lifestyle, causing us to be "EAGER TO DO GOOD" for the Savior.

Much like he did with Timothy (1 Timothy 4:12), Paul had to encourage Titus to not give up in the face of others rejecting him (vs. 15). Titus may have been a younger man who was sometimes intimidated by those older than he was or maybe he shied away from confrontation, to the detriment of his ministry. Church leadership and disciple-making both sometimes require hard conversations with those we are trying to lead. In this case, Titus had "FULL AUTHORITY," and Paul urged him to confidently and wisely use the appropriate methods to get his message across.

Chapter three concludes this short letter with two more exhortations to godly living. Building on the practical situations from chapter two, which were focused on our actions toward fellow believers, the first few verses of chapter three show that this extends to unbelievers and even governing officials as well (vs. 1-2). It seems that part of Paul's normal teaching was that Christians are not to be trouble-makers in this world. Instead, by praying for our governing officials and living out our increasing godliness, we will often enjoy peaceful, tranquil lives (1 Thessalonians 4:9-12; 1 Timothy 2:1-4).

The reason for this lifestyle was always the result and reflection of God's salvation and grace that we have received (vs. 3-7). "FOR WE TOO WERE

---

164 Paul explained how to do this in Romans 6.

ONCE" like the godless world around us, but "THE KINDNESS OF GOD OUR SAVIOR" came through Jesus and changed us thoroughly. Because we have the message that the same salvation is offered to all people, we who are saved are to model what God's grace can do in a person's life, even to the confident hope we have both now and into eternity.

Verse eight again ties godly living to sound Christian doctrine (vs. 8-11). If we truly believe God's Word and submit to it as the final authority in our lives, it should be obvious by our obedience. Arguing over non-essentials, even among believers but especially with unbelievers, does more harm than good and encouraging a believer in his or her ungodly living by overlooking it is wrong. Bad behavior should be pointed out, in love, for the purpose of repentance and restoration to the local fellowship (see Galatians 6:1-2).[165] Even in his final greeting, Paul gave a perfect example of how the Christians under Titus' care can help their fellow believers (vs. 12-15).

This short letter is a wonderful reminder that right living can only come from, and should be the natural result of, right learning. Doctrine drives practice, so it is essential for Christians to know Christian truth so we can practice Christian life.

---

165 For those Christians who think the Bible teaches "we are not to judge others," one only needs to look at the many passages like this which explicitly call us to make judgments in our dealing with Christians who are not living up to God's biblical standard.

Philemon

The short letter to Philemon is the most personal of all of Paul's preserved writings. In his three decades of ministry, Paul certainly wrote many other short notes and personal letters, but God chose to preserve only this one for our benefit. Although nowhere does this letter give the location of Philemon, Colossians 4:7-18 provides a list of names almost identical to those in Philemon, including Philemon's slave, Onesimus. It seems that Paul sent Tychicus and Onesimus back to Colossae from Rome with two letters – one for the whole church (Colossians) and one for Philemon.

The purpose of this letter was three-fold. First, because Onesimus had run away from Philemon (presumably having stolen something), Paul needed to return him to his rightful master (vs. 12, 14). Regardless of our beliefs about slavery, this was the right thing for him to do, given the culture in which they lived. (The comment in Colossians 4:1 about how Christian masters should treat slaves is not coincidental.) Second, Paul wanted to vouch for Onesimus' conversion to Christianity personally.[166] He had been saved through Paul's ministry while Paul was under house arrest in Rome

---

166 Roman slaves had the right to go to one of their master's friends to serve as an arbitrator, and it seems that was what Onesimus had asked Paul to do here.

(vs. 10, 15-16; Acts 28:16, 30-31), and Paul insisted that he be the one to tell Philemon. (Philemon may not have believed Onesimus, thinking it was only an act to secure his pity.) Third, Paul wanted to ask for Philemon to pardon Onesimus for his crimes. Although Philemon owed Paul a great spiritual debt, Paul promised that he would personally repay Onesimus' financial debt, should Philemon choose to pursue it (vs. 18-19).

Many people have argued that Paul should have done something more to secure Onesimus' freedom since slavery (in their minds, anyway) is wrong. Opponents of Christianity point to Paul's silence and condemn the Scriptures for condoning slavery. In reality, Paul acted exactly as he should have in this matter. Slavery is never called a sin in Scripture and was often mutually beneficial to both the master and the slave, depending on the circumstances.[167] The sin was always in how masters would treat their slaves, something that Paul clearly addressed both here and in Colossians 4:1, as well as in other letters. However, verse 21 is often overlooked though it contains an implication that Philemon should treat Onesimus far better than Roman law required. While we cannot say that Paul necessarily meant that Philemon should completely pardon and free Onesimus, the suggestion is certainly there, and Paul allowed the Holy Spirit to place that conviction on Philemon if that was what God wanted.

Thus, this brief letter demonstrates that even our social and economic decisions are to be ruled by biblical truth. It also provides an example of how believers can tactfully and lovingly point out truth and error to help our fellow believers live godly in this world.

---

167 Slavery in the first-century Roman Empire was much broader and more nuanced than the forced slavery that most modern readers think about. Many people even chose to live as slaves because it provided a much better life than they could have on their own.

Hebrews

Hebrews is the only letter in the New Testament with an unknown writer. However, this does not mean he was an "anonymous" writer, because the readers knew exactly who he was (13:18-19, 22-24). Although Paul has been a perennial favorite, several factors seem to rule him out. First, the lack of a clear greeting was certainly not his style. Second, Hebrews 2:3-4 implies that the writer was a second-hand witness to Christ and did not do miracles, whereas Paul often insisted that his message came personally from Christ (Galatians 1:11-12, 15-17) and that he did miracles to authenticate his apostolic authority (2 Corinthians 12:12). Third, the language of the text itself does not match Paul's normal style or vocabulary, yet there are enough similarities that a close associate of Paul's is likely. Several men (and even a woman, Priscilla) have been suggested over the centuries, but they are all speculative, though some have more merit than others.

We also do not know the identity of the readers, although the heavy reliance on the Greek Old Testament (Septuagint, LXX) strongly implies Greek-speaking Jews. Additionally, in 13:24, the writer sent his readers greetings from "THOSE AWAY FROM ITALY" (the basic meaning of the preposition ἀπό, *apo*), implying that the readers were *in* Italy, possibly in Rome. The fact that Clement of Rome quoted from Hebrews in the A.D. 90s gives credibility to this consideration.

The main theme of Hebrews is that Jesus – including everything he is and everything he did, is doing, and will do – is better than anyone and anything that came before him. Because of this, the writer gave five warnings (the first four increasing in severity) about the great loss of inheritance that a Christian will suffer if he chooses to turn away from Jesus and follow anything or anyone else.

Although many scholars and teachers have attempted to interpret these warnings to mean that a Christian can lose his or her salvation, this interpretation is not valid. The key to the correct meaning is found in the warnings themselves and the use of the word "salvation" in its historical, Old Testament usage – the very context that the writer's entire teaching is based on. This will become apparent in chapter two.

Chapter one introduces Jesus as the final and ultimate revelation from God. Most importantly, it presents Jesus as the Son. Although God had previously spoken through prophets, "IN THESE LAST DAYS HE HAS SPOKEN TO US IN A SON" (vs. 1-2). So Jesus, the eternal Son, is better than all the Old Testament prophets, dreams, visions, etc. and provides a better revelation of God than they did. This was John's point three decades later when he wrote, "NO ONE HAS EVER SEEN GOD. THE ONLY ONE, HIMSELF GOD, WHO IS IN CLOSEST FELLOWSHIP WITH THE FATHER, HAS MADE GOD KNOWN" (John 1:18).

The writer listed seven characteristics or roles that Jesus has (vs. 2-3), with emphasis on his Sonship, followed by seven Old Testament passages supporting his deity and Messianic role, including his first quote from Psalm 110 which is the most-often quoted psalm in the entire New Testament (vs. 5-13). (This gives the contextual key that the writer would rely heavily on the Old Testament to support his arguments throughout the book.)

Not only is Jesus better than the prophets, but he is also better than angels. Angels were highly respected in Judaism as God's personal servants. But angels are *only* servants. Even though they are sometimes called "sons of God" (Genesis 6:1-4; Job 1-2; 38:7), Jesus is **the** Son, King, and Creator – even of the angels (vs. 4, 14).

Chapter two continues the writer's comparison between Jesus and the angels and introduces the first of five warning passages in the letter. The writer's concern was that the readers' situation would cause them to "DRIFT" from "WHAT WE HAVE HEARD" (vs. 1-2), referring to the revelation that came through Jesus. Drifting could result in "NEGLECT," which would bring some sort of punishment. In fact, the writer pondered, if the old message delivered by angels[168] resulted in punishment for those who rejected it, how much more will the new message, delivered by the One better than angels, bring punishment on those who reject it?

As noted in the introduction, vs. 3-4 hints that the writer was not an apostle, someone who "HEARD HIM" and did "SIGNS AND WONDERS AND VARIOUS MIRACLES," but rather a second-hand witness. This seems to eliminate at least Paul from consideration as the writer. However, it also reinforces what Paul wrote in 2 Corinthians 12:12, that signs and wonders were limited to true apostles, not made available to all believers.[169]

After this brief, first warning, the writer returned to the Old Testament and the subject of Jesus' superiority over angels, this time expounding on Psalm 8. He also shifted his emphasis from "Jesus the Son" to "Jesus the Man." Although Jesus was and is superior to angels, he underwent an experience that placed him "A LITTLE LOWER THAN THE ANGELS FOR A LITTLE WHILE."

Verse five contains an essential key to the proper interpretation of the whole book. "HE DID NOT PUT THE WORLD TO COME, ABOUT WHICH

---

168 This verse is one of three often-overlooked passages that mentions that God used angels to give the Law to Moses at Mt. Sinai. The other two passages are Acts 7:53 and Galatians 3:19.

169 These two passages should be strongly considered when discussing whether signs and wonders should be normative for believers today, as various Pentecostal denominations teach.

WE ARE SPEAKING, UNDER THE CONTROL OF ANGELS." With this statement, the writer clarified that the "salvation" (and later "inheritance" and "rest") that was the subject of his teaching was "THE WORLD TO COME." In historic Judaism, "the world to come" refers specifically to the Messianic Kingdom, not eternal life or forgiveness of sin (a typical understanding of "salvation").[170] Thus, the warnings about what these believers might lose in salvation refer to the Kingdom, not eternal life.

In the rest of the chapter, the writer gave four reasons that Jesus' humanity was so great. First, it enabled him to regain man's lost rule (vs. 5-9). During his earthly life and ministry, the Son-King of chapter one seemed to have no control, and the Creator "SUFFERED DEATH," but both of these were only "FOR A LITTLE WHILE."

Second, it allowed him to restore our relationship with God (vs. 10-13). Third, it equipped him to disarm Satan and deliver us from death (vs. 14-16). Fourth, it enabled him to become a sympathetic high priest for his people, "ABLE TO HELP THOSE WHO ARE TEMPTED" (vs. 17-18). This is the first mention of "HIGH PRIEST" in Hebrews, a subject that will dominate the rest of the letter.

Because of his temporary lowering and suffering, Jesus is "NOW CROWNED WITH GLORY AND HONOR...BRINGING MANY SONS TO GLORY," so he can finally "DESTROY THE ONE WHO HOLDS THE POWER OF DEATH...AND SET FREE THOSE WHO WERE HELD ... BY THEIR FEAR OF DEATH."

Chapter three continues the writer's subject of Jesus the Man and introduces his next major comparison. Not only is Jesus better than the angels, but he is also superior to Moses (vs. 1-6). For the Jewish readers, this was a significant claim, because no one in Jewish history is greater than

---

170   Only about 12% of all uses of the Hebrew and Greek words for "salvation" throughout the Scriptures refer to eternal salvation. The far more normal use is personal or national "deliverance" tied to God's promises to bring Israel into the Kingdom. This is the predominant meaning of "salvation" in both the Old and New Testaments.

Moses.[171] He was the great law-giver, the one who faithfully led the Israelites from Egypt, oversaw the building of the Tabernacle, and mediated the Law between God and Israel. Until the Law system was established, Moses effectively served as prophet, priest, and king over Israel, the only one to do so until Jesus reigns in his Kingdom.

However great Moses was, the writer conceded that he was, like the angels, still only "A SERVANT." Moses may have served in God's house, but Jesus is the "SON OVER GOD'S HOUSE." Moses may have overseen the building, but Jesus was the builder.

Preparing for the second warning to his readers, the writer once again opened the Hebrew Scriptures to exposit a psalm, this time Psalm 95 (vs. 7-11). The context is Israel's coming to Kadesh-Barnea after leaving Egypt (Numbers 13-14). Instead of believing God and following Moses into the land, they rebelled and lost their promised inheritance, also called God's "REST."

This example led the writer to warn his readers of the danger of having "AN EVIL, UNBELIEVING HEART THAT FORSAKES THE LIVING GOD" (vs. 12-19). He reminded them that God punished those who rebelled and disobeyed against him by their "DEAD BODIES [FALLING] IN THE WILDERNESS." They were kept out of God's rest (their promised inheritance in the land) because of their "UNBELIEF."

Chapter four continues the second warning by expanding on the concept of promised rest from chapter three. Under Moses and Joshua, the Israelites thought that reaching the Promised Land was the extent of their rest. However, the promise was not limited to the rest from slavery that "JOSHUA HAD GIVEN THEM" because "THE PROMISE OF ENTERING HIS REST REMAINS OPEN," both in the writer's time and until today (vs. 1-9). Coming

---

171 This is true in its context. Abraham, the father of the Jewish people, is also a significant figure as is David, the great king. These three – Abraham, Moses, and David – are each most significant in their own contexts.

back to Psalm 95, the writer warned the believers in his audience to not "COME SHORT OF IT" themselves, because "A SABBATH REST REMAINS FOR THE PEOPLE OF GOD."

Thus, the writer furthered the contrast between Jesus and specific Jewish heroes, this time comparing him to Joshua. Although Joshua could provide only temporary, physical rest, Jesus provides eternal rest. However, this rest is available only to those who do not "FALL BY FOLLOWING THE SAME PATTERN OF DISOBEDIENCE" (vs. 10-11) as those at Kadesh-Barnea. This is an early indication that the rest/inheritance that will come up throughout the letter is not a reference to salvation, which cannot be gained or lost by obedience or disobedience. Additionally, using the pronoun "WE," the writer repeatedly included himself in the group who could potentially lose access to this rest.

Lest anyone think he could sneak into the rest, the writer assures all his readers (including those in the present day) that God sees and knows everything and that his word of judgment can determine even "DESIRES AND THOUGHTS" (vs. 12-13).

Chapter five should begin with 4:14-16, as the writer moved from his second warning to his third emphasis on Jesus. Picking up from the end of chapter two, the writer opened a long section on "Jesus the High Priest." Although God's people have not yet entered into rest, we do already have full access to God through Jesus. The last three verses of chapter four contain two more exhortations with the formula "LET US" do something. Because Jesus is our High Priest, "LET US HOLD FAST TO OUR CONFESSION" (as opposed to drifting from and neglecting it, first warning) and "[LET US] CONFIDENTLY APPROACH THE THRONE OF GRACE" (rather than rebelling against it, second warning).

The reason we can do this is because of Jesus' ministry as our great High Priest. In 5:1-4, the writer mentioned some significant points about the

Aaronic priest – he was a human, representing the people before God with compassion because he was subject to their same weaknesses. Additionally, a priest was called by God to minister in this way, offering freewill gifts and sacrifices. The major weakness is that they were also sinners.

Using this as his comparison, the writer showed that Jesus met all of those requirements (except the weakness of sin) and that he did minister on behalf of the people through his sacrifice, which made him completely able to save all who come to him (vs. 5-10). He is now serving "AS HIGH PRIEST IN THE ORDER OF MELCHIZEDEK." The reference to Melchizedek is so significant that the writer will address it more in chapter seven; however, it is now clear that Jesus is also better than Aaron, in addition to the prophets, angels, Moses, and Joshua.

The final four verses of chapter five set the stage for and lead into chapter six and the third warning passage. The context is maturity. More specifically, a Christian's level of spiritual maturity, which is dependent on Bible study and Christian practice, will determine how much he can understand about spiritual matters. The writer thought he could not go much further in his discussion of Melchizedek because his readers lacked maturity. However, this lack of maturity was not because of lack of instruction. They had "BECOME SLUGGISH IN HEARING." Old enough to be mature and teaching others, they had regressed to a state of spiritual infancy, probably due to the unintentional drifting he had warned them about in chapter two.

Chapter six continues the theme of maturity from the end of chapter five and provides the third warning. The first eight verses are one of the most debated sections in the book because of the strong warning of judgment. However, all of chapter six is part of a parenthetical section in the middle of the 5:10 and 7:1 teaching on Melchizedek. Simply put, a believer (which the writer assumes all the readers were) who chooses to not "MOVE ON TO MATURITY" has the potential to regress to the point of no return where maturity and ministry are no longer possible (a kind of permanent spiritual infancy). This would result in both a physical punishment (possibly even death) as well as loss of reward or inheritance in the future.

Notice that "FALLEN AWAY" was not simply a momentary lapse of judgment. The believer described here had the "RAIN" of God's Word and blessing and power "OFTEN FALLING" on him, and he "EXPERIENCED GOD'S GOOD WORD AND POWER." This person was once on the path toward spiritual maturity, but he began to backslide until he passed the point of a spiritual infant (where some of the immediate readers had fallen, 5:11-14). The falling away is an attitude marked by spiritual apathy resulting in the rejection of the Savior. Paul wrote that this type of immature believer "IS WARPED AND SINFUL; HE IS SELF-CONDEMNED" (Titus 3:11, NIV).

However, this result is not inevitable. The writer was sure that his readers would take his letter to heart and not regress in that way (vs. 9-12). The fact that the writer used the same word for "SLUGGISH" in both 5:12 and 6:12 emphasizes the theme of maturity, not salvation, in the whole section. This warning does not teach or imply that a believer can lose his salvation.

The final paragraph of chapter six leads the topic back to Melchizedek. The writer pointed to the promise his readers were expecting to inherit because of God's promise to Abraham (vs. 13-20). He capitalized on that thought, showing that God made a significant promise to Messiah as well, that he would be "A PRIEST FOREVER IN THE ORDER OF MELCHIZEDEK" (another quote from Psalm 110). To show the significance of the promise, God made it with an oath. However, because there is nothing higher than God by which he could swear, he swore on his own name (reputation).

Chapter seven returns to the theme of "Jesus the High Priest," picking up the teaching on Melchizedek left off in 5:10, with a specific focus on the nature of his priesthood (as opposed to the Aaronic priesthood) and how Jesus fulfills it. Proving yet again that Jesus is better than an Old Testament hero, the writer showed that Melchizedek was greater than Abraham because he received a tithe from Abraham and blessed Abraham, something that only someone greater can do (vs. 1-10). Using the seminal argument that Levi (Abraham's grandson) was in his grandfather's "LOINS," Levi (who received tithes under the sacrificial system) had also paid tithes to Melchizedek.[172] The writer's point was that the Levitical priesthood was inferior to Melchizedek's; thus, Jesus' priesthood is also greater than the Levitical priesthood, because of God's promise that Jesus would be "A PRIEST FOREVER IN THE ORDER OF MELCHIZEDEK."

The very fact that God promised a greater priesthood proves that the Levitical priesthood could not accomplish everything the people needed (vs. 11-28). However, because the priests mediate the law, if the priesthood is inferior, so is the law. Thus, with Jesus' new priesthood came a new law that only Jesus can mediate. Unlike the old law which was useless for making anyone spiritual, Jesus introduced "A BETTER HOPE...THROUGH WHICH WE DRAW NEAR TO GOD." Additionally, because the old law was based on an old covenant, Jesus has become a mediator of a better covenant as well. All of this was to prove that Jesus now offers something that the old priests, old law, and old covenant could never offer – complete salvation with everything it includes. Strengthening this position is the truth that Jesus ministers as a priest forever since he will never die.

Chapters eight through ten shift the focus from the better High Priest to the better covenant itself, expounding one primary Old Testament text – Jeremiah 31:31-34. This is exceptional because it is the longest Old Testament passage quoted in the New Testament in its entirety.

The writer first noted that everything that Moses had built was simply a "SHADOW" of the archetype in Heaven, including the tabernacle, altar,

---

172 This seminal argument is often used to show how the sin nature can be imparted to all of Adam's descendants, because when Adam sinned, "ALL SINNED" in and with him seminally (Romans 5:12).

and sanctuary (vs. 1-6). Even though the New Covenant had not yet been promised at that time, Moses himself knew that what he was setting up, including the covenant, was not the final form. Jesus' ministry, then, also includes "BETTER PROMISES."

Chapter eight ends with the writer quoting the primary New Covenant passage (Jeremiah 31:31-34) and noting that the coming of the New, by necessity, invalidates the Old. Within conservative dispensationalism there is much debate over 1) whether the New Covenant is in full effect right now for Church Age believers, 2) whether there are separate "New Covenants" for the Church and Israel, or 3) whether the New Covenant applies only to Christians who are Jewish. Each position has godly men and women who support it, and this book cannot explore all the details, but it is an important topic that should be investigated further.

It is significant that the writer used three keywords in chapters eight through ten to describe the inferiority of the old sanctuary, promises, system, etc., and all of them are found in 8:5. Compared to what Jesus accomplished, Moses' system was only a ὑποδείγμα (*hupodeigma*; "sketch, outline"; 8:5; 9:23); a σκιά, (*skia*; "shadow"; 8:5; 10:1); and a τύπος (*tupos*; "copy, pattern"; 8:5).

Chapter nine continues the exposition of the Jeremiah text by describing the ancient Tabernacle that Moses had built in the desert. It is noteworthy that the writer continued to refer to the ancient Tabernacle, not the Temple in Jerusalem (either Solomon's or Zerubbabel's/Herod's). This may be another indication that the original readers were not as familiar with the Temple because they lived outside the land of Israel.

Although he knew the details were not that important, the writer mentioned several of the articles and furniture from the Tabernacle (vs. 1-10). The point was that Jesus' better priesthood, better covenant, and better promises required a better sanctuary in which he could offer a better sacrifice. Instead of offering the blood of bulls and goats repeatedly, including to cleanse the sanctuary and the priests, Jesus entered Heaven with his own blood (vs. 11-14). With this he mediates the new covenant and, unlike under the old system, he can "PURIFY" even "OUR CONSCIENCES." His sacrificial death was so inclusive that it provides forgiveness even for those sins "COMMITTED UNDER THE FIRST COVENANT," which were only covered (but never fully cleansed) by animal blood (vs. 15-28). This also makes his sacrifice better, because it was made "ONCE FOR ALL" time and people. Unlike the old priests who made sacrifices repeatedly when they were on duty, when Jesus returns, it will be to "BRING SALVATION" (in the sense of inheritance and rest in the Kingdom), "NOT TO BEAR SIN."

Chapter ten begins with the note that, not only did the repeated sacrifices under the old system not truly purify anyone's conscience from sin, these continual sacrifices actually served as "A REMINDER OF SINS" (vs. 1-4). Thus, the old law system was unable to do what Jesus did, proving again that Jesus offered a better sacrifice. Quoting from Psalm 40, the writer argued that God never intended for "WHOLE BURNT OFFERINGS AND SIN-OFFERINGS" to be the final payment (vs. 5-9).

Jesus provided further proof of his superior sacrifice when "HE SAT DOWN AT THE RIGHT HAND OF GOD" (vs. 10-18; cf. 1:3). The writer noted that the Levitical priests never sat down because their work was never done. However, because Jesus "OFFERED ONE SACRIFICE FOR SINS FOR ALL TIME," his sacrifice was perfect and complete, offering full forgiveness as the New Covenant promised.

The second half of the chapter begins with three exhortations which parallel the final three chapters of the letter (vs. 19-25). Chapter eleven will show us how to "DRAW NEAR WITH...FAITH." Chapter twelve will focus on "THE HOPE THAT WE CONFESS." Chapter thirteen will offer practical examples of how to "SPUR ONE ANOTHER ON TO LOVE AND GOOD WORKS." These are all possible because of the work of our great High Priest, who ministers for us day and night in Heaven. The famous triad of faith, hope, and love is also an obvious nod to Paul's use of them in 1 Corinthians 13:13 and 1 Thessalonians 1:3, showing the Pauline influence on the writer of this letter.

The chapter ends with the fourth, and harshest, warning (vs. 26-39). It is so strong that many have used it to support the possibility of loss of salvation. Even those convinced that a believer could never lose salvation have difficulty dealing with the strong language and often interpret it that those under this judgment are professing believers only but not true Christians.

However, if we understand "salvation" to refer to the full inheritance promised to those who persevere and stay firm in the faith, instead of just forgiveness of sin and eternity in heaven, then loss of reward and loss of eternal blessing satisfies even the harshest warning and can easily be applied to a true believer without requiring him to spend eternity in hell. This is the best understanding of the text in the context of the whole letter, and it has support throughout the New Testament. To think that our Heavenly Father cannot or does not punish his children when they sin or to think that punishment must equate to a loss of eternal salvation is naïve; indeed, chapter twelve insists that punishment of his children is exactly what we should expect from the Father.[173]

Chapter eleven expounds on the nature of persevering faith, providing examples of many great heroes from Israel's history. The readers would have been well-versed in all the stories recounted (which is why the writer could simply give names or broad details toward the end of the chapter, knowing the readers would understand), and the faith of the fathers would have bolstered their own.

The writer chose the only three faithful patriarchs from before the

---

173 It is the use of "fire" here and in the third warning (6:1-8) that leads people to conclude the loss of eternal salvation, because they automatically interpret "fire" to mean "hell fire." However, 1 Corinthians 3:13-15 is clear that believers will face a judgment of fire for their works, and even those who lose all reward will still "BE SAVED, BUT ONLY AS THROUGH FIRE." Thus, God's holy judgment fire will apply to both believers and unbelievers, albeit with different results.

flood (vs. 1-7). Abel sacrificed in faith, Enoch walked with God in faith, and Noah built the ark and saved his family and the animals in faith. No one else in Genesis 1-6 merited recognition as a person of faith.[174] Yet, "WITHOUT FAITH IT IS IMPOSSIBLE TO PLEASE" God, something the original readers were in danger of giving up.

Between the Flood and the Law, the writer elaborated on the great patriarch and matriarch of Israel: Abraham and Sarah (vs. 8-19). It was their faith, exhibited multiple times over, that God rewarded.[175] Isaac, Jacob, and Joseph basically receive honorable mentions (vs. 20-22). Isaac was a mostly faithless man. Jacob started poorly, lived with a modicum of faith, but finally died in great faith. Joseph learned to live in faith through suffering and was allowed to give a prophecy about Israel's exodus from Egypt.

It is important to note that the writer did not mention the Law at all in this chapter. Again, possibly due to Paul's influence, there is no Law in the chapter on faith, as the two are mutually exclusive. In the section on Moses' life, the writer recounted Moses' birth (which was more accurately his parents' faith), his intention to live as a Jew rather than the Pharaoh's son, the establishment of Passover, and the Red Sea miracle (vs. 23-29). Each one of these is a significant foreshadowing of Jesus himself. Jericho and Rahab are the final examples mentioned before the writer simply listed names and events (vs. 30-40). His point was that the readers must not give up in their suffering when so many who had gone before had died in faith without ever yet receiving their promises. Persevering faith transcends this life.

Chapter twelve addresses "THE HOPE THAT WE CONFESS" (10:23). Continuing from chapter eleven, the writer pointed to Jesus, the true pioneer

---

174 Interestingly, this includes Adam. After Genesis 1-2, Adam is never mentioned in a positive way in Scripture. Rather, he is always set up as the progenitor of the sin and destruction that Jesus had to correct. Whether he was a true believer or a life-long rebel is never clarified.

175 Verses 17-19 answer the question that Genesis 22 never does: what did Abraham expect to happen when he offered Isaac as a sacrifice? Genesis 22 reveals Abraham's faith, but not the basis on which his faith rested.

of our faith, who endured what he did because of hope (vs. 1-3). Whereas faith believes in the truth of the unseen, hope is the confident expectation that it will certainly be fulfilled. Because our hope is in something that cannot be shaken, the writer encouraged that we do not "GROW WEARY...AND GIVE UP" when suffering and persecution comes. In fact, the writer said, what seems like persecution may in fact be God's hand of discipline, which causes pain in the short-term so that we may grow maturity in the long-term (vs. 4-12).

Rather than seeing suffering only as a judgment on unbelievers, the writer quoted Proverbs 3:11-12 to confirm that God "DISCIPLINES THE ONE HE LOVES AND CHASTISES EVERY SON." Discipline from God is a confirmation of sonship. As Jesus endured his suffering and learned obedience in the process (5:8), so should we.

The second half of the chapter offers the fifth warning, much more gentle than the last two (vs. 14-29). The writer encouraged his readers to not become a poison to those around them, causing others to give up. He also warned about becoming like Esau, who gave up what was rightfully his for short-term satisfaction. If we ignore the warning and "REFUSE THE ONE WHO IS SPEAKING," we will suffer loss. The Israelites suffered earthly consequences (death) because of their rebellion, but Christians will suffer an eternal consequence in loss of relationship with God and blessing in this life and relationship and inheritance in the next. The immediate readers who rejected these warnings also suffered loss in A.D. 70 when many of them died in the destruction of Jerusalem and the Temple.

Paul's influence is unmistakable in this warning: "So WE MUST NOT GROW WEARY IN DOING GOOD, FOR IN DUE TIME WE WILL REAP, IF WE DO NOT GIVE UP" (Galatians 6:9). "FOR OUR MOMENTARY, LIGHT SUFFERING IS PRODUCING FOR US AN ETERNAL WEIGHT OF GLORY FAR BEYOND ALL COMPARISON" (2 Corinthians 4:17). Instead of giving up and losing our inheritance, "LET US GIVE THANKS" because "WE ARE RECEIVING AN UNSHAK-ABLE KINGDOM," where we will enjoy not only the presence of God himself, but also "MYRIADS OF ANGELS," the whole Church, and "THE SPIRITS OF THE RIGHTEOUS, WHO HAVE BEEN MADE PERFECT" (Old Testament saints).

Chapter thirteen ends the letter with final instructions about carrying out "THE GREATEST OF THESE" (1 Corinthians 13:13) – love. The writer insisted that "BROTHERLY LOVE MUST CONTINUE" (vs. 1). Without giving a lot of detail, the writer offered some very practical ways that we can love one another – in-home hospitality (vs. 2)[176]; believers in prison (vs. 3); strong, godly marriages (vs. 4); contentment, rather than greed and covetousness (vs. 5-6); support of church leadership, especially those who teach faithfully (vs. 7-9, 17); and sharing with the poor (vs. 16).

Most of these instructions deal directly with our local church communities.[177] We will not live well in an increasingly wicked and hostile world without close relationships in our local churches. The writer already emphasized the increasing importance of Christian gatherings as we get closer to Jesus' return (10:25). Christians who do not prioritize gathering with their church community do damage to their spiritual maturity.

The writer finished his letter with specific prayer requests (vs. 18-19) and a benediction, praying that God would grow them in the outworking of his will (vs. 20-21).

The closing description of Jesus as "THE GREAT SHEPHERD OF THE SHEEP" is an appropriate conclusion for this letter. As the Son (chapter one), Jesus is Jehovah "MY SHEPHERD" (Psalm 23:1). As the Man (chapters 2-4), he was the "GOOD SHEPHERD [WHO] LAYS DOWN HIS LIFE FOR THE SHEEP" (John 10:11). And as the High Priest (chapters 5-10), he is the one who

---

176 "SOME HAVE ENTERTAINED ANGELS" is often linked to Abraham's hospitality in Genesis 18, but there are other occasions in the Hebrew Scriptures where this occurred as well (see Genesis 19 and Judges 6 and 13 for other examples).

177 Throughout the New Testament, "brotherly love" and "one another" always refer to fellow Christians, not unbelievers. Although Christians should certainly serve unbelievers when possible (Galatians 6:10), our primary responsibility toward them is to share the gospel, whereas ministry is always directed toward other believers.

provided life and sustains his sheep by offering his own life, instead of sheep and goats, to "EQUIP [US] WITH EVERY GOOD THING TO DO HIS WILL."

"TO HIM BE GLORY FOREVER. AMEN."

James

James was probably the first or second (behind Matthew) New Testament writer (approximately the early- to mid-A.D. 40s). He followed the pattern of Old Testament exhortation (especially the prophets and proverbs), and his letter has been compared to Jesus' Sermon on the Mount for that reason. James wrote this letter to Christian Jews who had been dispersed from Israel during the early persecution of the Church (see Acts 8) to encourage them to live out their Christian faith, especially in the face of their trials. Thus, the major theme of the letter is the active demonstration of faith through good works.

The main question of James is not about the content of the letter (although a few passages have generated quite a bit of debate) but about James himself. There are three James named in Scripture who were connected to the Early Church, yet since the writer did not attempt to give specific identification, the question of "who" has been long-debated. Only one of the three, however, has the best support.

Two of the twelve apostles were named James, which would naturally lend credibility. However, both are consistently mentioned in Scripture with descriptions. One was "JAMES, THE SON OF ALPHEUS." The other was "JAMES,

THE SON OF ZEBEDEE" often connected to his brother, John (Matthew 10:2-3). Neither is mentioned even once without this type of clarification.

The third James, however, is referenced differently. He was not one of the Twelve, so he did not always need identification, yet when he was distinguished, it always was done in such a way as to elevate him. In his resurrection account, Luke called Jesus' mother "MARY, THE MOTHER OF JAMES" with no other clarification (Luke 24:10). After "JAMES, THE BROTHER OF JOHN" was martyred (Acts 12:2), Peter, Paul, the other apostles, the Jerusalem church elders, and many others deferred to James' leadership on several occasions (Acts 12:17; 15:13; 21:18). Paul told the Corinthians that James was granted a special appearance by Jesus on his resurrection day (1 Corinthians 15:7). Finally, in Galatians 1:19, Paul clarifies that this James was "THE LORD'S BROTHER," matching Luke's identification of his being Mary's son (see Matthew 13:55). Thus, it seems that Jesus commissioned his half-brother (son of Joseph and Mary) to become one of the "PILLARS" – probably the "Lead Pastor" or "Chief Elder" – of the Jerusalem church (Galatians 2:9). For this reason, he would have had no need to further identify himself to those believers who had scattered from Jerusalem. This James was most likely the writer.

Chapter one begins very abruptly with a short greeting and quick encouragement. These believing Jews had been displaced from their homeland and had lost their close-knit Christian family. Even though their immediate persecution had stopped, they found themselves facing a new persecution that was both anti-Semitic and anti-Christian. They were certainly tempted to give up their faith to blend into their new communities as much as possible.

James offered them three reasons to not give up and, instead, to embrace the trials they were facing. First, he knew that their trials would cause them to become stronger in their faith and more dependent on God (vs. 2-8). This dependence, visible by their growing wisdom in approaching that persecution, would continue to stabilize them and their faith. Second, even though their persecution was temporary, he knew that their spiritual growth would be eternal and will be rewarded by God himself (vs. 9-18). He reminded them that God does not tempt us with evil intent; that comes from our innate sinfulness. Instead, God gives good gifts to help us grow, which is his unchanging plan. Third, he wanted these trials to drive them back to the Scriptures, which would point out specific areas in which they needed to grow (vs. 19-27). James warned them to not get angry over their circumstances and ignore this reflection, but instead, use the opportunity to live out Scripture teachings, especially in their interaction with each other. Loving their fellow Christians in tangible ways would help them grow in and through their difficult times.

Chapter two continues James' focus on doing good works, especially to the poor mentioned in 1:27. There is no place for class warfare within the Christian community (vs. 1-13). What a person owns or wears should not affect his place in the assembly. Wealth was often considered to be God's favor on a person, but James meant to correct that mistaken concept. James gave Moses' and Jesus' command to "LOVE YOUR NEIGHBOR AS YOURSELF" the title, "THE ROYAL LAW" (vs. 8). There is no higher love than that of unselfishness and watching for the interest of others (see Philippians 2:1-8).

Verse ten is often misunderstood to mean that "all sins are the same in God's sight." James' point that "ONE WHO...FAILS IN ONE POINT HAS BECOME GUILTY OF ALL OF" the law does not mean that all sins are equal. The law itself, with its levels of punishment, proved that some sins are weightier than others. James' point was that a person could either be completely right with the law or a law-breaker, but not both, and that not loving one's neighbor is as much a violation of the law as adultery and murder, even if they did not carry the same punishment. Lesser crimes, like prejudice, were still violations of God's perfect standard.

The rest of chapter two contains one of the most debated passages in the New Testament. Having been saved because of Paul's teaching of justification through faith alone in Romans, Martin Luther famously disregarded James as apparently teaching justification through good works. The key to proper interpretation is found in verses 22 and 23. By quoting Genesis 15:6, James and Paul both agreed that a person is saved through faith alone; however, God did not mean for faith to stand alone. Genuine saving faith should produce life change that results in good works (although not every saved person matures as they should), which "perfect" or "complete" that faith (2:22). Thus, faith and good works work together, not *for* salvation, but *in* salvation. Faith is just the first step in the life-long process of spiritual maturity.

Chapter three's teaching on the power of the tongue seems to be disconnected to its context (vs. 1-12). However, its "size-to-impact ratio" concept could point back to chapter two, where not loving one's neighbor (a "small" sin) has a profound impact within the Christian community. Likewise, the tongue, a small member of the body, can greatly affect those around us, either building up for good or tearing down for bad. The life change that faith should bring (end of chapter two) should harness the power of the tongue for good. James could not understand how a believer could use his tongue for both good and evil, blessing God yet cursing his people.

The end of chapter three and the first paragraph of chapter four go together, bridging the power of the tongue to practical teaching about Christian speech. Each of these paragraphs begins with a question. The first is "Who is wise and understanding among you?" (vs. 13-18). Godly wisdom is to exhibit itself in good works done in gentleness toward those around us. Bitterness, jealousy, and the like demonstrate selfishness, the opposite of the royal law, leading to discord within the assembly. Godly wisdom, however, leads to peace and righteousness.

Chapter four opens with the second bridge question (starting in 3:13): "WHERE DO THE CONFLICTS AND WHERE DO THE QUARRELS AMONG YOU COME FROM?" (vs. 1-3) The obvious answer would be, "From selfishness," which is exactly what James answered. Even in our prayers, if we ask with selfish motives, God is unlikely to grant what we desire.

Reminiscent of the Hebrew prophets, James called his readers spiritual "ADULTERERS," those who cheat on God by chasing the world and its ungodly suggestions (vs. 4-10). Probably just a few years later Paul would write, "THE FLESH HAS DESIRES THAT ARE OPPOSED TO THE SPIRIT, AND THE SPIRIT HAS DESIRES THAT ARE OPPOSED TO THE FLESH, FOR THESE ARE IN OPPOSITION TO EACH OTHER" (Galatians 5:17). James gave only one solution – the same as Paul's: submit wholly to God, humble oneself completely to him, and confess sin. ("Clean hands" is a common metaphor in the Hebrew Scriptures for confession of sins.)

James concluded this section with another focus on specific speech (vs. 11-17). Speaking against a fellow believer is to judge where God has not judged. Paul would later expand on this in his teachings on a believer's conscience (see Romans 14, for example). Where God has not spoken, a believer does not have the right to speak. This submission to God and his Word applies to our own decisions as well. A life of full submission will hold plans with an open hand, allowing God to lead as he desires. Ultimately, any decision or action that is not done in faith is sin.

Chapter five concludes this letter with a series of topics, all designed to be final encouragements to James' readers. Verses 1-6 contain a two-part negative encouragement, patterned after the Hebrew prophets who would encourage their immediate listeners by prophesying judgment on their oppressors (e.g., Amos and Nahum). First, James' oppressed readers would certainly be encouraged to know that God knew of their suffering. Second,

James' oppressive readers would be encouraged to change their ways (do good deeds) in light of God's view of their current actions.

Considering God's awareness of their situation, verses 7-12 emphasize patience in this life. James used some form of the words *patience, wait,* and *endurance* at least seven times in this paragraph. He used examples of a farmer waiting for his crop, the prophets enduring through their suffering, and the perennial favorite – Job, a model of endurance. James was intentional to point out that Job's suffering was in line with God's purpose, and that God repeatedly shows himself to be compassionate and merciful.

The final verses refer to prayer, specifically prayer of confession and spiritual restoration (vs. 13-20). Although some teachers attempt to use this section to guarantee supernatural healings, that is not a legitimate interpretation. The emphasis is on the believers' spiritual state (the Greek words behind both "ILL" and "SICK" can mean either physical or spiritual illness, vs. 14-15), confession (vs. 16), and wandering from the truth (vs. 19-20). So, James concluded his letter encouraging his readers to pray for each other so they may stay true to their faith and complete it by an outworking of godly lifestyles.

1 Peter

Peter's intended recipients were people scattered throughout Asia Minor. The word διασπορά (*diaspora*, "dispersion") is used elsewhere in the New Testament only twice. In James 1:1 the "TWELVE TRIBES" are specified, and in John 7:25 it refers to Jews dispersed "AMONG THE GREEKS." Although 1 Peter contains principles available for all Christians of all time, since Peter was acknowledged to be the apostle to the Jewish people (Galatians 2:7) and since the word διασπορά was used to refer to Jews outside of Israel, it is likely that this letter was originally written specifically to Jewish believers.

However, this possibility has been debated and at least two solid arguments support the view that Gentile Christians may have been in view. First, διασπορά does not have an article ("the"), meaning that it does not necessarily refer to a specific "dispersion." It could easily refer to all Christians scattered throughout the pagan world. Second, Peter stated that his readers were once heavily involved in pagan lifestyles (4:3-4), which would have been unlikely even for unsaved Jews.[178] Thus, although Peter may have intended

---

178 As the Hebrew Prophets show, idolatry was the overarching reason Israel was taken into captivity by Assyria and Babylon. The Israelites knew this and, after the exile, idolatry and paganism never again became a national problem for Israel. It is possible or likely that some individual Jews participated in it again by Paul's and Peter's time, but they would have been the exception, not the rule.

this letter for Jewish believers, he probably knew that Gentiles would read it as well. Again, there are certainly principles that still apply to all believers in the Church Age.

Peter's final greeting (5:12-13) includes three important pieces of information. First, Peter wrote this letter "THROUGH SILVANUS." This name appears alongside Paul and Timothy in the greetings of 1 and 2 Thessalonians and 2 Corinthians 1:9 and is almost unanimously acknowledged to be the man Luke called Silas throughout the book of Acts. (The name "Silas" appears only twelve times, all of them in Acts 15:22–18:5, and all of them in conjunction with Paul or Paul and Timothy.) Silas was a Roman citizen (Acts 16:37), a leader in the Gentile church in Antioch of Syria (Acts 15:22), and a prophet (Acts 15:32). He was Paul's co-worker and probably an outspoken preacher since he and Paul were imprisoned together in Philippi while Luke and Timothy were not. It seems possible that Silas/Silvanus had a hand in composing Peter's letter as well as Paul's Thessalonian letters.

Second, Peter sent greetings to his readers from "THE CHURCH IN BABYLON." This has generated a great deal of debate over the centuries. The tradition that Peter ended his ministry in Rome has given rise to the speculation that "Babylon" is meant to be code for "Rome." If he wrote during the early stages of Nero's persecution of Christians, it would certainly be advantageous if the Emperor did not know that the great apostle was within his grasp. The letter's primary theme of bearing up under persecution gives weight to this timeframe.

Another option is that Peter used Babylon figuratively to mean any place of exile. For Jewish readers, Babylon would invoke memories of their national exile in Babylon in the 7th century B.C. This option has support in the concept of the "DISPERSION" (1:1), that he called them "FOREIGNERS AND EXILES...AMONG THE NON-CHRISTIANS" (2:11-12), and his reference to "YOUR BROTHERS AND SISTERS THROUGHOUT THE WORLD" (5:9). Some have insisted that he literally went to Babylon in Persia (Iraq) and while that is the natural reading, there is little in church history or tradition to support it. Regardless, there is nothing in the text itself to solve the issue satisfactorily.

Third, Peter mentioned that Mark was with him and called him "MY SON." This Mark must refer to John Mark, who traveled with Barnabas and Paul for part of their first missionary journey (Acts 12:25). Although he deserted them (Acts 13:13; 15:37-38), Mark continued his spiritual growth and ministry with Barnabas (Acts 15:39-40) and eventually became very useful to Paul (2 Timothy 4:11). Church tradition records that it was this Mark who wrote the Gospel of Mark during his time with Peter. It is possible that he became to Peter what Timothy was to Paul. Peter's use of "MY SON" is reminiscent of Paul's feelings toward Timothy (1 Timothy 1:2; 2 Timothy 1:2) and Titus (1:4). Mark must have had a significant ministry after his time with Paul and Barnabas for him to have been known to the believers throughout Asia Minor reading Peter's letter.

Chapter one begins with a celebration of our salvation in Christ. Peter called it a "NEW BIRTH," a "LIVING HOPE," and "AN INHERITANCE IMPERISHABLE, UNDEFILED, AND UNFADING" that "IS RESERVED IN HEAVEN FOR [US]" (vs. 3-4). Additionally, those who are believers in Christ "ARE PROTECTED" for a deliverance that will come in the future (vs. 5). It was important that his readers knew of God's eternal protection because Peter reminded them that it might be necessary to suffer in this life (vs. 6-9). This suffering, however, is only temporary and accomplishes a spiritual purification leading to the final salvation of our souls.

Similar to Paul's insistence that the Church was a "MYSTERY THAT HAS BEEN KEPT HIDDEN FROM AGES AND GENERATIONS," Peter noted that the ancient prophets could not understand everything they spoke about, no matter how hard they tried, and that even angels "LONG TO CATCH A GLIMPSE OF" this salvation that was never offered to or provided for them (vs. 10-12).

Because of God's current focus on the Church, Peter insisted that his readers live out God's grace as experienced through the indwelling Holy Spirit and become what God has designed us to be – holy like himself (vs. 13-16). Our special relationship with God as Father motivates it (vs. 17). Our redemption through Jesus' blood demands it (vs. 18-21). What does this type of lifestyle look like? First, we should treat each other with God's own love (vs. 22). Second, we should remove what is obviously evil from our lives (2:1). Third, we should feast on the Scriptures, which will cause us spiritual growth (2:2-3).

Chapter two best starts in verse four. (The first three verses connect to chapter one.) Here Peter laid out the reason to live properly in this world and gave some practical examples of what that should look like. His reason is very simple: our relation to Jesus. Peter portrayed Jesus as a stone lying on the ground. For unbelievers, he is "A STUMBLING-STONE AND A ROCK TO TRIP OVER" (vs. 8). For believers, however, he is a foundation on which we "AS LIVING STONES, ARE BUILT UP AS A SPIRITUAL HOUSE" (vs. 5). Because we are "NOW…GOD'S PEOPLE" who "HAVE RECEIVED MERCY" (vs. 10), we should "MAINTAIN GOOD CONDUCT AMONG NON-CHRISTIANS, SO THAT…THEY MAY SEE [OUR] GOOD DEEDS AND GLORIFY GOD WHEN HE APPEARS" (vs. 12).

Practically speaking, this means that, even though we are in this godless world, Christians are to obey governing authorities (vs. 13-17), using any freedoms we have to serve God and each other. In those situations when we do not have freedom, we must live under subjection of the human government but in the fear of God, obeying them even if they persecute us for our faith (vs. 18-20). Peter considered that kind of persecution to be an honor because it would imitate Jesus, who suffered though he lived perfectly (2:21-25).

Chapter three continues Peter's examples of living out Christlikeness, beginning in our marriages. Believing wives should let their Christian nature be their defining feature, especially in how they treat their husbands. This testimony is so powerful that it could turn unbelieving husbands to the gospel. Husbands, on the other hand, are to be worthy of their wives' respect and treat them respectfully as full partners in this life. Peter warned that mistreating one's wife is actually a hindrance in a man's relationship with God.

Peter wrapped up his exhortation toward godly practice with general statements like Paul's in Romans 12. As his basis Peter quoted from Psalm 34, emphasizing again that our prayers to God are affected by the way we choose to live. Christians who are not in line with God find him standing against them. Rather than God standing against us for living wickedly, it is better to have unbelievers stand against us for living righteously. Because not every unbeliever will persecute a believer, a godly lifestyle can be a catalyst to sharing the gospel with those who are open, so we should share our "HOPE... WITH COURTESY AND RESPECT." Finally, Peter reminded his readers that even Jesus himself suffered for doing what was right, and he still fulfilled everything God called him to do, including our present and future salvation.

Chapter four picks up immediately with the practical application for Christians based on Christ's suffering: stay focused on God's will rather than our fleshly desires. Peter's audience had been saved long enough that their lifestyles should have reflected the life change (vs. 3-6). Another encouragement to live in a godly manner is that Jesus' return is imminent. This lifestyle should include prayer, hospitality, and Christian service.

Verse 11 ends with a benediction leading many scholars to believe that it was the letter's original closing. The final paragraph of chapter four and the entirety of chapter five could mean that 1) Peter came back and added it later, 2) he began closing the letter at 4:11, or 3) someone else added everything after 4:11. Either of the first two options are acceptable, with neither affecting the interpretation or intent of the letter.

The final paragraph, verses 12-19, contains an encouragement to all who were and are suffering trial of some kind because of their faith. Peter's encouragement was three-fold: 1) his readers were not alone (vs. 12), 2) their reward will be proportionate to their suffering when Christ comes (vs. 13), and 3) suffering for Christ is proof of the Holy Spirit's indwelling (vs. 14).

Chapter five opens with an exhortation to local church elders (vs. 1-4). Although Peter called himself a "FELLOW ELDER," there is no indication in Scripture that he served in that role in a local church.[179] He could have meant that in a comparative meaning, because, although he may have functioned in a pastoral role in various churches, being one of the Twelve would have granted him more apostolic authority than typically granted an elder. Peter's encouragement to elders complements what Paul wrote in 1 Timothy 3 and Titus 1.

Peter closed his letter with a series of final exhortations for those not leading local churches (but they apply to all believers). First, we are to submit ourselves to church elders (vs. 5a). Second, we should act humbly toward fellow believers (vs. 5b-7). Third, we must resist the enemy by remaining strong in the faith (vs. 8-9). Fourth, we are to remember that God uses suffering to strengthen us (vs. 10-11). We explored the final greeting in detail in the introduction (vs. 12-14).

---

179 Acts 15 shows that there was a clear distinction between the apostles and the elders in the Jerusalem Church.

2 Peter

No New Testament book was more disputed by the Early Church regarding authorship and authenticity than 2 Peter. The similarities between chapter two and Jude's letter have caused scholars to question whether Peter borrowed from Jude, Jude from Peter, or if they both borrowed from another common source. There are at least three strong reasons that support Peter as the genuine author of this letter and that he wrote before Jude.

First, there is some difference in the language used between 1 and 2 Peter. On the one hand, if 2 Peter were a forgery, someone simply using Peter's name for credibility would have attempted to make it sound as much as possible like the letter already received and trusted. The difference in language, in fact, supports its authenticity. On the other hand, the differences are not so great as to obviously come from two different people. A comparison of 2 Peter with Peter's sermons recorded in Acts reveal similar language, although he preached them twenty years earlier. Thus, the similarities point to an older, more mature version of the same speaker/writer.

Second, Peter's account of the Transfiguration in 1:16-19 seems to be a personal reflection, not just a repeat of the accounts in Matthew, Mark, and Luke – each of whom wrote about that second-hand.[180] Since there is nothing like that in Acts or 1 Peter, it seems unlikely that a forger would try to credit that to Peter, supporting the case that this is Peter's own letter.

Third, like the other later writers (Hebrews, Jude, John, and even Paul's later writings), Peter was concerned about the false teachers that would certainly infiltrate the church (2:1-3; 3:3-4). However, whereas in Peter, Hebrews (13:9), and Paul (Acts 20:28-30) these teachers were still future, Jude and John referred to them as already present in the churches (Jude 4, 17-19; 1 John 4:1-6). Thus, it is reasonable to conclude that Jude followed Peter and that he quoted from Peter in Jude 6-13 and 17-18, as he fought against those Peter only prophesied.

This last reason also points to the primary theme of 2 Peter: **truth versus falsehood**. Throughout this short letter, starting even in the second verse, Peter repeatedly emphasized the importance of growing in our knowledge of God and Jesus. Though knowledge itself is not the only step in our spiritual growth, we have no recourse against false teachers without the full knowledge of God as revealed in the Scriptures (1:20-21). This "FULL KNOWLEDGE" (1:2, 3, 5, 8) is not to be confused with the cultic ideas of "secret" knowledge accessible to a select few. All believers (1:1) have access to the full knowledge of God because God has made it readily available to us.

Chapter one begins by presenting the path or process of spiritual growth in a succinct way. After stating that God had already granted believers "EVERYTHING NECESSARY FOR LIFE AND GODLINESS" (vs. 3), Peter commanded that we add to our saving faith seven qualities, each one cementing and building on the previous and producing the next (vs. 5-7). This process is based on our pursuit of truly coming to know Jesus better and love him more, without which we wander through this life blindly, forgetting God's

---

180 Even though Matthew was one of the Twelve, he was not at the Transfiguration, and Jesus told Peter, James, and John to not talk about it until after the Resurrection (Matthew 17:9).

past grace and unable to see his promised future (vs. 9-11).

Knowing that he would die soon (vs. 14-15), Peter wrote this letter to make sure that his followers focused on the one thing that matters: knowing Jesus. (Some scholars believe Peter's "TESTIMONY" also meant Mark's Gospel, which is traditionally understood to have been Peter's account.) For them to accomplish this, Peter insisted that they not rely on personal testimonies, even his own eyewitness account of Jesus' Transfiguration (vs. 16-18). Instead, he pointed them to the Scriptures, the timeless account that was created by the Holy Spirit himself (vs. 19-21). Peter called these "AN ALTOGETHER RELIABLE" witness, something that they all had. Not only were the Hebrew Scriptures complete and available, the Greek apostolic writings were becoming more and more available (see Peter's comment on Paul's letters in 3:15-16), verifying that the older prophecies had come true in Christ: "IN THESE LAST DAYS HE HAS SPOKEN TO US IN A SON" (Hebrews 1:2).

Chapter two paints a picture of false teachers and their teaching as opposed to the true teaching presented in chapter one. Essentially, chapter two is one long excoriation of those that Peter predicted would eventually make their way into the church to pervert it. Using well-known stories from the Hebrew Scriptures, Peter compared the coming false teachers to "THE ANGELS WHO SINNED" (vs. 4), "THE ANCIENT WORLD [OF] NOAH" (vs. 5), and "SODOM AND GOMORRAH" (vs. 6), all of whom suffered extreme judgment by God. He called them "BRAZEN AND INSOLENT" (vs. 10) and "CURSED CHILDREN" (vs. 14), comparing them to "IRRATIONAL ANIMALS" (vs. 12) and "WATERLESS SPRINGS" (vs. 17), and stated that they would have been better off not knowing the truth than turning away from it (vs. 21).

The reason for all this is because their teaching cuts out the very heart of truth, "EVEN TO THE POINT OF DENYING THE MASTER WHO BOUGHT THEM" (vs. 1). Though their message promotes freedom (vs. 19), their lives exhibit greed (vs. 3), adultery (vs. 14), debauchery (vs. 18), and immorality (vs. 19). They even practice what they preach, encouraging their followers to throw off the demands of Christ and wallow in "THE FILTHY THINGS OF THE WORLD" (vs. 20) like dogs and pigs (vs. 22). Peter said these would be accepted into the church and praised rather than condemned. There is no doubt that prophecy has proven true.

Chapter three begins with the same phrase as in 1:13. Peter's goal was to "STIR UP" his readers "BY WAY OF REMINDER," cementing in their minds the correct method of spiritual growth (1:5-7), the source of truth (1:20-21), and the dangers of being weak in truth (2:1-22). In wrapping up his letter, Peter noted that standing firm for the truth of Scripture would draw the attention of those who mock the truth (vs. 3-4). Like Paul's assessment in Romans 1:18-19, Peter wrote that this mocking comes from a deliberate suppression and rejection of the truth that God has made clear to everyone (vs. 5).

One of the arguments the mockers will use is that nothing seems to change[181], that God does not seem to move so he must not truly exist, and believers are simpletons for believing such nonsense. Peter comforted his readers by reminding them that God is not bound by time, and, because of his infinite longsuffering and desire for all to be saved, he will hold off his judgment until just the right time (vs. 8-9). However, when that time does come, his judgment will be swift and strong, and nothing will be able to stand against it. This should cause all believers to follow the path of spiritual growth God has given us, as we await the fulfillment of his promises (vs. 10-13). Peter mentioned that even Paul's letters were already being misused and misunderstood, just like the other words given by God. By saying this, Peter publicly acknowledged Paul's apostolic authority and placed him on the same level as the Hebrew prophets who spoke from God (cf. 1:21). He

---

181 This is the same argument used by evolutionists today called "uniformitarianism." They hold that "the present is the key to the past," so whatever is happening today must have always occurred the same way. It is this belief, ignoring the miraculous events of an instantaneous Creation and catastrophic global Flood, that allows them to promote a theory that the Earth is billions of years old and that evolution accounts for what we observe today.

closed with a final encouragement to hold fast to the truth and a command that we should grow in both the grace and knowledge of Jesus, a balance that is not always well-maintained.

1 John

Since there is no name given, the authorship of next three letters has been debated. However, they traditionally are attributed to the apostle John for several good reasons. First, the language of the letters and the gospel is overwhelmingly similar, in some ways more so than even between Paul's letters. Second, the issues addressed reflect a period late enough in the Church's life that some doctrines were already considered "old," yet early enough that the attacks on doctrine were still relatively new. Third, some of the Early Fathers who were personally close to John connect these letters to him.

Again, without a greeting, no recipients are mentioned in either. Second John is addressed to "AN ELECT LADY AND HER CHILDREN," while 3 John was clearly written to Gaius, a dear friend. Technically, then, at least two of these are not "general" epistles, a classification often given to the books of Hebrews through Jude, because of their general nature and unknown recipients.

First John is notoriously difficult to outline, because, rather than flowing from one thought into the next, John carried multiple themes throughout, blending them together. However, that does not mean there is no structure at all; there are, in fact, three keys to understanding this letter. First, four times John declared, "I [OR, WE] AM WRITING THESE THINGS TO YOU" for a stated purpose, primarily that we can know that we know God (1:4; 2:1, 12; 5:13). Second, based on the theme that we can truly know God, John gave a series of "tests" to determine how well we know God. Each of these is set as a contrast between knowing God and not knowing him (1:6-7, 8-9; 1:10–2:2; 2:3-6, 9-11, 15-17, 24-27; 3:4-10, 15-17; 4:7-10, 15-16; 4:20–5:4). Third, based on these "tests" of how well we know God, it is important to understand that 1 John presents the Christian ideal in a series of black and white statements. Many people have been tripped up by this short letter because of its harsh commands, leaving no gray areas. These will be explored further in each chapter. Suffice it to say that the one who would truly know God completely would also truly live in complete perfection. However, even John acknowledged early on that this was impossible, yet something to strive for (2:1-2).

Chapter one, with no introduction, jumps directly into arguing two primary points. First, it seems that John intended to debunk the fledgling Gnostic ideas regarding the spirit and the flesh. Based in Platonic dualism, Gnostics taught that the spirit/immaterial was good, but the flesh/material was bad. Some had even started teaching that Jesus did not and could not have come in the flesh and physically died (see 4:1-6). John opened with a series of phrases arguing that not only had Jesus come in the flesh, but John was also one of those who "HEARD...[SAW] WITH OUR EYES...LOOKED AT... HANDS TOUCHED" the genuinely physical Jesus (vs. 1; John 1:14). Jesus became everything we are to reveal God to us (vs. 2; John 1:18).

Second, John presented the gospel message: who Jesus is and what he did/does. He is the eternal light of the world that expels darkness (vs. 5-7; John 1:4-10; 8:12). Those who believe in him are to walk in his light to remain in fellowship with God and other believers. The first few tests of knowing him have to do with the recognition of our own sinfulness. When we are walking in his light, he will continue to cleanse us, as we confess our sin. Not confessing, on the other hand, is the same as claiming perfection, which is essentially the same as calling God a liar.

It is best to include 2:1-2 with chapter one. As much as John would have liked his readers to not sin, he knew that was an impossibility. Most English Bibles read "IF ANYONE DOES SIN" in 2:1, but this is a third class conditional sentence, which assumes that the hypothetical "if" could come true at some point in the future. Jesus' never-ending advocacy before the Father on our behalf when we confess our sin is meant to be an encouragement, so "WHEN ANYONE DOES SIN" seems to convey John's point more appropriately than simply "if."

Chapter two, beginning with verse three, presents the first of six "BY THIS WE [WILL] KNOW" statements (2:3, 5; 3:19, 24; 4:13; 5:2) demonstrating how we know that we know God or are in him. In chapter two we know this "IF WE KEEP HIS COMMANDMENTS...[AND] OBEY HIS WORD" (vs. 3, 5). Obedience to the Savior (not just obedience to a set of rules) is a clear indication that a person truly knows God because an unbeliever walks in darkness, not in the light. However, again, verse six encourages that the believer "OUGHT TO WALK" this way. Those who require that the spiritual ideal presented in 1 John must be the continued real experience for all believers at all stages of growth as proof of salvation are misusing the Scriptures. Even as he presented the ideal, John did so with grace and encouragement, knowing that we do not always live up to that standard.

In verses 7-17, John insisted that believers are to love God and that love should extend to fellow Christians. Not loving (or "HATING") other believers is likened to stumbling and groping around in the dark because that Christian is not walking in Christ's light. Jesus himself said, "EVERYONE WILL KNOW BY THIS THAT YOU ARE MY DISCIPLES – IF YOU HAVE LOVE FOR ONE ANOTHER" (John 13:35).

Another proof that a believer does not love God properly is shown in his love for "THE WORLD OR THE THINGS IN THE WORLD" (vs. 15). Because "THE WHOLE WORLD LIES IN THE POWER OF THE EVIL ONE" (5:19), spiritual growth should cause us to love God more while we love this world less. This reflects a worldview based on eternal things rather than temporal things.

Like several other writers before him (Paul, Peter, and Jude), John knew that false teachers are devastating to Christians. Because of how late he wrote (probably in the A.D. 90s), John saw these false teachers no longer just sneaking into the Church (Jude 4) but boldly teaching false doctrine from within the Church. He said there were "MANY" of them (2:18) who had exerted their influence strongly enough that they had left the Christian fellowship and had drawn others away with them. John insisted that there is one "litmus test" of basic orthodoxy (2:22; 4:1-3): **Jesus is the Christ (recognition of deity) who had come in the flesh (recognition of humanity).** Although much other doctrine is important, nothing else matters if there is disagreement on this point. This truth was the teaching of Jesus himself, the apostles, and the indwelling Holy Spirit (vs. 27).

Chapter three, especially the first half, is the most troublesome part of the letter for many people. John's declarations are bold, even harsh, and leave no room for mistakes. "EVERYONE WHO SINS HAS NEITHER SEEN HIM NOR KNOWN HIM" (vs. 6). "EVERYONE WHO DOES NOT PRACTICE RIGHTEOUS-NESS...IS NOT OF GOD" (vs. 10). However, as chapter two proved, the ideal is not always the real. John knew that his readers would continue to sin, but he did not want them to think that was to be shrugged off as "human nature." No, those fathered by God are not bound by "human nature"; we have a divine nature that is at work in us. John insisted that God's goal be our goal, even though we continue to fail miserably. Another consideration is the truth that when we are remaining in Christ (see John 15:1-8), we will not sin, because the Holy Spirit never leads us to sin. Thus, John could legitimately write, "EVERYONE WHO REMAINS IN HIM DOES NOT SIN" (vs. 6).

If the first half of the chapter is the negative side – what the Christian life should not include, the second half is the positive side – what it should include, namely, love for our fellow Christians. Using Cain as his example, John wrote that hating a fellow believer ("BROTHER") is akin to murder. Again, this makes sense. Murder is wrong because God made people in his image (Genesis 9:6). Hate separates people, essentially throwing a believer – someone in Christ's image – back to the world which hates him (vs. 13); it is spiritual homicide, something that cannot be done by someone who is actively living out God's love. This includes shutting off help in time of need (vs. 17). Christian love must necessarily be more than a kind word, something it was already devolving into in John's day.

Chapter four picks up on John's mention of the Holy Spirit in 3:24. Paul wrote that the Spirit is God's seal of salvation (Ephesians 1:13-14) and assurance of our relationship with God (Romans 8:16). John agreed. The Spirit is the internal evidence that we know God, while our obedience is the external (3:24). One of the primary ways the Spirit works is that he changes our understanding and beliefs. In verses 1-3, John gave the test of "who Jesus is" as proof of the Spirit's indwelling. Only a believer can fully agree with Jesus' full deity and full humanity, and John wrote that anyone who fails that test comes from a spirit of antichrist, not the Holy Spirit. Our basic beliefs reveal our spiritual state (vs. 6).

Coming back to the theme of loving one another, John gave another proof of genuine salvation. Only those who are God's children can exhibit God's love (vs. 8). The reason is that because a person cannot give what he does not have, and only a believer has experienced God's love and saving grace (vs. 10), only a believer can share it. Thus, because we are recipients of God's love, we are obligated to share that with fellow recipients (vs. 11). Not only is hating a fellow believer likened to murder (3:15), this ungodly action proves to be a lie because we cannot love God while hating his family (vs.

20). Again, this is the standard that God calls us to, even though we do not always fulfill it faithfully. So, following the blunt ideal, John couched it in the language of obligation: "THE ONE WHO LOVES GOD SHOULD LOVE HIS FELLOW CHRISTIAN TOO" (4:21).

Chapter five continues the themes of obeying God's commandments and loving one another because of God's love for us (vs. 1-4). Adding to this, John introduced the concept of the opposing world system. This system, he declared, wholly "LIES IN THE POWER OF THE EVIL ONE" (vs. 19). This should not be cause for alarm, however, because our faith in Christ "IS THE CONQUERING POWER THAT HAS CONQUERED THE WORLD" (vs. 4). John had written earlier that Jesus came "TO DESTROY THE WORKS OF THE DEVIL" (3:8), so we have no need to fear him or his world, "BECAUSE EVERYONE WHO HAS BEEN FATHERED BY GOD CONQUERS THE WORLD" (vs. 4) and "THE EVIL ONE CANNOT TOUCH HIM" (vs. 18). Instead, we can rely completely on Christ's promise, namely that "GOD HAS GIVEN US ETERNAL LIFE, AND THIS LIFE IS IN HIS SON" (vs. 11). In fact, this was John's final major reason for writing: "THAT YOU MAY KNOW THAT YOU HAVE ETERNAL LIFE" (vs. 13).

The final section includes three parts. First, John quoted Jesus' words from John 15:7. When we are remaining in him, we can ask anything in his will, and it will be granted (vs. 14-15). These requests and answers are proof that we are remaining close to him. Second, there will be some who leave the fellowship because of unrepentance. Rather than bearing fruit (John 15:1-8), their sin brings them down, possibly even to death (vs. 16-17). Third, once we acknowledge the only true God, anything that takes his place in our value system in an idol. "LITTLE CHILDREN GUARD YOURSELVES FROM IDOLS" (vs. 20-21).

2 John

Unlike 1 John, which had no clear recipient, 2 John was addressed to "AN ELECT LADY AND HER CHILDREN" (vs. 1). There are three common interpretations of this greeting. First, John could have been writing to all believers. However, this does not explain the difference between the lady, her children, and her sister (vs. 13). Second, the "lady" could be a specific local church or group of churches. In this case, the "children" would be the Christian members of that church or region, and the "sister" would be a different church or region. Third, the recipient could have been a literal "lady" with "children." She may have been wealthy, even hosting a local church in her home. This could explain how "ALL THOSE WHO KNOW THE TRUTH" (vs. 1) may have known and loved her. Some proponents of this view believe "ELECT LADY" could reflect her proper name, *Kyria* or *Electa*, or even a title *Lady Electa*. One of these options may best explain her sister mentioned at the end.

Following his opening greeting, John clarified something that he seemed to leave open in 1 John. His first letter frequently commanded that believers love one another. In this letter, he defined what that means: "Now THIS IS LOVE: THAT WE WALK ACCORDING TO HIS COMMANDMENTS" (vs. 6).

When we obey God, we are showing our love for him by living out his love toward other Christians (John 13:35).

The middle section is a warning against false teachers, much like 1 John 4:1-3. The spirit of antichrist drives those who deny who Jesus truly is. Because these teachers were on the loose, moving from city to city and church to church, John warned that this lady not welcome them into her home (probably where the church met) or give them a platform to spew their demonic message. Christian hospitality does not extend to wolves who are looking to devour the sheep. In fact, she would be complicit in their error if she knowingly allowed them access to that congregation (vs. 10-11). For those who insist that Christians are not to judge others at all, this passage is a great encouragement that we are to examine the doctrine that people bring us to determine whether it is healthy or harmful.

The closing is a wonderful reminder that this is a letter from one real person to another. More than just an ancient, faceless apostle, John was a man who loved God and loved the Church enough to pick up "PAPER AND INK" to warn from a distance and to "COME VISIT...AND SPEAK FACE TO FACE" (vs. 12). From our perspective, what an honor that must have been!

3 John

Like 2 John, this letter was addressed to a specific person, this time a man named Gaius. It appears that this name was common in the first century, so pinpointing the correct man is impossible. There are several men even in the New Testament who had this name, and we cannot be sure if any one of them was the intended recipient.

John referred to Gaius with great affection in verses 1-2. It seems from verses 3-4 that he was either a new believer or possibly someone who had recently returned to living faithfully. In this short letter, John wanted to point out that godly living extends to how believers treat one another, "EVEN THOUGH THEY ARE STRANGERS" (vs. 5). It seems that Gaius needed a little prodding to support some traveling missionaries John had sent his way.

The second issue John needed to deal with was concerning a man named Diotrephes. He was apparently a narcissistic, arrogant man in the church who was bold enough to slander John and would not welcome the traveling missionaries. He even went so far as to unilaterally excommunicate those who tried to help them! This may be the reason John had to encourage Gaius to continue his help.

The statement about Demetrius, that he "HAS BEEN TESTIFIED TO

BY ALL" (vs. 12), may have been John's way to refute some of Diotrephes' slander. Paul did something similar when he put his reputation on the line to Philemon on behalf of Onesimus (Philemon 17). Third John ends like Second John, with reference to "PEN AND INK" and the desire to "SPEAK FACE TO FACE" with Gaius (vs. 14).

Jude

As is the case with James, the identification of Jude has caused much debate. Jude and Judas were popular names honoring the great tribal patriarch, Judah. However, because Jude called himself "THE BROTHER OF JAMES" (vs. 1), with no clarification of *which* James, it is best to see this as a reference to the most well-known James at that time, Jesus' half-brother, the leader of the Jerusalem church.[182] This would also make Jude Jesus' half-brother. (The other two named in Matthew 13:55 were Joseph and Simon, also named after patriarchs.)

Although Jude's letter was never officially rejected by the Early Church, some were hesitant to recognize it as inspired, primarily because of his references to other Scripture (2 Peter) and extra-biblical literature. His quotation from the book of *1 Enoch* in verses 14-15 and the reference to the body of Moses in verse 9 has caused some to question its integrity. However, Paul quoted Greek poets, philosophers, and traditional sayings multiple times within his inspired letters, so this is not automatically cause for disqualification. In fact, there is nothing in Jude that contradicts other Scripture or creates new doctrine. Even the specific account in verse 9 about Moses' body simply

---

182 See the introduction to the book of James for an explanation of why that James was Jesus' brother.

adds new revelation without changing anything else already in Scripture. Ironically, rather than contradicting earlier Scripture, Jude is a short, yet strong, reminder of our need to maintain doctrinal accuracy and integrity.

Jude had intended to write a longer letter on the doctrine of salvation, but the influx of false teachers in the church (vs. 4; likely the same ones Paul and Peter warned about earlier) caused him to set that aside for a quick memo on doctrinal integrity. Specifically, he wrote, believers must "CONTEND EARNESTLY FOR THE FAITH" (vs. 3). It is important that we do not simply "believe" or "uphold" the faith. We must fight for it, knowing that our opponents will certainly fight for their side. Jude seems to quote 2 Peter 2:1 when he referred to those "WHO DENY OUR ONLY MASTER AND LORD, JESUS CHRIST" (vs. 4).

Showing a penchant for cadence in his oratory, Jude created four lists to describe these false teachers. First, he compared their coming judgment to the plagues of Egypt, the angels of Genesis 6, and Sodom and Gomorrah (vs. 5-7). Second, he compared their attitude toward God to Cain, Balaam, and Korah (vs. 11). Third, using visuals from nature, he compared their activity to dangerous reefs, waterless clouds, fruitless trees, wild waves, and wayward stars (vs. 12-13). Fourth, describing their spiritual state, he called them divisive, worldly, and devoid of the Spirit (vs. 19).

In contrast to this dangerous threat to local churches, Jude provided two lists for believers as well (vs. 17, 20-21 and 22-23). First, regarding ourselves, we must: 1) remember this was prophesied; 2) pray in the Holy Spirit; 3) maintain ourselves in God's love; and 4) anticipate Christ's mercy. Second, regarding others, we must: 1) have mercy on those wavering in the truth; 2) rescue some from the fire; 3) have mercy on others, while paying attention to ourselves (see Galatians 6:1).

Jude's final exhortation reminded his readers – and us – that succumbing to false teaching is not inevitable. Not only can God keep us from falling, but he can also cause us to stand, "REJOICING, WITHOUT BLEMISH BEFORE HIS GLORIOUS PRESENCE" (vs. 24) for eternity.

Revelation

There are four primary theories concerning how to understand the Revelation. The **preterist** theory holds that the Revelation symbolically refers to events that took place around the time of its writing (usually considered to be during Nero's reign), and the early Christians understood the symbolism because they lived those events. The **historical** theory is similar, except that the events happened throughout church history, rather than just during the first century.

Both of these theories are plagued with the problem that none of the events in the Revelation have actually happened, even symbolically. There has been no demonic global ruler, no cataclysmic judgments, no return of Christ, and no utopian kingdom (although some who hold these views do acknowledge the kingdom and eternity are still future). These must be rationalized away for any theory that views the Revelation as past tense. The **spiritual** or **idealist** theory skirts this problem by arguing that the Revelation uses symbolic language to explain a spiritual reality. In other words, the "events" recorded are not and will not be real events at all.

Standing in contrast to these, the **futurist** theory recognizes that the Revelation is clearly identified as "prophecy" or prophetic literature (1:1, 3;

22:10, 18-19). (The Greek name, ἀποκαλύψις, *apokalypsis*, means "uncovered, revealed" not "hidden, secret"). Specifically, this prophecy was given by Jesus himself to John (1:1, 17-19; 22:16). Since the Scriptures are full of prophecies that have been fulfilled literally, the Revelation must not be considered to be figurative, symbolic, or spiritual simply because the events have not yet taken place. Instead, its interpretation must be based on the concept that these are prophecies yet to be fulfilled literally. Even this view, however, is represented by a variety of interpretations of the specific timeline and events (as will be shown in these notes).

Although the book is not necessarily chronological throughout, it does provide a concise outline of its contents. In 1:19 Jesus told John to "WRITE WHAT YOU SAW, WHAT IS, AND WHAT WILL BE AFTER THESE THINGS." What John "SAW" must refer to the vision in chapter one. "WHAT IS" seems to be the then-existing churches named in chapters 2-3. Chapter four begins with the statement "AFTER THESE THINGS" (twice in vs. 1 and six times throughout the rest of the book) implying that everything from that point was John's vision of the future.

There is a great deal of imagery in John's vision, which has led to some of the theories mentioned above. However, "imagery" does not necessarily mean "symbolism" in a spiritual or non-literal sense. When we realize that much of the imagery comes from the Old Testament, the meanings tend to come into better focus. Interestingly, although the influence of the Hebrew prophets is prominent in the Revelation, it tends to come via allusions rather than direct quotes.

The Revelation begins with a blessing and ends with a curse. The blessing is upon those who read and obey the things written in the book (1:3). The curse is upon anyone who would add to or subtract from this "REVELATION OF JESUS CHRIST" (22:18-19).

Chapter one presents both the introduction to the book (including what has already been mentioned) and the singular event at which time John received this revelation. John began by explaining that what he was about to write came to him from Jesus, not any other source. Technically, this book was sent to seven major churches on a circuitous route throughout western Asia Minor (modern southwest Turkey), with a cover letter for each congregation. We assume that it was not intended to stay in these churches, but rather they would be the hubs from which it could circulate in their regions.

The "main event" of chapter one is John's vision of Jesus. John claimed to be on the island of Patmos due to persecution against Christians. This, along with the statements of many Early Church Fathers, helps place the writing of the Revelation to be in the mid-90s A.D. John was released from his imprisonment after the death of Emperor Domitian in A.D. 96.

While on Patmos, John saw a vision of the risen Christ. His response – falling down as dead (vs. 17) – was significant, because he had seen Jesus many times after his resurrection (see Acts 1:3) without that response. This time, Jesus appeared as the one who would judge, the Son of Man and Ancient of Days seen by Daniel (Daniel 7:13). The detailed description of Jesus given in chapter one has a double purpose. In addition to simply describing what John saw, Jesus used several of his different visible characteristics in the letters of chapters two and three to illustrate his messages to the individual churches.

Chapter two contains four of the seven messages to the churches. It is imperative to recognize that these messages are from Jesus, not John. Although much of the Bible is not a direct dictation, these chapters are. John directly recorded the messages that Jesus dictated to him. Even as an apostle, John did not have the authority to make the statements that Jesus made to these churches.

The seven messages each follow a similar template or pattern. First, Jesus introduced himself using one or more of the characteristics from John's vision in chapter one. Second, he gave a word of commendation to the congregations (all but one), followed by a word of condemnation (to all but two). Third, he gave a command to those who needed to rectify something. Fourth, he promised a specific reward to "THE ONE WHO CONQUERS." The reward was usually closely tied to something specific to each city.

Ephesus was commended for their good works, but they had left their first love – Jesus. They were to repent and return to where they started.

Smyrna was commended for their faithfulness, especially in persecution. Jesus had nothing to say against them.

Pergamum was commended for not denying their faith in the face of persecution. However, they tolerated false teachers in their assembly, specifically those who celebrated sexual immorality and idol worship. They were to repent from their sin and tolerance.

Thyatira was commended for their deeds as well, yet they, too, allowed false teachers and were plagued with sexual immorality and idol worship in the guise of authentic worship. Unlike Pergamum, Thyatira also had people engaging in witchcraft. They also needed to repent, but Jesus already previewed the judgment that was to come. Those faithful Christians were told to hold on until he came.

Chapter three continues the messages to the churches.

Sardis was commended for a few of their members who pursued godly living, but the majority of the church was dead. Jesus commanded them to wake up, repent, and strengthen what little bit they had left.

Philadelphia was the second church for whom Jesus had only praise. Although they were not numerically big or strong, they were faithful, even in persecution. The promise in verse ten that they would be kept "FROM THE HOUR OF TESTING THAT IS ABOUT TO COME ON THE WHOLE WORLD" does not promise how they would escape the coming Tribulation, only that they would. First Thessalonians 4-5 give more detail about why and how Christians will escape it.

Laodicea was the single congregation for whom Jesus had nothing good to say. They were proud of and dependent on their wealth instead of Jesus. In fact, he said that he was on the outside of their church trying to get in. Their only option was to repent, let Jesus back into their assembly, and accept his loving discipline and care.

The threat to all of the erring churches (back then and today) was that, if they did not change their ways, their influence (symbolized by the lampstands in Jesus' hand) would go out. That none of these churches is in existence today proves that Jesus was not simply speaking figuratively.

Many scholars see seven periods in church history represented by these long-gone local congregations. If this is accurate, Laodicea seems to represent today's church at large, what Paul prophesied as "MAINTAINING AN OUTWARD APPEARANCE OF RELIGION BUT WILL HAVE REPUDIATED ITS POWER" (2 Timothy 3:5). In Revelation 3:20, Jesus claimed to be on the outside of this church trying to get in. While that accurately represents some local churches today, it certainly does not reflect all of them. It is probably best to see all seven types of churches represented throughout all of church history. Thus, even today, there are both good and bad churches who, in one way or another, take after the characteristics of these seven. In effect, these chapters provide Jesus' personal insight and evaluation on our local assemblies.

Chapter four begins with the third phrase from 1:19 – "AFTER THESE THINGS." There are some who believe that 4:1 refers to the Rapture of the Church. In 1 Thessalonians 4:16, Paul wrote that the Rapture will take place "WITH A SHOUT OF COMMAND, WITH THE VOICE OF THE ARCHANGEL, AND WITH THE TRUMPET OF GOD." In Revelation 1:10 and 4:1, John described Jesus' voice to be like a trumpet, commanding, "COME UP HERE." Although we cannot be definitive that this does reference the Rapture, it is worth noting that the Church is not mentioned again after chapter three until Jesus returns in chapter 19. This is one support for the dispensational teaching that the Church is completely absent from Earth during the entire Tribulation period.[183]

What John saw in heaven can be described in three parts. First, he saw God himself, as much as an unglorified human could. He saw God's throne emanating with light (vs. 3). Second, in front of and around the throne, John saw three groups of beings - the 24 elders, the seven spirits, and the four living creatures (vs. 4-8). Third, John saw these beings in continuous worship of God.

Much has been written about each of these groups as scholars have tried to explain and identify them. Unfortunately, opinions are widely varied resulting in little agreement. The four living creatures seem the most obvious. Their description has great similarities to the cherubim described in Ezekiel 1 and 10, but they seem to say the same thing as the seraphim in Isaiah 6. It seems the beings in Revelation 4 could be either, although they are more like Ezekiel's cherubim.

John had already mentioned the seven spirits in 1:4. In his address to Sardis, Jesus described himself as "THE ONE WHO HOLDS THE SEVEN SPIRITS OF GOD" (3:1). They appear once more in 5:6, described as seven eyes that are "SENT OUT INTO ALL THE EARTH." Although this is not enough information to be definitive, most conservative scholars see these spirits as a reference to the Holy Spirit himself. Another theory, based on Isaiah 11:1-2, is that the seven "spirits" are seven characteristics of the Holy Spirit.

The twenty-four elders are described as sitting on thrones around God's throne. One common understanding is that these elders refer to the Church, who will reign with Jesus during his kingdom. The teaching that believers will offer their rewards back to Jesus seems to come from 4:10. The trouble with this is the number "24," which seems to have no connection to the Church. Another theory is that they represent both Israel and the Church,

---

183 See the comment in chapter three about the church at Philadelphia and 1 Thessalonians 4-5 for more detail on the Rapture of the Church.

since the New Jerusalem will contain the names of the 12 Jewish tribal families and the 12 apostles (21:12-14). In this case, both groups add up to the twenty-four elders. The problem with this view is that proponents often use the phrase "all the people of God," but Israel and the Church do not take into consideration believers from before Israel existed or Tribulation and Millennial saints. Again, with no further information about the 24 elders, it is important to not be dogmatic.

Chapter five seems to be a continuation of the scene in heaven. As the groups praised and worshiped God, John saw that God was holding a scroll closed by seven seals, but no one in all of heaven was worthy to open it. This caused John to weep until one of the elders pointed to the only one worthy of this task. He was described in the ancient terms "THE LION OF THE TRIBE OF JUDAH" (Genesis 49:9-10) and "THE ROOT OF DAVID" (Isaiah 11:1), and the reason he was worthy to open the scroll was that he "HAS CONQUERED." This is a clear reference to Jesus' death and resurrection as shown in the fact that John saw him as "A LAMB THAT APPEARED TO HAVE BEEN KILLED" and the fact that the song of the four living creatures and the twenty-four elders refer to the redemption through his blood. Jesus said the same thing when John first saw him in 1:17-18.

The worship scene in chapter five is similar to that in chapter four but much larger. In addition to the four living creatures and twenty-four elders, now John saw and heard "MANY ANGELS" that he did not mention earlier. In the Greek text, John wrote, *"The number of them was myriads of myriads and thousands of thousands."* A *myriad* means 10,000 when used as a number in the New Testament, so this has been taken to mean "10,000 x 10,000" or 100,000,000 angels. While this could certainly be true, the fact that John put *myriads* and *thousands* together seems to indicate that he did not intend it to be a precise count (as opposed to the 200,000,000 in 9:16 where he "HEARD THEIR NUMBER"). Instead, we could take this to mean just a large countless throng of angels.

Not only were the angels praising, though; John "HEARD EVERY CREA-TURE - IN HEAVEN, ON EARTH, UNDER THE EARTH, IN THE SEA, AND ALL THAT IS IN THEM" praising God as well (vs. 13). This is reminiscent of Paul's declaration "THAT AT THE NAME OF JESUS EVERY KNEE WILL BOW - IN HEAVEN AND ON EARTH AND UNDER THE EARTH - AND EVERY TONGUE WILL CONFESS THAT JESUS CHRIST IS LORD TO THE GLORY OF GOD THE FATHER" (Philippians 2:10-11). At issue is the timing of the worship John saw. Because of the events that are yet to happen in the Revelation, it seems out of place to say that every creature will worship Jesus before the Tribulation, which begins in chapter six.

A major key to interpreting the Revelation is understanding that it is not strictly chronological. Throughout the book, John wrote down what he saw. However, "then I saw" is not necessarily the same as "then this will happen." Several of John's visions are clearly out of order when it comes to the timeline of the future events. Because the only connection between 5:9-10 and 5:11-14 is "THE LAMB WHO WAS KILLED," it may be that the latter refers to worship that takes place at the conclusion of all things rather than at the beginning of the Tribulation. Noticeably absent from the second worship is the reference to the scroll, which is the main theme of chapter five to this point. However, since chapter six returns immediately to the scroll (and since there were originally no chapter and verse divisions), we must not take too strong a stance about this.

Chapter six reveals what was in the scroll of 5:1. As Jesus broke each of the seven seals, the scroll opened a little more to reveal its contents. As mentioned above about the chronology of the Revelation, it is probable that this scroll was meant to provide a summary overview of the events and judgments that will happen throughout the seven years of Tribulation, rather than the seals themselves representing specific judgments at the beginning of the Tribulation period.

As Jesus slowly opened the scroll, one seal at a time, John saw something that represented what will take place. *The first seal* revealed a rider on a white horse, carrying a bow (vs. 1-2). This seems to represent a time of relative peace, although he is called a conqueror. The rider is often identified as the Antichrist, but he likely refers to the entire early one-world, religious government system, in which Antichrist will be a key leader. *The second seal* revealed a rider on a red horse (vs. 3-4). This is clearly identified as the removal of the peace that the first rider brought, probably world war. *The third seal* revealed a rider on a black horse, which would be increased food prices, a natural result of the war (vs. 5-6). *The fourth seal* revealed two riders, Death and the Grave, on a pale horse (vs. 7-8). Lack of food leads to famine, various illnesses and diseases, and death. At this point, a quarter of Earth's population will be dead as a result of these riders. These four certainly run in succession, but there is no indication how long each of them lasts. Many dispensational teachers place all the seals in the first half of the Tribulation, but they are probably a summary representation of most, if not all, of the whole seven-year period, rather than individual events or judgments during the Tribulation.

The fifth seal shifted from Earth to Heaven and set its focus on souls "UNDER THE ALTAR" (vs. 9-11). These souls belong to people who had been martyred for their faith. They cannot be souls of Christian martyrs, because all Christians will be resurrected in the Rapture[184], so these must be people who were martyred before (Old Testament martyrs) and/or after the Church (Tribulation martyrs). If the governmental persecution of Tribulation saints may not start until the second half of the Tribulation (12:11-12), the timing of this seal is difficult to determine. Additionally, their martyrdom may not have anything to do with Antichrist, as there are plenty of groups intent on killing believers that may have free rein once the Church is gone. The souls

---

184   This assumes a pre-Tribulation Rapture of the Church, when Jesus will rescue all Church Age believers before the Tribulation begins (1 Thessalonians 1:10; 4:13-18; 5:9).

under the altar were asking for vengeance, but they were told to wait, because many more would be killed first.

The sixth seal revealed plagues that will come upon the Earth (vs. 12-17). The description of the sun, moon, and stars comes from Joel 2:31 and is either repeated or expanded upon in Revelation 8:12 and 16:8-10. Jesus also referred to them in the Olivet Discourse (see Matthew 24:29) and indicated that this would be near the end of the Tribulation. This seal also refers to major topographical changes on Earth that seem to occur throughout and near the end of the Tribulation. Whether these are all distinct judgments or this seal looks forward to the others is debated. As with the fifth seal, the exact timing of this sixth seal is difficult to determine. However, whenever it occurs, the people on Earth will be well aware that these judgments are from God, and many would rather kill themselves than have to suffer at his hand (see 9:20-21 and 16:9, 11).

Chapter seven seems to be the first major parenthesis in the vision chronology. Rather than seeing judgments, John saw two distinct groups of people. The first is described as 144,000 people (vs. 1-8). These will somehow represent Israel's twelve tribes (with Manasseh listed in place of Dan[185]) – 12,000 from each tribe. These people are called "THE SERVANTS OF OUR GOD." They each will receive "A SEAL ON THE FOREHEAD" before "THE EARTH OR THE SEA OR THE TREES" are damaged by the coming judgments. What their role is during this time is not specified, but they will certainly be marked out

---

185 The "twelve tribes of Israel" is not a fixed list. Instead, they appear in different combinations, depending on the situation surrounding the lists. 1) Jacob's biological sons were Reuben, Simeon, Levi, Judah, Zebulun, Issachar, Dan, Gad, Asher, Naphtali, Joseph, and Benjamin. However, Jacob adopted Joseph's two sons, Ephraim and Manasseh as him own, giving Joseph a double portion (the birthright inheritance; Genesis 48:5-6, 8-20). 2) Because the tribe of Levi did not receive a property inheritance in the land of Canaan/Israel, in the property passages Levi and Joseph are replaced by Ephraim and Manasseh. 3) When Ephraim is mentioned alone, he is usually the representative of Joseph. 4) In the list in this chapter, Joseph is named instead of Ephraim, but Manasseh replaced Dan. This is probably because Dan was the most ungodly of all the tribes, as shown by their swift and unrepentant fall into idolatry. As a tribe, Dan was the first to worship idols and never followed Jehovah (Judges 18:27-31).

for a reason. However, it is important to recognize them literally as enumerated groups of Jewish people from each of the named tribes, rather than a figurative number (12x12x1000) or any group of believers.

The second group will be comprised "OF PERSONS FROM EVERY NATION, TRIBE, PEOPLE, AND LANGUAGE" (vs. 9-17). Contrary to the previous group, this multitude will be too numerous to count, which helps confirm that the 144,000 will be literal, ethnic Jews. Additionally, it seems this group must also include Jews, again making the 144,000 a distinct group with a special purpose. This throng of people will join the angels, living creatures, and elders from 5:11-14, offering the same praise found in that section. When John could not identify this new group, one of the elders told him that they were "THE ONES WHO HAVE COME OUT OF THE GREAT TRIBULATION" (vs. 14). They are often assumed to be martyrs because they have "LONG WHITE ROBES" similar to the martyrs of the fifth seal (6:11). However, all the armies of heaven will return with Jesus in white linen (19:8, 14), and the believers in Sardis were promised white clothing, even though there is no mention of martyrdom (3:5), so these may simply represent all Tribulation believers. Whatever we cannot say about these people, we can say that they came to faith in Jesus during the Tribulation.

It is possible that these two groups are meant to show the state or number of believers at the beginning of the Tribulation (144,000 Jews) and the end (innumerable from all people groups).

Chapter eight resumes where chapter six ended, with the opening of the seventh seal. The traditional understanding is that the trumpets described in chapters 8-9 connect to the seventh seal. However, there seems to be a parallel between the fifth seal with the prayers of the saints on the altar (8:3-4) and the sixth seal with some of the trumpet judgments. The trumpets of chapter eight will cause physical effects on the earth and sky. How long each of these effects will last and if they overlap is not stated, but they will be literal judgments that also preview even worse judgments later (chapter 16).

The first trumpet will result in hail and fire (similar to the seventh plague on Egypt, Exodus 9:23-24), "so that a third of the earth ... a third of the trees ... and all the green grass was burned up" (vs. 7).

The second trumpet will result in "a third of the sea" turning to blood, affecting a third of all sea life and a third of naval commerce (vs. 8-9). As the third trumpet will show, this judgment will be specific to saltwater seas.

The third trumpet will affect fresh water as the second trumpet did saltwater (vs. 10-11). This will be similar to the first plague on Egypt, when the Nile River turned to blood (Exodus 7:19), except rather than turning to blood, one-third of all fresh water will be poisoned, possibly by a meteor.

The fourth trumpet will affect the celestial bodies (vs. 12). Following the pattern established by the first three trumpets, a third of all natural light will be affected, as the sun will be somehow diminished. Scholars debate whether this will be the result of a change in the rotation of the Earth itself, shortening the number of actual daylight hours, or an atmospheric condition that will limit the time light will be available.

The chapter ends noting a distinction between the first four trumpets and the last three. The upcoming trumpets are called "woes."

Chapter nine begins immediately with *the fifth trumpet* (the first "woe"). Whereas the first four trumpets are "natural," the next two are completely supernatural. At the sounding of *the fifth trumpet* the "shaft of the abyss" ("bottomless pit" in some translations) will be unlocked and opened (vs. 1-12). Outside of the Revelation, ἄβυσσος (*abyssos*, "abyss"), is used only in Luke 8:31 and Romans 10:7. In Luke, when Jesus cast the demons out of the pigs, they begged that he not send them into the abyss. In Romans, Paul quoted Deuteronomy 30:13 (substituting "into the abyss" for "beyond the sea") to refer to Jesus' resurrection. Since it is compared to a great furnace, it is possible that this abyss should be interpreted as hell or the lake of fire.

From this abyss came locusts, yet they were unlike normal locusts. Instead of destroying grass and plants, their mission was to torture "THOSE PEOPLE WHO DID NOT HAVE THE SEAL OF GOD ON THEIR FOREHEAD" (vs. 4). This obviously refers to the 144,000 Jews of chapter seven, and probably includes all who will come to believe in Jesus during the Tribulation. Unlike the previous trumpets, which have no time frame given, we are told that this judgment will last for five months (vs. 5). The torturous sting of these locusts will cause people to want to kill themselves; however, part of this judgment will be the inability to die.

To clarify that these are not just natural locusts with unnatural bites, John described what they looked like in verses 7-11. Each of the parts of the description may represent a characteristic: a man's face, intelligence; a woman's hair, beauty; lions' teeth, ferocity; iron breastplates, indestructibility. Additionally, they will have scorpion-like tails with stingers that they will use to torture people. Their "KING" is an angel or demon, whose name in both Hebrew and Greek means "Destroyer."[186]

The sixth trumpet (the second "woe") will also release demons upon the Earth, this time in two sets. The first set is described as "FOUR ANGELS WHO HAD BEEN PREPARED FOR THIS HOUR, DAY, MONTH, AND YEAR" (vs. 13-15). The only thing we know about them is that they "ARE BOUND AT THE GREAT RIVER EUPHRATES." There is nothing else in Scripture that points to their identity or the reason for their imprisonment or timing of it. Their purpose is "TO KILL A THIRD OF HUMANITY."

The second set of demons unleashed are likened to "SOLDIERS ON HORSEBACK" (vs. 16-19). In contrast to the nebulous "MYRIADS OF MYRIADS AND THOUSANDS OF THOUSANDS" of angels that John heard in chapter five and the "ENORMOUS CROWD THAT NO ONE COULD COUNT" in chapter seven,

---

186 It is not uncommon for a name to reflect a certain characteristic, which is carried into later languages. In this case Abaddon and Apollyon both mean "Destroyer." In another example, the Hebrew, *satan*, and Greek, *satanas*, sound alike and both mean "Enemy, Adversary, Prosecutor." (Although "Satan" has come to be used as his name, it is more accurately a descriptive title.)

he heard the number of this army to be 200,000,000. Although these soldiers are not called demons explicitly, their appearance is similar to the locusts earlier in the chapter but different enough to recognize them as distinct beings. Because this army also killed a third of humanity, it is likely that the four angels are the commanders of the army, in a similar way that Abaddon/Apollyon is the "KING" of the locusts. Whereas the locust plague lasted for five months, no time limit is given for this demonic army.

Even after these horrible plagues and demonic attacks, those who survive will refuse to repent and turn to the Lamb of God (vs. 20-21).

Chapter ten starts the second major parenthesis in the Revelation timeline, and it ends in 11:14. Rather than being in Heaven watching Earth, it seems as if John were back on Earth during this vision (vs. 2). A powerful angel was holding a scroll that had already been opened, and he stood on both the land and sea, probably signifying that the prophecy in the scroll would have a global effect.

Based on the fact that John was prohibited to write down what the seven thunders roared, it seems that there may be judgments and events during the Tribulation that God chose to not reveal (vs. 4). However, the seventh trumpet is clearly connected to the end of the Tribulation (vs. 7), so that does help fill in the timeline a little bit. It seems that, although the seals and trumpets will take some time, the coming bowl judgments will happen very quickly and in rapid succession. The phrase "HIS SERVANTS THE PROPHETS" occurs six times in the Old Testament to refer to the Hebrew prophets, so "THE MYSTERY OF GOD" must refer to things the prophets spoke but were not yet fully revealed until John's vision.

John was commanded to "TAKE THE LITTLE SCROLL AND EAT IT" (vs. 9). After eating it, John was told that he would have to prophesy again. It seems that the little scroll contained the prophecy that John was about to reveal. Since the next prophetic section deals with the rise of the Beast, some have linked this little scroll to what Daniel wrote and had to "SEAL...UNTIL THE TIME OF THE END" (Daniel 12:4), after his prophecy of the coming Antichrist. If this is correct, then Daniel may have already seen and recorded some or all the events of Revelation 11-13.

Chapter eleven continues the break in the judgment timeline as John learned about the coming of two unique witnesses. (There is nothing in chapter eleven to indicate that he saw them in a vision but rather was told about them.) These two witnesses will "PROPHESY FOR 1,260 DAYS" (vs. 3). This period is also referred to as "FORTY-TWO MONTHS" (vs. 2) and "A TIME, TIMES, AND HALF A TIME" (Daniel 7:25; 12:7; Revelation 12:6, 14), all of which refer to the second half of the Tribulation. This gives strong support for the two witnesses preaching during that time as well, although this is often debated.

The identity of the two witnesses is never given and has undergone wide speculation. The most common guesses often include Elijah for four reasons: 1) he appeared with Jesus during his transfiguration (Matthew 17:3); 2) the miracles the two witnesses will do resemble Elijah's miracles; 3) Malachi prophesied that Elijah would appear "BEFORE THE GREAT AND TERRIBLE DAY OF THE LORD" (Malachi 4:5); and 4) Elijah did not die, but was raptured alive (2 Kings 2:11). Because of the Transfiguration account, Moses is sometimes suggested as the second witness, as are Elisha (making the duo Elijah and Elisha) and Enoch (because only he and Elijah are recorded to have not died, Genesis 5:24). A second major suggestion is Zerubbabel and Joshua from Zechariah 3-4, because they are called "THE TWO OLIVE TREES AND THE TWO LAMPSTANDS" (11:4; cf. Zechariah 4:3, 11, 14). Because the two witnesses will be killed and resurrected, perhaps the best option is that they will be people from that time (possibly two of the 144,000) rather than an ancient Hebrew hero, especially one who already died.

During the time of their prophecy, no one will have the power to stop these men, including the Beast (who has not yet been formally intro-duced). However, at the determined time, the Beast will kill them, and the entire world will celebrate their demise, leaving their bodies in the streets of Jerusalem for all to see and mock. After three and a half days, however, they will be physically resurrected and ascend to Heaven in plain sight of the whole world. This, plus an earthquake, will point people again to God.

The final section reveals *the seventh trumpet* (vs. 15-19). Rather than a specific judgment like the first six, the seventh trumpet is similar to the worship in chapter 5 and the crowd in chapter 7. In all three cases, the onlookers said that the end was imminent. Any judgments that come after this (e.g., the bowls/vials) must happen very quickly.

Chapter twelve provides a long-term look at the big historical picture. John made it clear in verse one that this was a "SIGN," so we are to read this as symbolizing other people or events. A natural reading shows three main persons: the woman, who represents the nation of Israel; the dragon, who represents Satan; and the male child, who represents Jesus. According to verse six, Israel "FLED INTO THE WILDERNESS" to be protected by God from Satan for 1,260 days, the second half of the Tribulation. Jesus said that this would happen after "THE ABOMINATION OF DESOLATION – SPOKEN ABOUT BY DANIEL THE PROPHET" (Matthew 24:15). Daniel wrote that this would take place "IN THE MIDDLE OF THAT WEEK" (Daniel 9:27), the 7-year covenant that Antichrist will confirm with Israel.

At the mid-point of the Tribulation, Michael and his angelic army will overpower Satan and his demonic army and will cast them out of heaven. Once confined to the Earth, Satan will "MAKE WAR ON THE REST OF [ISRAEL WHO DID NOT FLEE]" and on those who "HOLD TO THE TESTIMONY ABOUT JESUS" (vs. 17) for the remainder of the Tribulation. It is during this period that many will be martyred, possibly those already mentioned in the fifth seal and some of the multitude in chapter 7. This time is called a "WOE TO THE EARTH AND THE SEA BECAUSE THE DEVIL HAS COME DOWN TO YOU" (vs. 12).

Chapter thirteen finally introduces the main human antagonist of the drama – the Beast. He is never called "antichrist" in the Revelation; that term appears only in 1 and 2 John about a general deceptive spirit and anyone who denies Jesus. However, it is appropriate to consider him as the ultimate embodiment of the antichrist spirit. He is referred to by several other names and descriptions, including "THE COMING PRINCE"[187] (Daniel 9:26), "THE KING" (Daniel 11:36), and a "LITTLE HORN" (Daniel 7:8). In the Revelation, the term "beast" refers both to this human ruler and to his kingdom, so it is important to let the context determine which "beast" John meant each time.

The final verse of chapter twelve shows Satan standing "ON THE SAND OF THE SEASHORE," watching the beast "COMING UP OUT OF THE SEA" (13:1). This beast is the entire beastly kingdom, as evidenced by its "TEN HORNS AND SEVEN HEADS" and the comparative description in Daniel 7. According to Daniel 7:8 and 24-25, one of these horns will rule over the rest; this is the Beast-man or Antichrist. He will rule as Satan's pawn (Revelation 13:3), warring "AGAINST THE SAINTS" (vs. 7).

The Beast (both the man and system) will have a spokesman with the ability to perform miracles. This second beast will speak like a dragon, with cunning and deception, much like Satan and the Beast (see Genesis 3:1). He will create an image of the Beast, give it "LIFE," and require all people to worship the image and worship the Beast. He will also be the one to establish the infamous "MARK OF THE BEAST" (vs. 17), which he will use to regulate all commerce. It seems that deciphering this mark will be impossible until this time, and it will probably be encoded in such a way that it will not be obvious what it is (vs. 18). Because this will take place during the second half of the Tribulation, there is nothing today that can be considered this mark or that believers should be afraid of using.

---

187   Sir Robert Anderson's classic book by this title is a fantastic resource for end times study.

Chapter fourteen begins with John's vision of the 144,000 Jews from chapter seven. John saw these people standing with Jesus in Jerusalem (vs. 1-5). This means that the Tribulation has ended and Jesus' kingdom is being established. Whether they were martyred during the Beast's war on the saints or whether they survived is unclear. However, they will all stand together with the Lamb in his kingdom.

The next section reveals four messages or declarations that John heard. The first will be the eternal gospel[188] announced by an angel flying through the skies (vs. 6-7). There will be no one during the second half of the Tribulation who will not know the gospel, even though many will reject it. The second will be a second angel declaring the fall of Babylon (vs. 8). Whether the references to Babylon in the upcoming chapters should be taken literally or symbolically for the Beast's kingdom is debated, although there is good reason to believe they may be both, if Antichrist headquarters his empire out of a rebuilt Babylon. The third declaration will be the final pronouncement of judgment on all those who took the mark of the beast (vs. 9-12). It is important to note that this mark can be refused, but no one who receives the mark will be able to be saved afterward. It is the ultimate rebellion against God and his gospel. Those who are believers during the second half of the Tribulation will see the wicked prospering (even through God's judgments), and it will require all their faith to stand firm.[189] The final pronouncement will come directly from heaven, rather than from an angel (vs. 13). As opposed to those who will die under God's judgment, "BLESSED ARE THE DEAD, THOSE WHO DIE IN THE LORD FROM THIS MOMENT ON!" because they will not have to experience the destruction yet to come. The fate of those who will worship

---

188 There are several "gospels" (messages of good news) mentioned in Scripture. In the current Church Age, we preach the gospel of the cross (1 Corinthians 15:1-4). However, Abraham heard the gospel of Gentile salvation before that (Galatians 3:8). Jesus and the apostles preached the gospel of the kingdom before the crucifixion (Matthew 4:34), which will be preached again during the Tribulation (Matthew 24:14). The "ETERNAL GOSPEL" probably includes all the previous messages plus any new revelation given during the Tribulation (Joel 2:28-32).

189 Psalm 37 shows that this will not be new in the Tribulation but has been necessary for God's people of all time.

the Lamb and those who will worship the Beast could not be more different.

In the final section of the chapter, John saw the same vision as Daniel 7:13, where the Son of Man comes in judgment (vs. 14-20). The visual was of a sickle being used to harvest grapes, which would be stomped in "THE GREAT WINEPRESS OF THE WRATH OF GOD" (vs. 19). The mass deaths of this judgment will produce enough blood to reach "TO THE HEIGHT OF HORSES' BRIDLES FOR A DISTANCE OF ALMOST TWO HUNDRED MILES" (320 km; vs. 20). The reference to the altar in verse 18 may connect this judgment to the vengeance promised the martyrs of the fifth seal (6:9-11). Because of the recurring use of the winepress illustration, this "harvest judgment" should probably be understood as the battles at Bozrah and Armageddon (Isaiah 63:1-6; Revelation 19:11-21) when Christ returns at the end of the Tribulation.

Chapters fifteen and sixteen return to the picture of judgments poured out during the Tribulation, before the Second Coming and the "harvest" described in chapter fourteen. In chapter fifteen the scene is set. The seven plagues are called "FINAL BECAUSE IN THEM GOD'S ANGER IS COMPLETED" (vs. 1). Before this final judgment, John saw the Tribulation martyrs worshiping God for the vengeance they were about to receive (6:9-11). This worship scene is much like chapters 5, 7, and 14. As the people sang, the angels prepared the final judgments.

Chapter sixteen lists the final seven judgments of the Tribulation. John described these as "BOWLS CONTAINING GOD'S WRATH" that would be "POURED OUT...ON THE EARTH" (vs. 1-2). These judgments will be similar to the trumpets but should not be confused with them, as if they were the same judgments. As noted in chapter eleven and seen in the rapid mention here, the bowls seem to come very quickly upon each other, even overlapping each other to maximize their potency. *The first bowl* will produce sores all over the Beast's followers (vs. 2). This is similar to the sixth plague on Egypt

(Exodus 9:10). *The second bowl* will turn all saltwater to blood, whereas the second trumpet will change only one-third of the water (vs. 3). *The third bowl* will turn all remaining fresh water to blood (vs. 4-7). This bowl includes an explanation which calls it vengeance for the blood of the saints. There will be nothing naturally potable to drink from this point on.

The fourth bowl will intensify the heat of the sun, scorching every-thing it touches (vs. 8-9). *The fifth bowl* will finally extinguish the sun's light, immersing the world into complete darkness (vs. 10-11). John mentioned a couple of additional details here. First, this will affect only the Beast's kingdom; apparently, the saints will not be affected. Second, the sunburns and sores from the previous plagues will still be in effect, so people will be in pain in darkness, similar to the lake of fire where they will suffer for eternity.

The sixth bowl will dry up the Euphrates River, making a path for the human armies from the Far East to join the Beast in his final attack on Jerusalem (vs. 12-16). John noted that the command for the armies to gather will come via demonic messengers from the "unholy trinity" of the Dragon, the Beast, and the False Prophet.

The seventh bowl follows the pattern of the seventh trumpet – lightning, thunder, earthquake, and hailstorm (vs. 17-21). There are several descriptions that show this to be far worse than the seventh trumpet. The earthquake will be so great - "UNEQUALED SINCE HUMANITY HAS BEEN ON THE EARTH" – that Babylon, "THE GREAT CITY," and "THE CITIES OF THE NATIONS" will collapse, and all islands and mountains will be flattened. In the hailstorm, the hailstones will weigh "ABOUT A HUNDRED POUNDS EACH." Throughout all the bowls, though, those receiving these judgments will not repent, choosing to blaspheme God instead (vs. 9, 11, 21).

Chapters seventeen and eighteen record the fall of the Beast's kingdom, Babylon. In 17:7, John's vision of the woman riding the beast is interpreted, so it is clearly meant to be symbolic, yet its meaning is plain. In this vision, the beast is the entire satanic kingdom, dating back to the original Babylon, foreseen in Daniel 7. The waters are all the peoples of the earth, demonstrating that the entire earth will be under the control of the Beast and his kingdom (vs. 15).

The woman is called a prostitute. Prostitution is used throughout the Hebrew Scriptures to illustrate unfaithfulness to God, usually demonstrated by idol worship and often including literal sexual immorality (see Judges, Jeremiah, and Ezekiel for many examples). Jesus condemned the churches in Pergamum and Thyatira early in the Revelation for tolerating sexual immorality and idol worship in their congregations. For this reason, many scholars see this chapter as referring to the collapse of the Babylon religious system. John described her as being "DRUNK WITH THE BLOOD OF THE SAINTS AND THE BLOOD OF THOSE WHO TESTIFIED TO JESUS" (vs. 6); thus, this religious system will be intolerant of true believers to the point of murdering them. Whether this collapse occurs in the first or second half of the Tribulation is debated, but the victims will likely include those of the fifth seal (6:9-11).

Not only is the woman called "THE GREAT PROSTITUTE" (vs. 1), she is also called "THE MOTHER OF PROSTITUTES" (vs. 5). This probably points to an ecumenical coalition of false religions under one world religious organization, much like the heretical World Council of Churches. This coalition will teach that all religions are essentially the same and any one of them, or a personal combination of various parts of them (even if they are contradictory) will be acceptable. Today's postmodernism, which rejects absolute truth in favor of personal, relative truth, is certainly a precursor to this worldwide religion, which will thrive once the true Church is removed in the Rapture.

Chapter eighteen shifts the focus to the failure of the Babylon economic system. Verse three reviews the sexual immorality of the kings of the earth and introduces a second group, "THE MERCHANTS OF THE EARTH [WHO] HAVE GOTTEN RICH" because of their dealings with her.

Verse eight refers to Babylon's destruction in "A SINGLE DAY." This could be taken literally, i.e., that the final plagues will occur within a 24-hour period, or it could be that this happens suddenly in a short period of time. The description of the plagues in verse three do not have an exact parallel to the seven bowls, and verses 10, 17, and 19 state that this will happen "IN A SINGLE HOUR." Even if the bowls happened in one day, it seems unlikely that they all happened in one hour. Because this is in the middle of an already symbolic description, the day/hour statements are often understood to be hyperbolic. However, in each case the Greek text reads, "in one hour" or "in one day." So, the meaning could be that the collapse itself will happen in a moment, even though the events leading up to the collapse will take some time.

Verse 11 brings the focus back to the merchants introduced in verse three. When they see the destruction happening to the Babylon system, they will weep as they watch their wealth, and the source of their wealth, vanish. Smaller examples of this can be seen in history on October 28-29, 1929, and October 19, 1987, when the US stock market collapsed. People committed suicide seeing their financial lives disappear in an instant.

John's final view of Babylon reverts to future tense when he saw an angel say, "WITH THIS KIND OF SUDDEN VIOLENT FORCE BABYLON THE GREAT CITY WILL BE THROWN DOWN" (vs. 21).

Chapter nineteen picks up the chronology again with worship in heaven that approximates chapter 5:11-14, the enormous multitude in chapter 7, the seventh trumpet in chapter 8, and the 144,000 in chapter 14. A new detail is that this celebration is called "THE WEDDING CELEBRATION OF THE LAMB" (vs. 7) and "THE BANQUET AT THE WEDDING CELEBRATION OF THE LAMB" (vs. 9). That this "BRIDE" must be the Church is revealed in the fact that she has already "MADE HERSELF READY" before she returns with the King (vs. 14). Throughout the Hebrew Scriptures Israel is not called a bride but rather the unfaithful wife of Jehovah (see Ezekiel 16:32). The faithful Jewish saints (pre-Church) will be resurrected after Jesus' return as he prepares his kingdom (Daniel 12:1-3, 11-13). The Church will have already gone through the Judgment Seat of Christ after the Rapture (2 Corinthians 5:10; 1 Corinthians 3:11-15) and will already be resurrected and glorified (1 Corinthians 15:51-52; 1 Thessalonians 4:13-18).

Beginning in verse 11, John finally saw the return of Jesus as "King of kings and Lord of lords" (vs. 16). It will be at this time that "he stomps the winepress of the furious wrath of God" that John had already foreseen in his vision (vs. 15; 14:14-20). The Word that spoke everything into existence will be the Word that will finally strike down his enemies (see Psalm 2).

In verse 19 John saw the battles take place that he envisioned in the sixth bowl. Rather than a long, drawn-out war, Jesus will speak death to the armies (vs. 21). The Beast and False Prophet, however, will not die. Instead, they will be judged immediately and "thrown alive into the lake of fire" (vs. 20). The fact that they will be alive points to the physical torture that the lake of fire will present. It is not a spiritual place for souls but a place where physical bodies can endure.

Chapter twenty reveals some information about the long-anticipated kingdom of God that had remained a mystery to this point. First, Satan will be imprisoned during this period, unable to "deceive the nations" (vs. 1-3). Second, this kingdom should not be confused with the eternal state, as so many of the Hebrew prophets did. Not knowing this detail, they assumed the kingdom would last forever. Instead, John discovered that it would continue only 1,000 years (vs. 2, 3, 4, 5, 6, 7). The fact that John repeated this number so many times cannot be overstated. Third, whereas the Church saints will be resurrected at the Rapture, the Old Testament and Tribulation saints will be resurrected after the Second Coming, after Armageddon, but before the Kingdom (vs. 4; Daniel 12:1-3, 11-13). Fourth, this leaves only the unbelievers of all time still dead. They will be resurrected at the end of the Millennial Kingdom (vs. 5).

There are at least four descriptive names often used to depict Jesus' kingdom, each one emphasizing a different aspect. *Millennial Kingdom* emphasizes its duration. "Millennium" is Latin for "1,000 years." *Messianic Kingdom* emphasizes its king. Jesus is the promised Jewish Messiah, the only rightful king appointed by God. *Kingdom of God* emphasizes its source. This kingdom will be granted to Jesus by the Father for 1,000 years, after which time Jesus will turn everything back over to the Father (1 Corinthians 15:23-28). *Kingdom of Heaven* emphasizes its character. This phrase is found only in Matthew and reveals that Jesus' kingdom will be the same kingdom of peace and righteousness that the prophets foretold (Isaiah 11).

At the end of the 1,000 years, God will release Satan for one final revolt. He will gather together all the unbelievers who will live through the Millennium without accepting Jesus' Messiahship. They will attack Jerusalem once more and fail. At this point, Satan himself will be "THROWN INTO THE LAKE OF FIRE AND SULFUR" (vs. 10). An important note is that, even though it will have been 1,000 years, "THE BEAST AND THE FALSE PROPHET" will still be there (vs. 10). This verse strongly supports the doctrine of eternal, bodily punishment.[190]

The final judgment on all unbelievers of all time will take place in front of the Great White Throne (vs. 11-15). There they will be presented with all of their deeds and be judged for them. This will apparently affect the level of punishment in the lake of fire, but will not affect whether or not they go there. The only thing that determines their destination is if their names are "FOUND WRITTEN IN THE BOOK OF LIFE" (vs. 15). At this judgment, all unbelievers will be "THROWN INTO THE LAKE OF FIRE," where they will join Satan, the beast, the false prophet, and the wicked angels (Matthew 25:41) forever.

---

190 The other view is full or partial annihilationism, where unbelievers will either be consumed immediately or after a period of time in the lake of fire. In either case, the punishment is not eternal. Nothing in Scripture supports this view.

Chapter twenty-one commences the culmination of all things. After all the saints have been resurrected and all unbelievers have been banished in punishment, Heaven and Earth will be destroyed and re-created (vs. 1-2). It is in this eternal state that the promise of no tears, sickness, death, etc. will finally be realized (vs. 4). Most importantly, God himself will be with the saints, and we with him, for eternity – Immanuel, "God with us" forever (vs. 3, 5-8).

Onto this new Earth will descend a new Jerusalem, unlike anything this world has seen. The description of the city that John saw is how most people think of "heaven," but this is not the Heaven that now exists, that believers enter upon death.[191] This city is yet to come. The city's foundation and gates have the names of the twelve tribes of Israel and the twelve apostles embossed on them, confirming that there will be some distinction between Israel and the Church for eternity. How far that distinction goes is not revealed, but "THE NATIONS" are mentioned in verses 24-26 and in chapter 22. This is a normal term in the Hebrew Scriptures for non-Jewish people groups.

One significant point regards the size of the city that John had to measure. Some have confused this city with the vision Ezekiel had in chapter 48 of his prophecy. However, it is clear from the differences that, although Ezekiel did not know it, his prophetic vision was of the Millennial Jerusalem and Temple, whereas John saw the eternal city. This is also apparent from the fact that John specifically noted that there will be no temple in the eternal city, though there will be one during the Millennium (vs. 22).

Chapter twenty-two gives the final details we have about the future and end of all things. Contrary to what many would like to tell us, there is nothing left that God desires to reveal to us. The tree of life that was in Genesis 2 reappears in the Eternal State (vs. 2). What is meant by its

---

191 This is significant when considering the stories of those who claim to have been to heaven and back. They almost always describe heaven with details from Revelation 21-22. However, if this new city comes out of a new heaven that does not yet now exist, how could they see it now?

leaves being "FOR THE HEALING OF THE NATIONS" is highly debated and not explained.

Unlike twice before, where Daniel (12:4, 9) and John (Revelation 10:4) were required to seal up what they saw and heard, John was specifically commanded now to "NOT SEAL UP THE WORDS OF THE PROPHECY CONTAINED IN THIS BOOK" (vs. 10). The final verses contain a series of blessings on those who believe in the prophecy and act on it by believing in the Lamb, much like the blessing in 1:3 on those who obey it.

A curse is pronounced on all who would change the prophecy because to do so would be to make God out to be a liar (vs. 18-19), because the vision came to John from Jesus himself (vs. 16). This prophecy is essentially history written in advance, and John used the past tense throughout to record what he already saw as having taken place. To try to change the record would be as effective as trying to change history.

The final revelation and promise we have from Jesus is that he is coming soon. Anyone who has believed in him can pray with the ancient apostle:

"AMEN! COME, LORD JESUS!"

Trust Publishers House, the trusted name in quality Christian books.

Trust House Publishers
PO Box 3181
Taos, NM 87571

TrustHousePublishers.com